THE BOOK OF PSYCHOLOGICAL TRUTHS

THE BOOK OF PSYCHOLOGICAL TRUTHS

A Psychiatrist's Guide to Really Good
Thinking for Really Great Living

R. Duncan Wallace, MD

iUniverse, Inc.
Bloomington

The Book of Psychological Truths
A Psychiatrist's Guide to Really Good Thinking for Really Great Living

iUniverse books may be ordered through booksellers or by contacting:

iUniverse
1663 Liberty Drive
Bloomington, IN 47403
www.iuniverse.com
1-800-Authors (1-800-288-4677)

ISBN: 978-1-4620-1561-0 (sc)
ISBN: 978-1-4620-1559-7 (hc)
ISBN: 978-1-4620-1562-7 (e)

Library of Congress Control Number: 2012903619

Printed in the United States of America

iUniverse rev. date: 05/14/2012

Contents

Introduction

I recall at the start of my career an important comment that C. H. Hardin Branch, MD, Chief of Psychiatry and former president of the American Psychiatric Association, made to our group of inexperienced psychiatric residents in 1965 at the University of Utah Medical Center. "No matter how good our science gets and what it teaches us, no matter how good our medications become, they will never be able to tell us how to enjoy a sunset or experience any other part of life." He went on to say that as physicians of the human psyche, we were to not only offer good medicine and science but also offer solutions and solace to those unfortunates who are experiencing psychological pain, emotional distress, and difficulty making their way. I took those comments seriously, and they have been a guide to my professional life. That's why I've written this book to share psychological truths.

In 1975, I had an exciting discovery about our mind's signaling system while preparing to deliver a lecture on photographers' creativity. This discovery greatly increased the range of possibilities and opportunities for overcoming obstacles and growing capability. As I readied myself for the lecture, I realized that everything from my mind was a signal and therefore information that conveyed a message. By "everything," I mean all my emotions, sensations, ideas, mental images, intuitions, behaviors, and observations. Each conveyed a message from my mind through my perception to my conscious, aware self. Each message offered a new awareness about some important information useful to my life.

This discovery was strong evidence and impetus that growth and discovery could both help and evolve me. I believed they could help others and allow them to ably handle every situation they encounter, and I realized that all forms of information could be used to create more growth. Our signal awareness system was a vast source of continuously flowing information, a treasure of potential utility. The more knowledge, viewpoints, and definitions I possessed, combined with my greater ability and precision in accessing them, the greater my understanding, the more frequent my discoveries, and the more powerful my life-handling capabilities. This signal-sensing and awareness-producing element is part of our mind's extraordinary processing system. We sense and become aware (the signal), and then we interpret the message to receive its full information. Then we transform the information into ideas, understandings, new discoveries, or actions. A good example is that of a pianist. The pianist reads and comprehends a sheet of music, transforming the written notes into mental directives and mechanical energies (playing the keyboard), which transforms it to musical notes (sound energy) and results in beautiful music. Conversations that share ideas follow this general model—all human interactions do. We are truly information receivers, transformers, and transmitters.

For years I grew myself by challenging the uncertainties I encountered, eventually discovering solutions or methods that worked—processes of certainty, of capability, if you will. Sometimes the uncertainties were large and would stop me for a time, and I'd have to use all my resources: dreams, images, definitions, and questions of what it was and what it was not. What was its purpose? What capability did I lack that I needed? When I asked why it was like that, I would usually get enough of an answer that I could explore further, eventually getting to a full answer.

As each big uncertainty stopped me, I had a brief moment of doubt. What if I did not get that particular one? Pains in my mind would stop me, too, and I wondered if I would ever get beyond their unpleasant and unsettling effect. Though I would doubt, I was always successful and the process always worked. Now I could believe, know, and say that we are all set up for gain, that we increase throughout life. By 1983, I called this Increase Theory and employed it to describe a continuous process of self-growth, including obtaining solutions to problems through new growth. Mastery and discovery were merely two ways that aided increase best. Eventually I could see increase processes to be so universal that I began to say, "Increase simply is." The trick and the skill was to know how to use the increase force well so that I would have continuous, high-quality, valuable growth throughout my life-mastery and increase.

The term *mastery* as used in this book refers to our natural mastery (accomplishment) mechanism, wherein we do something often enough that we can do it well. Becoming a master or reaching a state of being masterful refers to something else. A masterful pianist, for example, has spent a lifetime acquiring expert skill and was probably born with a gift or talent for music. We are not concerned with this definition at this time.

Soon I learned that the increase phenomena did not have a morality of its own; it simply happened. I realized there had to be a way to define what good increase and bad increase were. This led to the development of a consideration ethic, a tool giving me a framework to guide and judge actions.

As a psychiatric practitioner, I confronted a myriad of problems through the years, in all kinds of people, from ages six to ninety. Eventually I saw unifying features to their problems and discovered that we all had similar general patterns. I saw, too, that occasionally we functioned at our very best through using certain patterns that provided the best functioning. These patterns are similar among us, and I have described most of them in this book. A number of them were so consistently present in so many patients, friends, and fellow discoverers that I began seeing them as universal psychological truths, verifiable patterns that produced good or best functioning, that were well aligned with actual reality. I saw, too, the problems resulting when these were avoided, disbelieved, or not followed. Most of my patients' psychological and emotional pains were products of illogical thinking (in otherwise logical people), or they were maintained by insufficient problem-solving methods to handle unwanted happenings and circumstances.

During these clinical years, I discovered not only pathological processes but also universal patterns of the mind—psychological truths. I found them in myself, in my friends, in creative photographers I studied, and in my think-tank members who met to explore new unknowns in our lives and in the mind. These unifying features were comforting, and I came to believe that our mind functions best when we use these patterns (psychological truths) well. We can all learn these patterns and apply them in our lives. Surprisingly, I found that each capability, each concept, each mechanism, each truth continued to work in handling ever greater numbers of life situations as we grew and developed further. The power of continuous increase was built into them, so they had lifelong utility. When we had enough of these valuable capabilities at our command, we cut through most problems quickly.

Psychological truths are verifiable patterns that produce good or best functioning, well aligned with reality. They will bring you a clear and tranquil mind that is free of mental pressure. They provide an avenue by which to remove your mental and emotional pains while converting the situations that cause them into new discovery and new ability. These truths put you in charge of yourself so that you both keep and increase your psychological strength.

Psychological truths have other marvelous properties. They will show you the best ways to grow and develop your capabilities. They will each be a tool of how to function at your best in any situation. They explore and reveal solutions to the many uncertainties encountered in life. They show you the meaning, value, and best use of situational anxieties. They conquer psychological depression and dangerous despair. They will assist you to regain any loss of meaningful purpose you may experience. Collectively they will give you the answers and methods to create enduring and durable quality of life, and they will continuously give you ever-increasing life-handling capability.

The psychological truths are instantly recognizable and usable, both for the short term and the long term. They will become your new and excellent common sense and will show you how your mind is your friend. You won't want to be without them.

Psychological truths are destined for a long and useful life in the human family. They will influence thinking and educational systems, philosophy, and societies at large as their power is recognized and applied.

Psychological truths are both inherent and natural. Some have been created to cause new and future self-evolution. Some are used at one time or another by all of us unconsciously and, at best, haphazardly. By knowing and then intentionally using them, we will greatly increase our practical wisdom and abilities. We will be as knowledgeable as many of the wise sages of history.

These psychological truths were discovered during a forty-eight-year psychiatric career working with thousands of people in psychotherapy who presented with a variety of problems and pains. These psychological truths cured them. What started out as correcting the illogical patterns of individuals eventually led to broadening these concepts to apply to others. Then they became mechanisms, two or more concepts working together. Finally they became the far-reaching bedrock truths that impact everybody's performance in life: causing best results when used, but pain and impairment when not known or not used.

I tested the validity of these truths for thirteen years in a weekly think tank of professionals and laypeople. They proved out and always worked. In a moment of great discovery, a friend and collaborator and I simultaneously realized that if one violated a psychological truth, one created a psychological pain. That discovery brought the realization that we all have a truth system within us, and it will work well for us if we listen to it and know how to use it. If we violate it, we get pain and inefficiency at the least—and life-restricting results, including misery, depression, severe anxiety, and a frightened existence at the most.

Join me and others in the great and continuous life adventure that these psychological truths bring.

SECTION 1

Remove Mental Pressure and Pain, and Strengthen Self-Power

CHAPTER 1

———◆◈◆———

How to Eliminate Mental Pressure and Personal Stress

You have the ability to release mental pressure and stress. When you learn to release mental pressure, your health and quality of life will improve dramatically.

Would you like to function without feeling mental pressure or stress? You can! You can remove all of your mental pressure and most of your personal stress immediately and, eventually, permanently. You know how bad it is to feel the pain of stress and mental pressure. At times, you have probably said, "I'm all stressed out. I hate this pressure and can't stand it anymore!" The good news is that you don't have to stand it anymore. When you know what to do, you can fix it.

This chapter shows you how to remove mental pressure quickly and decisively. When you do, you will be well on your way to possessing amazing ability and a free feeling that you never dreamed possible. Immediately your health, general well-being, and quality of life will be enhanced, and your energy will increase. You will feel lighter, laugh more, and love life more. You will be far more efficient and able to accomplish much more. It's true that you can enjoy a constant state of active tranquility.

Mental pressure is universal, causing most of our personal stress. Mental pressure develops in us naturally as we grow up. It is the most common psychological pain in our busy, frantic, modern-day life. Yet it doesn't need to be.

In this first chapter you will learn the cause of mental pressure, how to recognize it, and how to quickly remove it through your own releaser thought. Then you will see how to continuously bypass creating it through correcting the error that causes it, by using a subtle but powerful psychological truth.

When you remove your mental pressure, you will have much greater well-being and a continuous feeling of active tranquility in your mind. You will accomplish more with less effort; your efficiency and effectiveness will increase in everything you do.

The opening workplace example that follows will familiarize you with how a pressured and stressed employee thinks, feels, and functions, versus how one who is not mentally pressured or stressed goes about his or her work.

A Tale of Two Employees

It was already 2:30 p.m. Jim was feeling worried and harassed by all of the things he had planned on doing by 6:00, so that he could attend an important company function at 7:00, a dinner to honor employees with ten or more years of service. Jim was new to the company and wanted to make a good impression with management by attending, but he had so much to do; he had even skipped lunch. He fretted, *How will I ever get it all done by tonight?* He knew his boss wanted a report presented at the committee meeting tomorrow, and he estimated that he would barely make the deadline if he could get everything together. He silently talked to himself as he worked, pressuring himself to hurry.

Then the boss stopped by his desk and asked him to include one more analysis in his report. Jim smiled, said okay, and kept himself from blowing up. For the next ten minutes, he experienced fear that he wouldn't get it done, but he pressured himself with, *I have to. I've got to hurry. I've only got three hours left!* He did get it done but went to the dinner suffering from a headache. That night he fell asleep, exhausted.

George, who worked in the same department, had been with the company for three years. He, too, had reports to prepare for tomorrow's committee meeting—not one, but two reports. Yet George went to lunch that day with colleagues and attended the company dinner that night. Not only that, but George was friendly and open, had a smile for people, and generally appeared unruffled and calm. He had invited Jim to join the group for lunch that day, but Jim had declined due to his workload and his concerns about it.

At the end of the corporate dinner, they chatted briefly. Jim revealed how bad it had been for him that day—the pressure he'd felt, the worry he'd had, and how mentally taxing his job was. He asked George why he'd appeared so relaxed and unruffled during the day, and how he could take time off for lunch with reports due. "Don't you feel the stress too?" he asked.

"No, no I don't," said George. "But I used to until I learned not to. I rarely, if ever, feel pressure or stress anymore; I don't create it. My mind actually feels like I'm on a vacation most of the time. I can enjoy whatever I'm doing, wherever I am, and I accomplish far more than I used to."

Jim was stunned. *How is George able to do this?* he wondered.

Experiencing Mental Pressure

We feel mental pressure when we have deadlines to complete things. We feel it when we have a lot to do in a short period of time. We especially feel it when preparing for an important test, if the successful completion will have consequences on our future. Pressure often arises when we are trying to prevent an unwanted result. Mental pressure is simply a feeling of pressure in our mind. Though initially we may try to motivate ourselves using mental pressure, it soon becomes painful and unpleasant. We might say to ourselves, "I've got to get this done," or "I'd better hurry and get it done by four o'clock because I have to get to my meeting." How many times have you heard yourself say, "I have to—or else," or maybe even "This is a do-or-die situation"? How many of us worry throughout the day that we won't get everything done?

To complicate matters, we harbor all sorts of feared outcomes if we don't succeed, like, "What will happen to me? What will the boss think?" Or, "If I don't pass the test, I won't get into graduate school and my career hopes will be ruined." We even fret about our favorite sports teams: "If we don't win, we'll never amount to anything. We've got to win!"

Mental pressure exacts a toll. Many experience physical symptoms, such as headaches, elevated blood pressure, and tight muscles. Others become short-tempered, impatient, and hard to work with. When mentally pressured, we can become tense, critical, and even explosive. We go around and convey a "Don't bother me—I'm busy" message. Sound familiar? If left unattended, mental pressure can cause headaches, raise blood pressure, and produce anxiety and depression.

Mental pressure is described in different ways. We say, "I'm stressed" or "I'm all stressed out." We often describe our jobs as "high stress." The word "stress" and terms linked to it have become so widely used that, to a large extent, they have lost their precise value, though we often know what people mean when they use them. Mental pressure is a form of distress.

Some Background about Mental Pressure and Stress

Originally, the medical community used the terms *stress* and *distress* to describe the effect of external factors on our bodies and minds. Stress and distress had a central role in psychosomatic medicine and theory; they have been implicated in heart attacks, mental breakdowns, and various other illnesses.

The extent of the role that stress plays in various physical illnesses remains a subject of study and debate, but many experts suspect that stress and some illnesses are related. Attempts to define personality types (Type A and Type B) tried to show causation of cardiac illnesses in the Type A individuals who created a great deal of self-pressure with a "competitive and driven to accomplish" behavior pattern.[1] The original studies appeared more certain about this than more recent inquiries, but in the 1960s the general medical belief was that it had some validity. Thomas Holmes, MD,[2] produced some very important work, rating by severity the number of life stress events (divorce, loss of a job, death of a spouse, etc.) that people experienced and then correlating the number and severity with the onset of physical illness. The higher the point score, the more severe the illness he could predict. Until new evidence is presented, the debate about the correlation between physical illness, mental illness, and mental stress will invariably continue. Nonetheless, because of the likely ill effects of prolonged stress on health, medical practitioners believe it is good to reduce stress.

Concern about stress and its possible role in illness, and certainly its toll on quality of life, led to the rise of stress seminars, the popularization of transcendental meditation, and Dr. Herbert Benson's book *The Relaxation Response*.[3] Today, a thriving cottage industry has developed, offering a litany of ideas and programs designed to promote better health and well-being. Although some approaches have found success offering assistance in helping reduce stress, few if any have offered a realistic look into the exact central cause of mental pressure, or have offered workable solutions for increasing our internal capability to handle it or eliminate it altogether.

The Cause and the Cure, in General

Until recently, the syndrome of mental pressure, subsequently called mental pressuring, has been wrongly considered to have outside or external causes—things such as a hectic schedule, the pressure or forces of a fast-paced society, and the individual's need to find professional success and financial well-being. Though no one denies that modern circumstances play a part in this equation, the truth about mental pressure and stress is that it is self-created by a specific thought pattern.

Not surprisingly, when I challenged four hundred participants at a University of Utah Fall Conference in 1978 to tell me where their mental pressure originated, from outside forces or from inside forces, 390 believed it came from the outside; only ten said it originated from the inside. Two hours later, at the end of the conference, the figures were almost exactly reversed. Only seven people still believed mental pressure came from outside forces. During that two-hour period, I introduced a unique concept that eliminates mental pressure, and I offered simple tools that release mental pressure immediately, resulting in a clear mind and freedom from the ill effects of mental pressure. The audience cleared their minds of pressure and took away a valuable tool for future use. Each of us possesses the capability to achieve this transformation. With the proper tools and releasing techniques and practices, we can develop a form of psychological strength that defeats pressure and keeps us in charge.

Each of us exhibits some mental self-pressuring; some experience it occasionally, whereas others feel it constantly. There are some fortunate people who seldom experience mental self-pressuring, and they are easy to spot because almost always they are calm or appear at peace. We often call on them during emergencies. In my experience, they represent less than 1 percent of people.

A Case Example

When people are crucial about the need for a certain outcome, their faulty thinking creates mental pressure. Jennie, a thirty-six-year-old woman who makes financial programs for organizations, offers an excellent illustration of this causative shift in thinking. When she and I were discussing how people create mental pressure, she observed that many of her work colleagues quickly become upset and frustrated during problem-solving meetings. "They limit themselves," Jennie observed, "by getting very crucial and making absolute statements such as, 'We'll never figure this out in time!' or 'It's impossible!' or 'We've got to have a solution or we'll lose our jobs!' At the same time, they stubbornly hold their positions rather than being fluid and arriving at a solution, a synthesis based on all the data gathered at the meeting. They are not even aware they are doing it."

The Real Cause of Mental Pressure

I have often wondered why we get so crucial, or "all driven up," as a tough, streetwise patient called mental pressure during therapy. When we create mental pressure, we're usually reacting to an important situation by changing from realistic probability thinking to absolute-necessity thinking. Realistic probability thinking says, "Let's see how I can do this," or "I'll do this, trying these steps," or "I'll do it if I'm able." When we shift to absolute-necessity thinking, it's "I must do this," or "I have to," or "It's do it or die." We depart from logic and probability, acting as if there is no other possibility than the one we must have. We fear losing or not obtaining our tightly held goals. We fear not succeeding, so we essentially ignore or squeeze out all other solutions. We believe that crucial, absolute-necessity thinking helps us reach our goals and overcome any doubt or reluctance we have. We believe, erroneously, that we must pressure ourselves to accomplish the goal.

The Subtle Shift in Thinking

When we set goals and go about accomplishing them, we begin to talk to ourselves differently. We depart from reality and change to the crucial, absolute-necessity thinking. We focus only on the accomplishment and mentally try to force the result we want. This shift in thinking is so subtle that most people are not aware of it or the fact that it creates mental self-pressuring. Even for someone who is aware of the problem, like Jennie in the example above, this departure from reality happens occasionally. Luckily, when we release or correct our thinking, the problem disappears.

Mental Pressure in High Achievers

More typical and common than Jennie are the high-achieving people who characteristically live day-to-day in the throes of mental self-pressure. Diane, a college graduate student, came to me about issues concerning her emerging adult professional and personal life. As she described the pros and cons and pondered the choices and decisions she faced, I noticed she took everything very seriously. Everything was "crucial," and if she made a decision, she felt it closed off all others—so it had better be right. She was convinced that if she made the wrong decisions, all was lost. How could she ever know what to do? She had to make the right decisions because everything depended on it.

With guidance, Diane gradually worked though the choices and decisions and moved on. She learned that by making everything so crucial, so terribly important and so life shattering, if she made the wrong decision, she severely limited her choices and hurt herself. She lived in a state of perpetual mental pressure, which she created. After first becoming aware of her thinking patterns, she was then able to remove the pressure by employing a releasing technique. As a result, she was refreshed, clear, and tranquil. With minimal assistance, Diane devised her own releasing technique to help eliminate the pressure. By the end of her therapy, every time she caught herself making things absolutely crucial, she used her releasing thought to return to clarity and freedom.

Compounding Mental Pressure

Marilyn fit the profile of the harried school teacher, mother, and single head of household who has too much to do. She was always busy and goal-oriented, and she listed all her tasks at the beginning of each day and started her self-talk about them. "I have to stop by the post office, mail the letters, process the mail, make my phone calls, and then stop at the store and pick up a few items for school projects. I have to hurry so that there's time to start the students' projects in the morning. Then I have to go to the faculty meeting, attend Missy's performance this afternoon, fix dinner, and still find time to exercise. I must get started now, or I'll never get it all done."

As you can probably guess, Marilyn was exhausted at the end of each day. Granted, she accomplished a great deal, but she wasted precious energy by constantly making things crucial and pressuring herself. In part, she had developed this style as a girl growing up on a ranch. "The animals died or crops failed if we didn't handle things immediately," she told me. In that kind of environment, immediate problem solving was crucial to success in many situations. However, that was not so in her current daily life.

By discussing and analyzing her self-pressuring, Marilyn came to see the foible in herself. She told me, "I am like the family dog who runs all day long, and then at the end of the day I can only lie there looking up, occasionally beating my tired tail, wishing I could do more, but loyal to the end." When this bright woman reset her motivating self-statements from, "I have to do this and then this and then this …" to "I want to do these things, I will do what I can, and it will take the time it takes to do them," she found release and a sense of peace she did not have before. Like many others, Marilyn slipped occasionally and returned to her old pattern of pressuring self-talk, but when she realized it, she released it and kept her mind clear. Her freeing statement, based on reality and truth, was, "I will do what I can, and I will get done what I do, no more, no less." The result was that her life was no longer a daily race, she had far more energy at the end of the day, and she felt more at peace.

Mental Acceptance

Sean, a fellow psychiatrist, would get angry and irritable, and feel mental pressure and stress whenever his office phone rang while he was conducting therapy sessions. He changed the ringing to a flashing light so that his answering service could signal him about emergencies with quick, repeated flashing rather than ringing, but this did little to alleviate the mental pressure. If Sean received three calls per hour, he would feel significant pressure to get them handled in the ten minutes between patients at the end of a fifty-minute session. If calls piled up during the last hour or two of the day, and he had a dinner engagement or a class to teach, the pressure of this "time compression" became excruciating. Sean worried, "How am I going to get all this done in time? I've got places to go! What will I do? This is terrible." After he made the calls he felt some relief, but then he breathlessly rushed off to his next engagement, fretting he would be late and foul up other people's plans.

When we analyzed Sean's situation, we discovered that he was hoping ahead of time that the phone wouldn't ring so that he could avoid its problems. He concluded this was ridiculous because he was in practice to help people. Besides, he needed the phone for new referrals, for prescription requests, and to deal with patients' new problems or situations that could not wait. Sean's solution was to always mentally accept the phone calls and deal with each when he had the time to do so. He decided to quit pressuring himself over unreturned calls and over his belief that it was necessary to handle them immediately. Sean realized that in reality, he could only do what he could do. If he wanted to be on time for his evening engagements, he could either schedule them fifteen minutes later or deal with the phone calls later that evening or the next day, except for the emergencies. The result was that Sean stopped feeling pressure, except for the brief instant of the phone call's interruption prior to his consciously deciding to accept it. The mental pressure he had created was now reduced to an interrupting signal. When he quickly performed a release from it, he would go back into a smooth, mentally clear flow, a much-preferred state of mind.

An Example of a Mental Pressure and Anxiety Cycle

Some people—like John, a therapy patient—live in constant mental pressure, beset by anxiety every waking hour. His problem was classic: his anxiety created more mental pressure, and in turn the mental pressure created more anxiety. John is a successful attorney who owns a large law firm. He has a reputation for being very precise about details and for representing his clients successfully. John had little peace of mind and had no friends, though many attorneys and staff worked for him. Not surprising, he could negotiate well and be charming or tough when necessary. He was the son of a well-intentioned but critical and harsh father whom he could never please. In part, John was still trying to please his father when he came to see me.

John sighed frequently during therapy sessions. It eventually became clear that he was attempting to relieve mental pressure with his sighs or exhalations. When I mentioned it, he saw it also. We decided to employ the sighs as markers to his mental pressure, and we worked to discover what he was thinking at the time. As expected, he was being crucial and goal directed, fearing he wouldn't succeed but aggressively pursuing success at all costs. He approached every situation in his personal and private life with the same pressure-causing cycle. He would build the pressure from his crucial intention and absolute thinking, "I must do this now," then sigh and release some of it briefly, then start all over again. John desperately needed freedom and release from this cycle.

He felt anxiety that he wouldn't be successful at his firm's law practice, so he pressured himself on every case with which he was involved. Anxiety about whether he would succeed, and his great fear that he wouldn't, caused him to pressure himself unmercifully. Often he would ask himself, "What will my dad think if we don't win this case?" Then he'd say, "I can't let him be disappointed. I've got to succeed." This crucial and absolute thinking pattern created mental pressure, which he used to try to beat the fear and anxiety.

Eventually John learned to release his anxiety and pressure, but to rid himself of it, he had to see things realistically. He realized the folly of trying to please his father. His father's feelings were his father's, and John couldn't control those. Even if he did succeed, it was no guarantee that his father would be more pleased in the long run about an individual case. His father might be more realistic than he was and realize he couldn't win every case. Further, John and his lawyers should be succeeding for themselves and their clients, if they could; that was what they were being paid to attempt to do.

John later became even more successful, branched out into other endeavors, and felt good while he did it. We worked on the origins of his anxiety and pressure and changed the logic of his motivating thought patterns that had caused him to maintain the pressure. He achieved even more success, had more efficiency, and did it all with a greater sense of well-being. Fortunately he learned to have friends and take time for himself, and his life was greatly enriched because of it.

Releaser Thoughts—Breaking Out of Mental Pressure

Releasers are thoughts that people can use to break out of the mental pressure cycle, clearing or freeing their minds immediately. There are an infinite number of possible releasers, and each of us can customize our own. The only requirement is to change from the crucial, the absolute, the "one result only" necessity thinking to a type of reality-based, logical thinking. In essence, the pressure-creating thought has to be supplanted by a better thought.

Here is what to know. The reality or truth about whether any future task will be completed includes its probability, which is its likelihood of success, as well as its uncertainty, the part you don't know about because it has not happened yet (e.g., unforeseen impediments to a task's completion). There has to be enough capability if it is to be accomplished. What it can't be is certain ahead of time, though the mental pressuring thought attempts to claim, "I absolutely have to have this result!" It is illogical to employ this forced idea or notion when we want a certain outcome. Being logical instead will remove the pressure and remove the illogical thought, which is fighting against our innate sense of logic.

An excellent releaser, one that has worked for many patients and for me as well, is, "I desire to do it. It's important and worth it. I will do it if I am able." A shorter version is, "I will do it if I can." This example includes choice and motivation ("I will do it") and factors in elements of reality (the uncertainty, probability, and capability) by adding the idea "to the extent I am able." Say it to yourself, "I will do it if I can." Notice that it is quiet, clear, and agreeable. Now say this to yourself: "I have to do this. I have got to complete it." It feels tight and mentally pressuring; you can feel the tension. Your mind is neither clear nor quiet; you are not relaxed or tranquil. Now repeat again, "I desire to do it. It's important and worth it. I will do it if I am able." Notice again the clear and released feeling. Practice it, saying it again and again.

Remember the subtlety Jennie pointed out? She said, "My coworkers are not even aware they are doing it." *Awareness* is the pivotal component—the awareness that you feel mental pressure, and the awareness that you are creating the pressure during your illogical motivational thinking or self-talk. Once you identify the mental pressure, you can clear it by supplanting it with a good releaser. Here are some other examples of good reality and pressure-clearing thoughts, including my favorites:

"Nothing is necessary; some things are preferable."

"I will do it if I am able."

"It is worth it; I will attempt it."

Try it out. Change your self-talk and motivating thoughts. Practice using these releasers when you feel mental pressure. Develop your own releaser, one that suits you. Or give these a try:

- It is important, not absolutely necessary.
- I will attempt it. The results will be what they are.
- It is worth an effort.
- I will do it if I can.

The amount of benefit you experience will surprise you. Its beauty lies in its simplicity, yet it will have a profoundly positive effect on your well-being. What you say to yourself and how you say it really counts.

Attaining Mastery over Pressure

When I first started using releasers, I loved the free and tranquil feeling they gave, until I inadvertently slipped back into the habit of reflexive crucial thought, which brought mental pressure back into my mind. Each time this happened, I wondered why I couldn't put these crucial thoughts with their pressure to rest permanently. I wanted to be continuously pressure free. Why couldn't I just get so good with reality and truth thoughts that they became automatic? I struggled for more than a year. Was mental pressuring such an important human reflex that it had to arise? It was a vexing question.

Two years later, as I walked onto the floor of the psychiatric unit at my hospital, one of the nurses inquired, "Dr. Wallace, we nurses were wondering what it is about you. You are the only doctor we know who never gets stressed out and upset. You smile and laugh often. What is your secret?" I suddenly realized I had not consciously felt mental pressure for a long time; I had not even thought about it until the nurse commented. *What do you know*, I thought. *I've finally achieved it! I don't get crucial any more, and its release is now automatic. I have mastered it!*

I don't know how long it will take you to stop creating mental pressure, to automatically function without it. But it *will* happen, so keep using your releaser. You will stop the mental pressure each time you use it; that is reward enough. Someday you will find that you no longer create mental pressure in the first place.

Possible Origins of Pressure-Creating Thinking

What could be the origins of crucial thinking that creates mental pressure? When I tried to convince my teenage daughters to motivate themselves without pressure, my youngest, then a sophomore in high school, told me, "Dad, if I did not pressure myself, I'd not do my assignments. I have to make it crucial or I won't do it. I need the pressure to motivate myself."

For her at least, and for many others, the answer seems to lie in using pressure to overcome resistance to doing things we do not really want to do, like homework or chores. We know it is best to do them, so we overcome our reluctance through self-pressuring.

We learn early in childhood to acquiesce to our parents, our teachers, and other authorities when we would rather do something of our own choosing, like playing outside. We are often threatened, "You'd better, or else." "Pick up your toys, or you cannot go out to play." Or we are simply commanded, "You have to do this." "You have to do your homework, or you can't go to the game tonight." Their authority and the consequences of not doing what they say, coupled with our dependency upon them, instills the absolute, no-other-option type of thinking. We develop it as a habit and later use it consciously to motivate ourselves. There may be no way to arrive in life as an adult without this inoculation of crucial, absolutely necessary, illogical, one-option-only type of thinking. Fortunately you can now use releaser thoughts to stop it, and then eventually eliminate such thinking altogether.

Extreme Example

Nancy, a writer of children's books, took the "nothing is necessary" release technique so seriously that she stopped writing. Instead, she relaxed, watched a lot of TV, took naps, and in general luxuriated and pleased herself. She was relieved, and for the first time in memory she felt released from her taskmaster, her former method of pressure motivating. After four months, she wondered if she should be worried, but she wasn't.

When she told me of this development, she was happy to report that she was writing again. But now, she was far more happy and at ease than ever before; she was doing it now because she wanted to. Its true value and importance returned, and her work was better than ever. She had no resistance to doing it anymore and found she could do it better without pressuring herself.

A note of caution as you practice this release technique: do not let the releasing of mental pressure become crucial itself. While this might sound strange, it is a real pitfall. I once became so attuned to pressure building up I would admonish myself, "You must not create pressure! You have to think differently!" The result was I became crucial about being non-crucial—I created pressure instead of eliminating it. If this happens to you, step back and laugh.

Here is a revealing question: "How much energy is required for any task?" This Zen-like koan is hard for many to answer. A fair answer is to say, "Enough." The best answer I have found is, "The right amount. No more, no less." Zen koans are questions to make you think deeply, such as "What is the sound of one hand clapping?" In your mind, imagine how a basketball goes through a hoop and net with a swoosh. The net briefly holds the ball as it goes through, slowing its movement but not stopping it. The net holds just enough to give definition on the way through. Try to be like a basketball net: accept, define, and release, and do not hold on so tightly. When a new request with a time limit comes from a boss, or when you take on a task, size it up and see its components. Quickly plan how to handle it. Let go of any feeling of its being absolutely necessary, and go about doing the steps without the feeling of pressure. Observe, define, decide, release, and complete as able.

If you practice this, you will have a much smoother time in life. By using better thinking, you will have better living. Mental pressure uses up a great deal of energy, much more than is actually required to complete a task; it is a huge energy waste, perhaps our biggest.

"Protestations" and Resistance to Changing from Mental Self-Pressuring

The most common resistance to eliminating pressuring crucial thought is the belief, "If I don't pressure myself, I won't do it." I suspect this opinion is said quickly, without thinking clearly and fully. Many people grow dependent on self-pressuring and see it as helpful though unpleasant, the price of accomplishment. I always ask, "Is the goal important to achieve? Do you really want it?" When they respond, "Of course," I say, "Logically, if you truly desire the goal and it's important to you, you'll do it for those reasons, not because you pressure yourself." They always agree; they just never think of it that way. They have relied on a habit of having mental pressure instead of seeing the truth and using it—at the price of wasted energy and the unpleasantness of the pressure.

Remember that not pressuring yourself, not believing your goal is necessary, does not mean it is not important. By saying it is not necessary, some people mistakenly think I mean it is not important to do. I do not mean that at all. It is probably valuable to do and may be very important, but it is not absolutely necessary, the one and only possible thing to do. As we all know, we could be interrupted by an emergency or be technically unable to do what we set out to do. Therefore in a logical and practical sense, no matter how important some things are, changes in plans and priorities prove they were not absolutely necessary after all.

An attorney friend explained it this way to a colleague, who was stumbling with the idea. He said, "It is not absolutely necessary that I do my client's work. It is important that I do it for his sake and mine. If I didn't, I wouldn't last long in the legal profession, so I do it. But it is not really necessary that I do it, if I am willing to suffer the consequences." It is at the level of motivational thought and violating the pure truth that we create mental pressure by illogically thinking, "I absolutely have to, I must do it!" If instead we use true logic and say, "It's important, I desire to do it, and I will if I am able to," then we really do these important things (practically speaking) because of our desire and ability, and we do not create mental pressure while doing so.

Some people still have trouble thinking what they do is not absolutely necessary, in spite of the explanations of the difference between very important and absolutely necessary (a requirement). That is when I ask them if it is absolutely necessary to eat food and drink water. The answer is always yes. "No," I say, "not so, unless you want to live, and then it is an absolute requirement, necessary and crucial. After all, some choose to die. Some people try to make political statements by starving themselves. Others blow up themselves and others. Occasionally older people with serious illnesses or impaired quality of life quit taking food or water because they want to die; they want to get out of what has become a painful and miserable life." So, I conclude again, "It is not necessary to eat or drink water, unless of course you want to live. Then it is required." That explanation usually provides the convincing.

The True Uses for Crucial and Absolute Necessity

There is a true use for the concepts of crucial and absolute necessity; they have a place but not in direct motivational thought. They pertain, instead, to things already completed or to hypothetical situations. For any experience already completed, it was crucial, necessary, and a requirement that every element happened in the exact sequence it did; otherwise it couldn't have been that unique experience. There is no mental pressure generated from crucial thought, because the experience is already complete and true as it is. In hypothetical situations, the outcome is not a probability. It is already set, so crucial motivational statements are important to fulfill the preset outcome. There is no mental pressure with those statements because they support the definite outcome. For instance, a car dealer may say to an automobile manufacturer and supplier, "For us to have an adequate supply of cars to meet the projected demand, we need one thousand cars by July 1." Similarly, you can say that if your team is to win the championship, it must win tonight's game. It is only when the goal is future, desired but not yet reached (the outcome is uncertain), that crucial and absolute motivational statements create mental pressure. Prior experiences and hypothetical situations already have the outcome completed, so there is no mental pressure, just the required ingredients.

Mental pressure comes from a type of thinking used by most of us to help overcome reluctance or fear of not succeeding. By its nature, it is illogical because instead of using truth and reality as motivators, it relies on crucial, absolutely necessary pressure thinking. As we have seen, the result is a cycle of pressure and pain. We have also seen it can be eliminated by the use and practice of releasers, the "I will do it if I am able" or "nothing is necessary, things are preferable and important" thinking. Remember, there is a big difference between important and crucial; things are important, not absolutely crucial. When we align ourselves with the truth and the reality of a situation, the *psychological truth* of the logic of cause and effect, mental pressure disappears. It is surprising, but our minds are so exquisitely tuned to the truth that when we distort it, even a little, mental pressure results. When we violate this psychological truth of cause and effect, this powerful subtlety, we get the pain of mental pressure.

At a recent golf tournament my partner, a colleague and surgeon, told me this story. Its succinct and concise message communicates the essence of not having mental pressure. He said, "Sometimes, I am late to my afternoon office appointments because of complications during morning surgery. My receptionist looks out at the full waiting room and says, 'How will we ever see everyone? We are so far behind!' After this happened many times, I finally told her, 'Life is too important to get all stressed up about it.'" I loved how he put it so well. Life's quality and its value are so important that we should not ruin it with the needless creation of mental pressure.

Chapter Summary

1. Notice (become aware) that you have the unpleasant feelings of stress and pressure. This is the warning signal that you are thinking illogically, *violating the psychological truth of the logic of cause and effect.*
2. Notice what it is that you are saying to yourself that is illogical, absolute, crucial, and off-line with the logical truth. Compare it with

the logical statements presented in the text. Use the logical truth statements and the releaser thoughts, such as: "I have this to do. I'll do it to the extent I am able." "Nothing is necessary; some things are preferable." "It is important, not absolutely necessary. I'll do it if I can." Apply your own chosen *releaser thought* to remove the mental pressure instantly.

3. Replace the illogical statement you have been thinking or saying to yourself with a logical truth statement and notice that mental pressure never builds up in the first place. The way you say these things is what is really important. If you say the motivating statements as things that are necessary, you will have mental pressure. When you say them as things that are important and desirable, as things to do to the extent you are able, there will be no pressure.

4. Each time you make a correction, you immediately release the pressure and feel the rewarding tranquility. You may have to make these corrections a number of times before they become an automatic habit, a new and better way, the way of truth, which creates best functioning. You become better at it the more you do it, until eventually it becomes automatic.

5. Some of the illogical statements we make are so subtly off-line with the truth that they have gone generally unnoticed by everybody. Changing them to correct and true logical statements causes very dramatic changes in how our mind feels, removing mental pressure and personal stress and creating tranquility.

6. Follow the steps above immediately when you notice mental pressure or stress, or as soon as you hear yourself saying crucial and absolute, illogical things to motivate yourself.

Some Applications

Here is a small list of situations to which you can apply a corrective truth thought, a releaser thought. The actual number of such situations is vast. Eventually you will be able to say or think of motivational statements that do not create mental pressure in the first place.

- A harried mother with small children and constant interruptions who is feeling stressed and pressured could say, "Wow, this is a lot to do. I'll do the most important first, then whatever else I can get to."

- Students preparing for exams, who worry and pressure themselves while studying, could say, "I'll study it and do the best I am able to do."

- Anyone who works with deadlines and sees them as pressure could say, "I can only do what is realistically possible. It will only be done when I get it done."

- The single parent who is both breadwinner and caretaker and worries about how to get everything done could say, "I can only do the possible. I'll do the most important things first."

- Administrators pondering significant decisions and feeling worrisome pressure about the consequences could say, "I will make the best decision I can after weighing all the factors. That is the best I can do."

- When hoping strongly that negative outcomes will not occur, one could say, "I will work to prevent negative results, but I will accept whatever they are and work with them in the best possible ways."

- When you are running out of time and fearing that you might miss scheduled transportation, you could say, "I might miss the train. I'll try to get there, but if I don't, so be it."

- When you are believing and pressuring yourself that you absolutely must get something done by a certain time, you could say, "Things can be very important, but nothing is absolutely necessary. I'll give it my best."

- Professional athletes, particularly those in a solitary and slow-starting precision sport such as golf, who feel the pressure and the stress about a hoped for outcome, could say, "I will trust my skills, plan the best I can, and accept the result."

CHAPTER 2

---◆·▶◀·◆---

How to Deal with Painful Emotions and Make New Discoveries

When you learn to read the messages your emotions are sending you, you can use that information to free yourself of emotional pain and enjoy increased pleasure in life.

You can remove the pain from emotions such as anger, fear, disappointment, and guilt when you realize that your emotions are sending you situational truth messages. It's possible to learn the psychological truths of your marvelous emotional system and use that knowledge to increase the amount of pleasure in your life. In this chapter, I'll show you how to discover and use the psychological formulas that create satisfaction, joy, fulfillment, and well-being. Here's what you need to know first: *Pain always points to undiscovered truth; to truth that has been violated or fought against, if known; or to an ability not yet developed.* You can convert circumstances that evoke painful emotions into new discovery, new ability, and new mastery.

Being Sensitive to Our Emotions

When a professional golfer wins a major golf tournament, we witness his or her exultant joy of triumph. But when a golfer in contention finishes poorly, we see the agony of defeat, the same that we experience when we try hard and do not succeed at something we dearly want.

Who can deny the feelings of rapture and wonder at the first realization of being in love? Or how about the warm feeling of delight holding a newborn baby? When we pet a purring cat or play with a beloved dog, it feels good both to our senses and to our psyche.

When we are confronted by a disturbed bee, we duck, are filled with apprehension, and quickly attempt to get out of its way. How chagrined we feel when someone butts in line ahead of us. When we read of a kidnapping, we are outraged at the child abductor. And we can't forget the terrible, sinking feeling as we watched, again and again, the collapse of the World Trade Towers on September 11, 2001.

(For those who lost loved ones on 9/11, or who have lost loves ones through kidnapping, the following discussion is not meant to imply that feelings accompanying relationship losses can be dismissed lightly. On the contrary, because we are social beings and because relationships make up a substantial part of our lives, tragedies in relationships cause far-reaching effects. Dealing with this type of immense pain from major grief reactions is discussed briefly later in this chapter, but it is ultimately beyond the scope of this book.)

Emotions and feelings are universal. They are pleasurable or painful. They instantly ignite and excite us, getting our full attention and awareness. They are natural and automatic, serving us well and warning us with fear, anxiety, or frustration. Emotions enhance our experiences by giving us delight, joy, rapture, and satisfaction. These pleasurable emotions are rewards that make us seek similar experiences again.

Imagine how flat life would be without emotions. We wouldn't have joy or satisfaction. There would be no fear to warn us, or frustration to give us resolve. Whether pleasant or painful, emotions are positive forces we can use to aid us in living safely and well.

When a group of people has an experience that prompts strong emotions, whether painful or pleasurable, it strengthens the bond between them and creates a sense of belonging. These strong emotions also result in a shared feeling of connection and mutual empowerment, which can be used in a positive way to further motivate a team or any group with a shared aim. It strengthens resolve. Alternatively, hate and vengeful emotions can blind individuals, ethnic groups, or even nations and motivate one to retaliate for perceived wrongs.

Typically, most people take the expression of their emotions as a matter of course, utilizing them to justify and motivate their actions. We all try to avoid emotional pains and seek out more pleasure, but the truth is, our emotions are more than just an expression or litmus test of how we are feeling. They hold one of the secrets to understanding and learning how to handle life better, and to knowing what our true nature is. When we understand the wisdom of our emotions, we can then create a more productive and fulfilling life.

Emotions as Signals We Can Decipher and Use

The secret to learn is that beneath the surface of each emotion, there is an encoded meaning, a logic or truth that offers an important message. When we learn to decipher the underlying message that the emotion signals us about, and we use it in a conscious way, we are able to make wiser and more informed decisions and can more ably set the direction for our next move in life. We will have handled our situation better and developed new capability and wisdom through having creatively handled that situation. When we use our emotions in this way, each one is an opportunity for growth.

By tapping deeper into this powerful and elegant signaling and messaging system, we are able to successfully guide ourselves into the future, learning and mastering new and better strategies and capabilities for shaping our life. Our emotional signaling and messaging system is unique, designed for each one of us. It offers immediate, unmistakable, and unerring information, except in instances of misperception, which I will address later. It always tells us the truth of the evoking situation. We do not need to turn it on or off; it is always there to serve us. It is a wonderful psychological truth messaging system about what we encounter day by day, moment by moment, as we live life.

The Nature of Our Emotions

We experience emotions frequently, some pleasurable and others painful. Our species shares this characteristic with many, if not all, members of the animal kingdom. How many times have you seen your pet dog or cat react to territorial threats from other animals? Our pets snarl, show anger, attempt to dominate, and even occasionally attack. How about the way they respond with joy when we return from being away?

Each of us is equipped with an intuitive ability to sense what emotions other people are experiencing, reading it in their facial expressions and body language. Studies have shown that all peoples, from sophisticated and civilized to primitive and tribal, can correctly identify emotions when presented with photographs of different facial expressions. Of course we are more keenly aware of our own emotions because when they arise, they briefly fill our being and consume our consciousness. Whether we are observing others or monitoring ourselves, the expression of emotion is a way to communicate the personal meaning of a particular experience, an important means of communication. Emotions also play a major role in keeping us safe because they alert us with fear when in danger, and they evoke focused protective aggression within us. They enhance and enrich our lives through comfort, love, and care. They offer joy, fulfillment, rapture, and aesthetic enjoyment.

A Particular Emotion Is Tied to a Particular Happening

When we address the deeper meaning of our emotions, we realize they are the immediate, automatic interpretation and reaction to situations we encounter. These immediate reactions are not thoughts per se, though each has a logical formula and is experienced in part by our conscious awareness system. Emotions are information, however different, that inform and focus us. Each emotion has a distinct feel or specificity all its own, and each is evoked by a certain kind of experience. Emotions highlight and point to the specific truth of what we are experiencing; each has an exact definition.

Just like a winning athlete, triumph and satisfaction come for each of us in a winning experience. Also, anger surfaces when we are obstructed by something uninvited or not wanted, as when a car cuts in front of us and we have to brake or take evasive action to prevent a collision, or when someone yells at us and interrupts our peaceful moment. This specificity—that a particular emotion is tied to or associated with a particular type of happening—is a large part of the value they have for us.

As we grow from childhood to maturity, we become familiar with the different types of our emotions and have a general sense of what makes them surface. At the same time, we learn what they communicate and what we can do about them. Each of us handles our emotions and the situations or circumstances that prompt them in our own unique way, but in a larger, more general sense, we all handle them roughly the same way. One person's anger style may not be yours, but whether he or she rages and throws a tantrum while you quietly stew and hold it in, the anger-causing problem comes to light and stimulates people to solve the situation in some manner.

Emotions Motivate Us

A universal truth is that emotions motivate us. In the case of anger, it helps us remove an obstruction or solve the causal problem, or perhaps change direction, seeking solutions elsewhere. When we want pleasure, we actively seek it out through the experiences that create it, such as listening to music for serenity or seeing a funny movie for humor and enjoyment. By contrast, we try to avoid the painful emotions and the situations that may cause them, such as avoiding a presentation in front of a class so as not to feel or experience self-consciousness or embarrassment. This approach has merit but may be unwise at times, when the emotional pain is the frustration created by not really knowing how to deal with a situation.

Emotions Are Experiential, Situational Truth Messages

Emotions are valuable gifts—each has a specific meaning and offers a message we can depend on, reliable truth about what has just occurred. They provide us with an automatic and instantaneous signal. The beauty

27

is that we do not have to consciously do anything to receive these valuable signals, because they come as rapid-fire responses to experiences. They are the truth signals about what we encounter. Part of the hidden wisdom is that we can incorporate these messages into a guiding compass of truth of experiences whose direction pointer is unfailingly accurate. Pain points to the truth of obstruction, and pleasure points to the truth of smooth flow to the general nature of our experience.

Pain Is an Opportunity

Knowing that pain points to an obstruction, this gives us an opportunity. Though we tend to avoid the obstruction (pain), we do better to master it and remove the pain through improving our abilities. When we do that, the same obstruction with its pain will not happen anymore. It will have been mastered. It will take a new obstruction to create pain again. As for pleasure, we can continue to improve our ability to function smoothly and well, which in turn increases our pleasure even further. If you choose the paths of improvement you will increase in both pleasure and ability.

The Exceptions to Unerring Truth from Our Emotions

Although our emotions are unerringly accurate, there is a qualifying condition that must be present before its messages can be trusted. This qualifying condition is our perception of reality. Perception, the way we see, is the combination of incoming data and how we interpret it. Our perception of reality—of what truly occurred—must be in agreement with what has actually happened. Our perception of reality is critical to the accuracy of our emotional response; we cannot have one without the other. Occasionally we misperceive; we have all had the experience of misunderstanding someone and quickly assuming what that person was saying or doing that we didn't like. The person who was misunderstood usually feels angry or hurt (his or her wish to be correctly understood is obstructed). When he or she retaliates and accuses us, we may in turn feel defensive, angry, or even afraid. All this comes from the mistaken perception, the misunderstanding. Another familiar example is when we enter a room, and people are talking about someone else in a disparaging manner and then become silent to keep it private. We wrongly believe they were talking about us. Our perception is wrong, and we might react with suspicion, discomfort, or hurt feelings. Whereas our perception of the reality of the experience is wrong, our emotional response is perfectly appropriate to that wrong perception and is therefore inappropriate to the actual reality.

On another note, there are people with illnesses of the mind who distort reality. In many years of practicing psychiatry, I have treated paranoid people with suspicious fears who are unable to read reality correctly; the result is they have distorted and inaccurate emotional reactions because of their distorted reality. Because they cannot read reality accurately, they live in a world of misinterpretation and painful emotions. They tend to believe that others are against them or are persecuting them. These unfortunate souls cannot trust anyone. The point is, for us to have the full value of unerringly accurate emotions, we must have unerringly accurate perceptions. Fortunately for most of us, our perceptions and emotions are accurate and in tune with the real world a high percentage of the time.

The Emotional Alphabet Analogy, and Your Possibilities and Potentials

Each basic emotion, such as anger, fear, sadness, happiness, delight, or satisfaction, has a definition or a formula for the conditions that cause it. Each has a unique character, like a letter of the alphabet. Together, individual emotions can form more complex emotions, like putting letters together to form words. For example, disappointment is composed of both anger and sadness about a hoped for expectation that did not occur. Bewilderment's makeup is that of being perplexed and confused, uncertain, obstructed, and perhaps frustrated about something not understood. Frustration is anger and helplessness about something that did not happen, or about being unable to proceed because you do not know how, or you cannot because you do not have the means or supplies.

Creating Pleasurable Emotions

When we write or tell a story, we are creating an experience for others. We place words and ideas in a unique and meaningful way to prompt a certain response from our audience. In like manner, we can create emotional experiences by simply creating the particular conditions that evoke them. For example, if we want to feel joy, we can accomplish this by simply stimulating delight, pleasure, and satisfaction in ourselves or others. Or we can create joy when we give a desirable gift: a necklace to a wife or daughter, a surprise trip to a fun destination, or taking grandkids to a movie. To experience fulfillment, we might create something of value for others and ourselves by putting in effort, even sacrifice. When we solve a problem and in the process teach a method that works well for someone (solve a business, legal, medical, or psychological problem for them), we have fulfillment, a sense of accomplishment and satisfaction.

We all seek experiences that can give us pleasure and excitement. We attend an uplifting symphony concert, go to a film filled with suspense and adventure, or read an intriguing book that absorbs our attention and creates profound emotion. We don't consciously give the formula that creates the emotional experience much thought; we just participate. We see it, listen to it, or read it, and we experience it vicariously. Nevertheless, the true formulas, the specific emotion evokers, are at work to create the experience within us.

As we gain experience and understanding, we can utilize our power and capability to create the kinds of experiences we desire. We can, to some extent, become the architect of our emotional life, the composer of our own emotional symphony, the writer of our own emotional life story. Rather than simply reacting to our emotions, we can develop great range and versatility. With understanding and practice, we can even create the feelings we want to have by bringing about or remembering the circumstances that cause them.

The Differences between the Painful, Unpleasant Emotions, and Pleasurable Emotions

Unlike pleasurable emotions over which we have some control, we only get painful emotions when unwanted things occur. These unwanted emotions are reactions to situations or circumstance that obstruct us; they are so different from our preferred experiences that they create painful responses. We have all experienced the pain and unpleasantness of fear, anger, and frustration—for example, when we give genuine help to an older relative and then are wrongly accused that we were courting that person's favor, helping only for an ulterior motive such as inheritance; or how chagrined and unfairly treated we feel if wrongly accused of cheating on a test when we did not. Guilt and shame are also painful. Embarrassment and the fear of embarrassment are quite unpleasant. The pain of remorse and regret can deliver the additional pain of anguish. Rage and hatred are infamous for the pain they create and can be very unpleasant.

Given a choice of pain or pleasure, we easily choose pleasure. There are exceptions to this—for example, when a significant pleasurable reward is involved, like the marathon runner who struggles for hours in pain to complete the race, then experiences a form of ecstasy and profound pleasure at its conclusion. Or, when we learn a difficult but desired skill under the scrutiny of a perfectionist and, at times, tough taskmaster. We may experience pain from the criticism and critiquing, but the gain in capability and new skills make it worth it.

Not surprisingly, the duration of pain is much longer than that of pleasure. We can sometimes hold pain indefinitely, keeping it bottled up to re-experience again and again. It can even survive a lifetime if we never face it, understand it, and then solve the situation that created it. In contrast, we hold pleasure only for a brief time; it comes and then passes. The pleasures of thrills are even more fleeting, lasting only a few seconds. Although we can recall and reminisce pleasurable memories and emotions, in a sense reliving them, the positive and pleasurable effects do not last very long. Our pain and pleasure systems are very different with respect to how long they can last. Why?

Pain or unpleasantness often surfaces when we are stopped in our tracks by something that is not working or when something happens we do not like. We say, "I don't like it. I hate it. Why did this happen?" This type of pain arrives as disappointment or frustration. We may feel bewilderment, uncertainty, or confusion when we do not know how to proceed. Normally, after our initial frustration subsides, we figure out a new way to succeed, or we get professional advice or consultation. If we are not successful and fail to complete what we set out to accomplish, but then we do not analyze, try to improve it, or get new learning or advice, we will not develop any new ability to handle it better the next time. If we do not progress by understanding and mastering the situation, we continue to hold onto the painful situation, with its obstruction and our limitation, and we re-experience its pain or unpleasantness every time we think of it or experience something similar.

Solutions to Pain-Creating Situations

The solution for these and countless other pain-creating situations can be found in the following principle or truth: The things that we are uncertain about and do not know how to handle, that give us pain, and that we encounter often and think about—if we do not master them, they will eventually chase us down and narrow our life. If you keep avoiding public speaking or leading group discussions, and your job requires it, you will not be effective. Instead, you will be fearful and unconfident and have to give that particular job up, or else be removed by company management. If you avoid going out in public, you will become more and more reclusive. If you avoid doing things with friends, you will have fewer and fewer friends and will end up alone. Essentially, the longer we avoid handling the full weight of the pain-evoking situations in all its myriad forms, the more they obstruct our pleasant life. By not facing these painful situations, they continue to pile up, and we keep bumping into them. The only answer for good, quality function is to stand and master the situation. If we do this by creating unique solutions to each pain-producing situation, the pain is automatically released and we move on more capable than before, confirming the psychological truth that pain is the pointer to truth undiscovered and capability not yet developed. So, discover the underlying functional truth, the actual ingredients of the encountered situation and the truth of your emotional response, and then use these messages to think of a better solution. This is the capability you need to develop if you are to become master of the situation.

Gain and Mastery

It would seem that our mind is hardwired for gain and mastery. In all likelihood, this hardwiring is a result of eons of facing and overcoming problems that led to safety, survival, accomplishment, and satisfaction. While the obstructions and problems of pre-gain and pre-mastery are many times painful and unpleasant, it does no good to avoid them. Think of it this way: the next time you are faced with a painful or unpleasant task or experience, remember it is a pre-mastery message. For instance, if you have been asked to teach a class, yet you doubt your abilities, lack confidence, and feel anxious, nonetheless prepare and go through the experience. Do this several times, and it will become far easier; your skill and confidence will obviously increase. By facing the message, you ultimately gain and master. Conversely, by avoiding it you create greater pain and unpleasantness. The fact remains: master you will and master you must, if you want to handle life well.

Meaning of Pleasure

We really cannot speak of the meaning of pain and unpleasantness as pre-mastery signals without mentioning the role of pleasure. Though pain means we have a situation to handle or master, pleasure means we are capable and our capabilities are growing. With the exception of entertainment or pleasurable sensations, such as a tasty dessert, much of pleasure is the result of accomplishment. From our accomplishments we gain satisfaction and fulfillment, two important elements for healthy and successful living. The truth is, pleasure comes as a result of mastering a situation or problem by using our repertoire of life-handling abilities. Pleasure is a by-product of good quality accomplishing movement in life. By developing mastery skill and learning well from experience, the frequency and amount of pleasure we can have will increase.

The Mistake of Seeing Pain as Bad and Pleasure as Good

One mistake people make is seeing pain as bad or negative and pleasure as good or positive. This misconception makes us reluctant to tackle new learning and masterable situations. Which pains are suggesting that you master new skills? Pain and pleasure are both positive and directing signals; find their meaning, find their truth, and then proceed with conviction in the best way possible. Thankfully, we have pain to bring light to our unseen, unmastered areas.

As soon as we master a situation, we develop new confidence and capability to handle similar situations. I am sure we can all recall a task or problem that gave us great frustration until we mastered it. The card game of Bridge is one good example. Almost without exception, the game's complexity frustrates and defeats beginners until they gain experience and mastery. When they obtain mastery, the game becomes greatly satisfying and adds to their repertoire of accomplishment and pleasure. Furthermore, the new mastery of previous pain-signaling situations allows us to explore or enter new realms, realms that had been previously closed to us through our avoiding the great gatekeeper of pain.

Opportunities for Mastery

There are emotional or motivational obstructions that can cause pain. Each of these potentially difficult situations is really an opportunity for mastery. If we will look at pain as a pointer to truth undiscovered, and capability not yet developed, we will be less intimidated or obstructed when these pains occur, and with time, more experience, and improving technique, we will see them as opportunities.

Here is an example of how this applies. Consider a time when our progress or movement is stopped by a situation which truly obstructs us, such as a missing file that is important to completing the project. In this instance, the pain—anger, frustration, fear, or disappointment—is initially evoked from discovering that the file is missing. Most important, however, is the full truth of the situation that there is a problem to fix, and there is a best way to fix it. When we look at the situation more totally, we are able to see a fuller solution and not just be upset. When we analyze the problem, we realize we already know the situational truth that something needs to be fixed. When we just react with the emotions, it blinds us for a while from correcting the situation. For this kind of pain-causing problem, the solution is to think fuller, discover, and then strategize anew and handle the problem. If the file is never found, the project could be reanalyzed, new data could be developed, and the project would go forward.

Another example is a team sport where you, as the captain or coach, called a play that didn't work, and it lost you the game. You can either anguish about the loss, or you can analyze why that particular play didn't work and then modify it so it might work if you tried it in a future situation.

There was the artist who could not mix exactly the color she wanted to paint onto the canvas. She wisely went to an art store and selected the right variation of red that would work in the canvas. Rather than remain frustrated and continuing to mix, she sought the right color and found it by searching at the art store. The pain of frustration left and was replaced by the satisfaction of knowing she now had the right color.

Also take the example of a scout master out for a twelve-mile hike with a group of boys. Instead of constantly being frustrated and irritated at two or three stragglers who didn't modify their actions after encouragement, he inquired as to why they were going so slowly. He found out the reasons: the stragglers were emotionally upset with other troop members for teasing them. He called a meeting, and they all heard each other and talked about their feelings. Everyone felt more understood, and from that point on, the stragglers quit straggling and joined the main group.

The Pain of Fighting against an Unwanted Truth or Reality That Has Already Happened

Another kind of pain reoccurs when we know truthfully that something unwanted has occurred, such as our airplane flight being delayed, yet we do not like it and so continue to complain and hate it rather than accept the new reality. When we fight against a truth that has already happened with an emotional response such as, "I know it happened, but I hate it," we recreate the initial pain and dilemma we first experienced. In essence, we create a vicious cycle that brings us back to the beginning again and again, and we avoid the peace that acceptance or acknowledgement brings. Further, the longer we spend our energy and effort on hating it rather than accepting it and turning our effort to making new adjustments in our plans or strategies, the more inefficient we become, and the good solutions may elude us. Every time we fight the truth, we bring back the pain.

Though this seems logical and simple, aligning ourselves with reality is much harder when we're emotionally involved, wanting a different outcome. Remember that when preference and reality collide, reality always wins. If we use this more comprehensive logic and repeat it to ourselves, we will conquer these problems. The sooner we admit we are fighting truth and reality, the sooner we let go and the quicker our pain goes away. The best way to function is to acknowledge the truth and align ourselves with it, then attempt to succeed with different or improved strategies. When we do this enough times, it will become second nature and we will have gained in capability. We can add to the general psychological truth that "Pain is a pointer to a truth undiscovered, a truth not used if known, or a truth fought against or violated."

Pain from an Obstruction We Lack the Expertise to Handle

We can experience emotional pain evoked when we are blocked in a situation and do not have the expertise to handle it—we are not up to the task or we do not have sufficient capability. The emotions we usually experience are frustration, resignation, confusion, and bewilderment. For instance, if we have information access problems or communication problems in our business, we may need a computer program consultant to provide new software to solve the problem. The general answer for eliminating these types of problems (pains) is to get help. Though many of us are reluctant to seek help, there are many situations where it is absolutely necessary if we are to move forward. Getting help could come in the form of more education or a consultation with a professional or expert. With some assistance, we often become sufficiently able to handle the task ourselves. However, there are times we need expert help from an attorney, doctor, accountant, colleague, or a wise person when the problem is beyond our capability. We need to allow ourselves the option of relying on these experts to do it for us.

For another example, consider tax return preparation. The tax laws are so complex and voluminous that it often pays for us to get expert help. In this case mastery comes by managing and applying the skill of experts on your behalf. When you do, the pain goes away and the problem is solved.

Pain from Taking a Stand against What Will Likely Occur

Another type of pain comes from taking a narrow psychological stance. Instead of greeting whatever comes willingly and evaluating it realistically, we may instead try to ward something off by daring it to happen: "It had better not happen, or I will hate it," or "If that happens, it will ruin my day." This approach gives us too narrow a viewpoint and sets us up automatically for pain and defeat. For instance, a harried doctor being called for more emergency treatments than is usual gets frustrated, feels angry and pressured, and blurts out, "I'd better not get another call. This is too much, I've had it!" When the next call comes, as it inevitably does, he blows up and requires five minutes to calm himself. How much easier it would have been to acknowledge the extra busy day, accept the calls with humor, and even say something such as, "Today is really busy. I am going to keep track of the number of calls and see if I set a new personal record."

This could also play out when a young mother with toddlers says, "Nothing else had better happen!" after her oldest child skins his knee and requires first aid. Then her second child trips and bumps his head, causing a skin tear that requires stitches. Instead of being frustrated and angry, as she would have been in the past, she accepts the problem mentally and soothes her youngest child before taking him to the doctor.

The Pain of the Pessimistic Stance

Pessimists are people who believe, "It will never work out." Those who often have calamity think, "Oh no! All is lost! What will I do?" They create and suffer this self-defeating fear and discomfort frequently and needlessly. I suspect each of us has experienced this type of pain at one time or another. Pessimists often perceive themselves as victims and use phrases like:

- Poor me.
- I am always helpless.
- Nobody likes me any way.
- Why does this always happen to me?

These people presuppose and predict this type of pain. They suffer greatly but seldom acknowledge the truth so that it can assist them.

Unfortunately, they prevent the useful technique of acknowledging the truth from coming to their assistance or rescue. Stances that predict pain and suffering are self-fulfilling prophesies. They key to stopping them is to notice our self-talk. If we hear constricting statements that prevent our acceptance of what is forthcoming, we are most assuredly in a narrow stance, ready to mentally fight against what might happen. The only answer is to drop the narrow stance and replace it with a more open, accepting, come-what-may stance. It takes practice, but as we do it we will become more comfortable and adept at accepting what occurs in both the present and future. We will feel better because our repertoire, our capacity for handling what occurs, improves as we accept all of the possible realities of what can occur.

Long-Term Pains

There are other long-term or chronic psychological pains dealt with in chapter 17; these include the pains of guilt, remorse, regret, and psychological depression. Long-term pains are formed out of self-deceptive beliefs that become presumed causes of unwanted things that happen out of our control. As we empower these beliefs, particularly if we assume responsibility as being the cause when we are not responsible, we hold long-term pain and punish ourselves needlessly. I have seen this happen often when a parent, hurt and disappointed about a wayward child's activities, tends to blame him or herself for the adolescent's problem, as if it was the parent's fault. "Where or how did I fail?" the parent laments over things the child has been doing illicitly and for his or her own personal reasons.

Pain of Mental Pressure and Personal Stress

Another major type of pain is mental pressure and personal stress, covered in chapter 1. When we switch our motivational thoughts from the reality and the truth of how we accomplish tasks into the crucial, absolute type of thoughts, and when we attempt to force the desired result, we create the pain of mental pressure. Our inner mind is keenly attuned to logic and truth, and when we depart from it, we create mental pressure and stress.

When we are able to identify the kinds of pain and unpleasant emotional experiences we are having, and we are familiar with the structure and the nature of each type of pain, we can quickly analyze each pain's ingredients and provide a curative solution that reduces the pain's duration while mastering the situation. From that time on we will no longer experience pain or obstruction from similar situations. This takes a few repeats to learn, but mastery and peace of mind is the result.

A Great Example of Increased Competence

Recently a close friend shared an enlightening work experience with me. After years of exploring with me the ideas contained in this book, he had an opportunity to use the increased capability he had developed to help a client.

It seems that a highly valued individual in a public position at her corporation was about to renew her work contract. Although she enjoyed her position and did not want to consider other options, she faced a significant problem that needed to be addressed. She consulted my friend, frantically explaining the dilemma that was generating her distress—and to a large extent, impairing her ability to think clearly about her options. In less than two hours she was scheduled to go into a contract negotiating session, and she felt overwhelmed with worry and fear. The simple truth was, she didn't want to work with her partner any longer; she absolutely hated doing so. She also wanted more money and felt her request for a raise was justified. Prior to talking to my friend, she determined there were no other comparable and local positions available in her field. She loved her work except for her ongoing irritation about the partner; they made a successful team, but still she no longer wanted to work with him. "I don't know what to do," she frantically told my friend. "How will I handle this? I just can't work with him!" she exclaimed. Her emotions were running high, and she was getting visibly more anxious as the time neared for her contract negotiation.

My friend quickly sorted the elements of the situation into what was possible and what was not—what was required and what was optional and negotiable. Next, he asked her to observe the emotional reactions that overcame and blinded her logic. "Can you get out of the contract?"

"No," she replied, "I can't. There is nothing else available. If I could I would, but I can't get out of it. I hate the situation I'm in!"

He wisely showed her that she was fighting reality, instead of accepting it and going with it. There was no other option or recourse if she was to continue with the company, regardless of how much she disliked working with her partner. "So," he advised, "quit fighting that reality. Quit hating it, because it will only give you pain and confusion." Reluctantly she agreed. He told her it was okay to acknowledge her hate because it was true. But in spite of her hating it, she had to continue with the contract if she chose to work. That dose of the truth of that reality, and her acknowledging it, settled her down. "So," he said, "make a choice. Do you want to work or not?"

"Yes, yes I do," she offered plaintively, but now she was resigned. "I accept that. I acknowledge that I hate it, but nonetheless if I want to continue to work in the field, at this time and in this place, I must continue with the contract. I can't get out of it, though I could ask for a raise in pay."

Next, my friend dealt with her wish to work with someone else, suggesting this was something she could try to negotiate at a later date. For now she had to live with her current contract, though she had good reason to ask for more money. He reminded her that her partnership with her coworker was viewed in a positive light by both customers and fellow workers; she could use this popularity as a bargaining point.

Trying to understand her opposition, he asked, "Why is it that you hate working with this fellow?" She explained that he had some quirks and personality characteristics that bugged her. As she explained, he could see that she was getting all riled up just talking about the prospect of continuing to work with him.

He told her, "It's obvious that you are giving your power away to something you can't control. You are letting his mannerisms get to you." She stopped, took several deep breaths, and agreed. Calmed and more clearheaded, she described her intended salary negotiation strategies and what result she hoped for. He suggested how to present them, when to pause and wait rather than anxiously rushing in with her figures. She saw the wisdom of not putting everything on the table initially. For the first time in a week, she felt back in control. The consultation had lasted only twenty minutes.

My friend was pleased at his ability to help. He told me, "In just twenty minutes she went from frantic to calm and collected. In just twenty minutes she was reoriented to strength and clarity. By offering a viewpoint unclouded by crucial and absolute thinking, she quickly saw the truth and the reality, and she went into her meeting emotionally stabilized and confident."

Workplace Competence Using the Emotional Alphabet: A Comparison of Two Methods

Compare the two workplace examples below: the problems faced by two project managers are dealt with in different ways. Whose method of problem solving do you prefer? With whom would you rather work?

Bill and John both work for a large national construction company. Bill's project is a condominium conversion, changing a large apartment building into individual condominiums that can be sold. The building requires some slight remodeling and updating of plumbing and appliances.

There is a schedule to meet. Bill finds that the plumbing company he hired has a problem with another job, which delays them completing the work for the condominium project. He blows up. "How can you do this to us?" he yells, gesturing wildly and pacing. Then he demands from his two assistants, "Fix it!" His actions disturb everyone within earshot, and it takes him twenty minutes to calm down. Bill feels embarrassed after his display and apologizes. He probably lost a little respect, but he is a good project manager. Soon he and his assistants arrange for other plumbing groups to complete the job on time. Even so, when the CEO of Bill's company wants to fill a higher management position, he will probably look elsewhere.

John heads a hotel redecorating project for the same company. He finds that a major supplier has created a delay in getting the rugs for the hallways. Briefly surprised and bothered, he starts to get angry but realizes that solving the problem is the important thing. He understands that exploding with anger will not help anything and will probably make finding a solution more difficult. He also knows he does not want to carry an angry, emotional charge around within him. He quickly recognizes that he is being obstructed by the problem and understands it needs a solution. Because he felt a brief initial stirring of anger and frustration, he sighs and releases it with a deep breath. He takes a few quiet moments to comprehend, acknowledge, and accept the problem, and then he evaluates possible alternatives for a solution. By doing this, John's anger dissipates and disappears. He quickly assigns his assistants to do a cause-and-effect analysis, and then he sets a meeting for 10:00 a.m. the next day to discuss what they have discovered, brainstorm ideas, and then implement solution strategies. His assistants, coworkers, and superiors observe how he handles the problem and respect his work. He has exhibited good leadership abilities and has demonstrated a noticeable sense of self-command. He will probably get the higher management position when it opens up.

The Big Unwanted Happenings, Tragedies, and Catastrophes

Tragic or catastrophic events evoke tremendous emotional and psychological pain. Although profound in nature, the strategies and techniques needed to face this pain successfully are fundamentally the same as other situations we have already discussed. The emotional impact created by the death of a loved one, the breakup of a family through divorce, a severe injury to a family member, a job loss or a major business failure—all are deeply troubling and intense emotionally, and the pain can potentially be long lasting. The emotions we feel are confusing and conflicting; we might feel hurt, fear, uncertainty, sadness, and disorientation, and we might feel them simultaneously or in a series, one coming atop the next. In many situations, this flood of emotions overwhelms and stuns us psychologically.

Because of the importance and long-term effects of such devastating situations, they require significant time and effort for the process of grieving and the various elements of loss, including the "future together" that will now never happen. For example, if your spouse suddenly and unexpectedly dies, you will never retire together to the cottage on the beach that was a part of your future dreams; you will not grow old together. It will take time and effort to accept and revise your future expectations. Tragic or catastrophic events often require reworking the plan of your future expectations. Also, you must assess and evaluate what are the replacements for the very important talents and functions that the loss created. Even so, when you acknowledge the truth of what has occurred, if only for a brief moment, your mind goes into neutral and is momentarily free of pain. However, the enormity of the unwanted happening and its effect on the current structure and functioning of your life brings back the multiple pains and uncertainties that you will need to deal with to get your life fully back on track.

Here is something you can say to handle these situations: "Hard as it is to accept this unwanted circumstance, it really did occur; it is the truth." After you make this truth acknowledgement, then of course the emotions of hurt and loss can flow freely—and they should, if you feel them. You must grieve these more severe circumstances and their effect on your life—unwanted loss, sadness, hurt, rage, disbelief, briefly feeling sorry for yourself, and even feeling victimized. The grieving process over large losses can go many months, off and on. Periodically repeat to yourself that it has truly occurred and that you acknowledge the truth, regardless of it being unwanted. Say to yourself, "Nevertheless, it is the truth." You will feel the momentary neutrality of truth, the lack of pain.

I advise my patients in these circumstances to keep moving every few hours, mentally giving attention to purposeful, responsible work (such as parenting), and then have reflective time alone, followed by support time with friends, confidants, or therapists with whom they discuss the effects of the loss. I tell them to enjoy entertainment and lighthearted laughing with friends, and not to get frozen in only one type of activity. I advise them to move among the possibilities, staying in one for only four hours on average (except for work, if required to provide a longer time).

Eventually through the use of the principles of our pain and pleasure alignment system, the specific truth messages of our emotions; and the development of new or replacement structures and strategies—perhaps new relationships or new opportunities—we handle and eventually master these tragic circumstances. Through the use of these capabilities, our life goes on. These large and complex circumstances, often the stuff of psychotherapy, are beyond the scope of this book, but they are mentioned here briefly to show the momentary absence of pain when the truth of what has occurred is acknowledged, and how ultimately for full adjustment to be made, the truth of the actually reality must be fully realized and accepted.

Removing the Pain of Emotions: Creating Greater Self-Capability

Modern life is filled with situations and problems that cause painful emotional reactions. We experience them almost daily, and each has the potential to derail our short-term progress and even threaten our long-term peace of mind. We are wise to develop powerful methods to handle our emotional reactions and our own situations, or others' with whom we are concerned. For instance, we can experience painful emotions when a person we are close to is having problems or doing wrong things that are leading him or her to disaster. We can help to an extent, but if we worry too much or try too hard to help, we create too much frustration for ourselves. The person in question whom we are concerning ourselves with must ultimately choose his or her life path and live with the consequences. It is wise to remember the true objective of our emotions, even if painful or uncomfortable. First they alert us, and then they cue us to offer the proper response. Here are some innovative ways to handle some of the most frequent yet problematic pain-producing emotional reactions we experience. The solutions offered here teach new problem-solving methods and will help you build new strategies for handling your emotions.

How to Handle Anger

Anger impacts each of us. There are many causative factors for the emotion of anger, and in our fast-paced, goal-oriented world there is ample opportunity for it to surface and create pain. An operational definition of anger is a surprise signal to a perceived obstruction in our path, to our movement, to our current, smooth, and ongoing pattern or sequence. Something has stopped us. We all know the feeling, for example, of being involved in a project to fix something around the house, when halfway to completion we suddenly realize we do not have the right tool or materials to finish the job; the instant response is irritating anger. Another example is when we are driving, and someone cuts in front of us, forcing us to brake in order to avoid a collision; we are first startled and then angry. The best way to handle these vexing situations is to shift from the anger as soon as we are able and attempt to understand the situation. Take a brief moment to observe and analyze, sizing up the nature of the impediment, interruption, or obstruction. Review the smooth pattern of movement we were in just before the anger. Devise a way to either get the pattern back, change direction or approach, or drop the goal altogether for the time being and choose something else. In the first example, accept the truth and go get the tool. In the second, understand, keep cool to stay safe, accept the situation, and drive on. Do not stay angry and start cussing or chasing the other driver down because that does not solve anything. Those tactics will only inappropriately command your attention, making you a less than safe driver.

As you learn to handle anger-evoking situations in this manner, you will find that eventually you will not experience anger for more than a second or two, and perhaps not at all, as you gain experience at this. At first, however, it is important to know you are angry, to even feel it in your mind and body so that you can discharge its power rather than suppress it and pile it up. Piling up your anger before learning to understand it is not healthy, but discharging it destructively is unwise also (hurting others, losing control, making inappropriate statements, etc.). So discharge it nondestructively. One method is to blow all your air out forcefully, and then try blowing out once or twice more without taking in a new breath. You may find the anger charge is gone. Another method is to forcefully but silently scream or yell while looking upward or while looking into a mirror. These techniques remove the anger charge in your body. You don't want to suppress the charge because it is unhealthy, but you don't want to be unpleasant to others or engage in an enraged tirade. The mere fact that you recognize you are angry and are wisely discharging it so you can think clearly has already given you a measure of control you may not have had before. You can analyze the situation in a more cool-headed fashion and accept the truth: that the obstruction you got angry about really did occur. Then you can best figure out how to handle the situation, learn from it, and improve the possibilities for not being further obstructed and recurrently angry over similar situations. You will be on your way to developing new capability that will serve you well in the future, when you find yourself in situations you previously got angry about and never advanced past them. After a few of these experiences, you will probably notice your initial anger charge will be less, and your ability to understand your situation and decide upon a course of action will happen faster. Soon your ability at understanding will be so good that it will replace the anger almost instantaneously—and you will have a great new tool at your command.

Here's another example of how to handle the anger that comes from not liking an outcome and not accepting the result. When the anger is caused by fighting against the unwanted reality, the "I hate it when I put in all that effort and don't succeed" response, then you must acknowledge the truth of what happened to clear it. Do not fight the reality of the situation; we must acknowledge and accept it, and then the anger will subside and disappear. Then we should plan to make a better attempt with better tactics next time.

How to Handle Guilt

Feelings of guilt are known for causing nagging and unsettled turmoil within us, but these same feelings also carry important messages that we'd best not ignore. I like to define guilt this way: an elastic stretch signal that comes when we are considering breaking, violating, transgressing, or stretching a previous agreement (or considering doing so) with a person or a principle. Guilt happens when we are thinking of *doing differently* with something important, like changing or not adhering to a code of behavior, or a promise we agreed to, accepted, and adhered to in the past. For instance, if a job opportunity comes up in a distant city, you might feel guilty at the idea of moving and leaving your aging parents, though it could be the best thing for your career. So what do you do? The important agreement made in the past could be to a person (parents) or to a principle (honoring the parents and caring for them), and you are presently thinking of doing something contradictory or different. The feeling of guilt is the result. Most people quietly let the elastic snap them back to the old agreement, using it as a control mechanism: "I must stay and help out. I can't take the new job." Others rebel, get angry, and talk disparagingly about the former agreement: "Why do I have to stay and help out? It's controlling my life." Sometimes we even punish ourselves to alleviate the condemnation of guilt: "I am an ungrateful son (or daughter) for thinking of moving. I am not a very good person. I don't deserve a vacation, or that new car I was thinking about."

Why not do this instead? Let guilt help us discover the nature of the prior agreement and then evaluate its merit. If it still makes sense to continue and uphold our agreement, then reaffirm and rejoin it through a conscious and rational decision-making process. "I don't need the other job. Family is my most important value. It's worth it. I will stay." If instead the old agreement no longer makes sense to you, cut the stretching elastic, and make new decisions about that specific old agreement, choosing instead something more effective, useful, and practical for this time in life. "I can hire people to help my parents, and I'll fly back and visit at times and call to check on them. If I pass up this opportunity, it will affect my career too much. Besides, my parents would give me the go-ahead to move. They are proud of me and would feel guilty themselves if I stayed."

How to Handle Confusion

We have all experienced confusion. Confusion is the disarming experience of being suddenly consciously aware of not knowing what something is or how it works, causing us to feel momentarily overwhelmed by our lack of understanding. We all have experienced a modicum of confusion when faced with complex written instructions, or when we find ourselves in a totally new or unfamiliar situation or environment. I found in medical school that when I changed services—from medicine to surgery for instance—the procedures and types of care were different, and so were the routines. I always felt uncertainty and confusion for a day or two, but I found if I asked nurses, interns, and residents questions and devoted extra time and effort, I would be tuned in within days, able to handle the new tasks and routines, and no longer be confused. In order to avoid or clear any confusion that arises, it is important at the onset of any new endeavor to examine, explore, and learn the fundamentals about it first. Try picking the situation apart to discover its components or ingredients. This process of discovery nullifies the negative impact of confusion and helps clarify the true nature of what created it in the first place. Remember that confusion disappears as clarity is gained.

How to Handle Fear

Perhaps the most frequent and debilitating pain-producing emotional reactions is fear. Fear is a "gap" signal about danger sensed, combined with an element of immediate future uncertainty. There is a gap between where you are currently (in danger and afraid) and where you want to be (safe and away from the danger). An example is the fear some cross-country skiers experience when they realize they have strayed into a high-risk avalanche area. They want to be safe and avoid further risk, so they can retrace their exact path, keeping one or two hundred yards apart but remaining visible as they make their way back to safety. Careful evaluation and then a best course of action is the solution. Another common experience of fear occurs when the desired aim we wish for is in jeopardy because we sense there is a real possibility we will not succeed, such as when we apply for acceptance into a graduate or professional school, or we try for a job that has many applicants.

For the above examples and for the vast majority of fear-causing situations, the secret to disarming the pain response is to extract its true meaning and then take an objective look. We need to ask ourselves, What is the best way to jump the gap to safety or to reach the accomplishment we seek? Is it something we need to apply immediately (getting out of the avalanche zone) to remedy the situation? Do we need help or training or more assistance when it comes to reaching the accomplishment? If the answer is yes, then the solution is simple: obtain the help or assistance. Many times the best solution is to leave a particular troubling situation alone, to just let it be. Other times we may decide to stand and fight. Still other times we need to give it our best and then accept the consequences, as in trying to reach for an accomplishment. It does no good to worry and be constantly fearful. No one succeeds every time, but getting bogged down or swamped in fear, at the edge of the gap, never works. Wise action or waiting patiently, the product of our best judgment, is the appropriate route to take.

How to Handle Resentment

Resentment occurs when we react to a situation with anger or annoyed feelings about an outcome that is different from the one we desire. It arrives when we harbor ill will toward others because of how they affected an unwanted outcome, as when one of our basketball team members throws an errant pass that costs us the game. It can also occur when we have envy or even jealousy for something someone else has that we desire, such as a successful career, a new house, or some expensive possession. In the first case, the best use of this painful emotional response is to evaluate how the outcome occurred (e.g., the errant pass), and whether or not you had (or could have had) an influence over the outcome. If not, accept the reality that people make mistakes, and the team member's bad pass was only that. Use it to learn and perhaps construct another outcome in the future.

In the second instance, if resentment is directed toward other people for what they have that we do not, especially if we also have envy or jealousy, then it is best to explore our feelings to see if we want to attempt obtaining similar possessions or successes. Use the feeling of resentment as an indicator pointing in the direction of what we want. Then, if it is worth it and we are able, obtain something similar. One requirement is that we must be realistic and in tune with truth. We all might want a one-hundred-foot ocean yacht, like the admired billionaire, but it is better to acknowledge reality and let that one go. If we harbor resentment, envy, or jealousy we give ourselves a lasting pain that leads nowhere—except to ongoing unpleasantness, greater resentment, and feeling disadvantaged.

How to Handle Regret

The painful emotional response of regret relates to a former experience we had concerning our behavior that we wish we had done differently. For example, "I wish I had invested in that company's stock ten years ago. I would be a millionaire. I had an opportunity, and I regret not taking it." Or, "I wish I had been a better father (or mother). I should have been more involved. If I could only do it over again, I would do it differently. I regret it so much." In these instances, the moment of regret calls our attention to something which we truly could have done better. If possible, apologize and attempt to do differently. If this is no longer an option, we can do best by using the experience as a guide to help us to act more wisely in the future. Regret teaches us to do differently, not wallow in "if only" statements. Remember, apologize for the past and fix the present and future.

Also, we may falsely regret we did not do something different in the past because of how it now has turned out—yet we gave it our best attempt back then. It is only now with different knowledge that we retrospectively (but wrongly) regret it. We did not have our present knowledge, so we gave it our best based on our knowledge then; we would still make the same decision if we did not have knowledge of the new information and outcome. In those situations there is no room for regret. By the way, that is the reason for always making your best decisions and doing the best you can: so there is no room for future regret, only future learning.

How to Handle Disappointment

Disappointment, a compound emotion, is a combination of mild anger and sadness about an expectation (something hoped or planned for) that did not occur. We are all disappointed that we did not win the lottery or that the romantic relationship we really wanted to work ended unsatisfactorily. The strategy to disarm disappointment is to realize the truth: the desired outcome did not occur. Accept reality and make a decision of how to proceed next. We can decide to try again, to improve our tactics, or to set up a new and different potentially rewarding situation. When we stay in feelings of disappointment other than momentarily, we are stubbornly resisting the fullness of its message. We miss that we are fighting the truth, holding onto the wished-for result, and being angry and sad about it. We need to recognize, acknowledge, and release each feeling along with the missed outcome to clear disappointment.

How to Handle Anxiety

Anxiety is what I refer to as frightening uncertainty about a quality of life issue; another term is apprehension. It originates in our subconscious mind and warns us there is a threat to our quality of life on some particular thing that is at risk. We all have preferences for how we want things to be, whether we know it or not. Preferences reside in both our conscious and subconscious mind, stimulating hope and vying for successful outcomes or the continuation of what we like, what is comfortable. When a preferred outcome or continuation of something we perceive to be very important to our quality of life is threatened, we feel the pain of anxiety. We are concerned about whether or not we will be able to have it or keep having it. The pain of anxiety is a warning, a wake-up call usually from our subconscious mind, so that we can rally and do our best to retain or bring about our preference if possible. But there are no guarantees. For example, we hope our company will get the next lucrative contract from a company with whom we have done previous successful business. However, this time there is a new company in the bidding, and they are fiercely competitive. Which company wins of course affects us differently. When we do not get what we perceive to be important, maybe even essential to our quality of life, it is wise to adjust our thinking, accept the result, and make the best of it. After all, we are more than our specific preferences. All is not lost. On the other hand, if we succeed in keeping or obtaining our preference (the contract), we feel successful and happy. In either instance, if we tell ourselves we desire a certain preference and will do our best to bring it about, but in the end we are willing to take whatever happens, our anxiety will diminish. Even if we lose the desirable contract, we can find other work; the warning pain of anxiety will have served its purpose, and we will be prepared to handle the immediate future in the best way possible. In the example of the contract, anxiety will help us and our company prepare the best possible offer we can. When we accept the possibility of all outcomes, we can adjust if we lose our preference. We can accept the truth, make the best of it, and go on living. For example, when we have a tax audit, we usually get anxiety. We can use that anxiety to help us prepare most fully ahead of time to go through the audit. We can do the same when experiencing normal anxiety about taking tests.

How to Handle Panic

Panic is a special form of anxiety that arrives unexpectedly in a circumstance where we feel overwhelmed psychologically and believe we will be unable to function. We feel defenseless and vulnerable. Our heart pounds rapidly from the adrenalin release in our body, and we are alarmed and scared. We don't know what is happening. We may think we are dying, having a heart attack, or having a stroke. In my work with patients, the belief that underlies panic at its deepest level is the fear of losing our psychological identity, our sense of being and self, our self as an entity. What causes such a catastrophic reaction?

Panic exposes an unresolved dependency upon something or someone on whom we have been relying. Further, we believe we need that reliance to keep from being totally helpless. When a circumstance threatens that dependency or actually removes what or whom we have been depending upon, we panic. The panic generally causes us to cast frantically about, looking and hoping for rescue from our dilemma. Disconcerting and frightening as it is, panic nevertheless has a value. It reveals exactly what our weakness is and points to the area of our life where we are vulnerable and need to grow some strength so that we can stand on our own.

This happens, for instance, when a love relationship breaks up, leaving us feeling lonely and lost. We feel hurt, helpless, and very sad. If we have been depending too much on the relationship, we will feel unsure how to proceed and handle life. We will think that we are nothing without the relationship (i.e., that we are losing our identity). Then we panic. If, on the other hand, we have had a more healthy relationship of mutual give and take, without a crippling dependency, we know that we will be able to go on. We realize we will eventually form a new fulfilling relationship after we have gotten over the current breakup.

There is a primitive precursor to panic that comes from an earlier time in life. In later infancy and early childhood, the fear of abandonment can evoke episodes of frightening uncertainty generally called separation anxiety. Later, the fear of being lost or actually getting lost can evoke fear and panic in a young child. I had an adolescent patient who could still recall the panic and terror of being lost at Disneyland for over an hour when he somehow got separated from his parents. The separation anxiety and fears of being lost help to protect a young child by keeping him or her close enough to parents or family to remain safe. A young child cannot well fend for him or herself. The child's true need and vulnerability, immaturity, and actual lack of capability, puts him or her at risk for harm or loss of life if lost or abandoned. The fear of death and the fear of being helpless to handle life are real issues in such situations. These early innate safety reflexes can be evoked in later life and can be experienced as panic when we feel overwhelmed and helpless psychologically. The good news is that we are not young children and will not die from the situation. Sometimes we merely need to reorient our thinking to handle the panic-provoking situation. Other times we may need to develop some new life-handling skills to replace the dependency that keeps us feeling weak and helpless.

Panic is often subjectively experienced as one of several catastrophic physical fears, such as the fear of dying, the fear of having a heart attack, or the fear of having a stroke. It can also be experienced as a psychological catastrophe, such as the fear of losing control, or the fear of losing our mind. Though panic has a strong physical element from the adrenaline outpouring—a rapid and loud pounding of our heart—its initial cause is psychological.

If and when you suddenly experience panic, take a moment to reassure yourself that you will not die, lose your mind, or have a stroke, and that you are not totally helpless. Say to yourself, "It's just a panic attack and will go away." After it subsides, observe, examine, and analyze the source of the panic. When we pinpoint a cause, we can then learn to identify the panic-provoking situation in advance, stopping it before it occurs or handling it better when it does strike. Panic will always tell us, even if obscurely, what it is about, and it offers us an opportunity to develop sufficient strength or strategies to avoid it in the future. Tell yourself, "I will not lose my identity or life." Our best answer or strategy is to reorient our thinking from panicking to comprehending and understanding our situation in a realistic and truthful way. Talk to yourself out loud if necessary. In cases where comprehending and understanding alone do not make the panic subside, the development of new capability or new understanding, and possibly medication, will be required. Consult with a doctor if panic persists.

How to Handle Subconscious Chronic Anger

Subconscious chronic anger, which has been suppressed and repressed into deeper layers of our mind, can explode and spew forth like lava from a sudden volcanic eruption. Jim is stewing about his marital situation, which is not going well. He becomes progressively more angry at the overall effect on his life. He has been holding this in when a coworker criticizes his performance on a small matter, and he explodes, yelling and swearing at her. It is clearly an overreaction, much more than the situation warranted. The person whose subconscious anger is erupting is experiencing the effects of the unsolved prior obstructions—in this instance, the marital problems and probably other things as well. The old anger hitches a ride on a new anger, causing obstructive situations, heightening the anger blast, and creating a much worse situation. This pressured anger response is evidence of an underlying, unresolved problem or circumstance. It has piled up from many old obstructions that we failed to properly deal with when they originally arose, and it is now being ignited by a new and current obstruction.

It certainly behooves us to deal with each anger-causing situation fully when it initially arises, to avoid piling it up and erupting in the future. Recall the methods I suggest. Notice the anger and then the obstruction that caused it. Discharge the anger charge nondestructively if you feel it surging through your body—silent yelling, yelling upward, snarling at a mirror. Then analyze the situation and figure out a best solution to avoid the build-up of anger. If you see yourself in this situation, and you are not easily able to discover what is at the source of your anger, obtain some professional help in the form of psychotherapy, which will allow you to discover the sources as well as release you from the grip of subconscious anger.

Use of the Truth of Our Pain-Pleasure Alignment System for Continuous Increase of Capability

As we become better at defining and using the situational truths behind our emotions, we see more generally that pleasure signals mean we are moving well with our current life-handling and accomplishing abilities. Further, we realize that the painful signals show us our momentary obstructions and impediments that we do not initially understand and have never developed ability to handle. It is wise and useful to master these obstructions by developing sufficient new abilities. When they are handled well, they no longer cause their type of pain—hence the psychological truth, "Pain is the pointer to truth undiscovered and capability not yet developed, or not utilized if already known." This truth is opportunistic; it converts obstructions and unknowns to developed capability, good movement, and accomplishment.

As we master more—either by using what we already know or by converting our pains and their obstructions into knowledge and capability, enlarging our repertoire—we have more pleasure and greater capability.

The method of converting the painful obstruction to capability bears repeating. When the pain is felt, stand back and define it with its underlying specific situational truth. Decide whether or not the goal or direction you were headed in is worth continuing. If so, devise a better strategy. If not, drop the goal and select a new objective. When you know these steps, you can apply them to all types of pain for best life handling.

Each pain, each obstruction is an opportunity for mastery and further increase. How many psychological and emotional pains do you have in a month? Some if not all are missed opportunities for precise learning and growth—for greater increase in abilities, understanding, and wisdom. I challenge you to start taking note of these pains and using them to spur personal growth.

Chapter Summary

1. Realize and know that for each painful emotion or feeling—such as anger, fear, frustration, guilt, or shame—there exists a formula of events or happenings, specific only to the individual emotion, that causes (evokes) that particular emotion.

2. There are many different examples that follow the general formula for each emotion. For instance, anger comes when the pattern of being—I call it the flow pattern one is in—is suddenly interrupted or obstructed. It could be the obstruction of someone cutting in front of you as you drive in a lane of traffic, or someone knocking books out of

your arms while walking in a school hallway. It may be another worker failing to complete a job in a timely manner when you are dependent on that job's completion before you can move forward on a project.

3. Recognize that you are starting to get angry or are in a situation where you might typically get angry.

4. Stop the anger from arising by shifting your focus from the anger to the conditions that are causing it.

5. Discover a new way to solve the situation that evoked the anger. You will have removed the pain and converted the situation to new discovery and new capability. Further, you will have mastered a situation that formerly obstructed you. It will no longer obstruct you or cause you pain in the future. You will have made a gain where you formerly had pain.

6. As you master new situations, increasing your life-handling ability, you will gain more often the pleasures of accomplishment.

7. Use the general formula, the situational truths of each pleasurable emotion, to create that pleasurable emotion when you desire.

CHAPTER 3

———◆◈◆———

Increase Your Self-Power and Know Its Hidden Values

You can be psychologically strong, always in charge of yourself.
Do not give your power to others unless there are good reasons
to do so.

When you understand what self-power is and how much self-power you have, you can become psychologically strong and always in charge of yourself. In this chapter you will learn how to unify your self-power to develop stronger willpower and to become better at negotiations. You will learn how to stop giving your power away and remove any feelings of vulnerability to others. You will learn the power of self-agreement with the truth and develop a strong sense of self-command. Your life will become much more under your own control.

Self-Power Has More Uses than Most of Us Realize
Few of us see ourselves as having much power. Even those who have a place of prominence in society and who are generally considered powerful do not see themselves that way. This powerless view can create problems, leading to impaired functioning and beliefs of inability. In fact, we all

have self-power; it is a basic psychological truth with which we are born. We develop it further both early and later in life. By not realizing we have self-power consciously—and more important, by not knowing how to use it well—we may give our self-power away and weaken our own position. It is far better to understand and develop this valuable force so that we can use it for our own best interest and for the best interest of those we love, not to mention those we may influence.

Whenever we make a choice to do something or agree to someone else's ideas, we are exercising our own self-power. This choosing or agreeing is an important part of the use of our self-power. Whenever we motivate ourselves to do something, or to fulfill any type of purpose, we are using self-power. Deciding and announcing that we plan to take a vacation to the seashore or to Disneyland is an exercise of self-power. Whenever we actively apply our thought or physical energy and strength, we are using our self-power. We automatically use it without really acknowledging it. Even a three-year-old uses his or her self-power, to agree and submit to a parental request, though it appears to be automatic. Even so, the three-year-old has the power to say no and suffer the consequences. In situations when punishment is given, that child may acquiesce and decide it is not worth it to say no. The child is not truly "conditioned" but instead has realized the value of agreement and therefore trusts the parental request. Imagine the chaos if children did not agree so often to parental guidance. There are well-known exceptions. Take, for example, the "terrible twos." During this stage, children often say no as they exercise their self-power in mastering developmental tasks to gain more of a sense of identity. The terrible twos lasts a short time, and then children become more agreeable again; from that point forward, they look to those who have the knowledge and certainties of how to live and follow their lead, just as we do. We let others, such as doctors, teachers, and ministers, inform us and guide our lives. We learn many lessons from personal experience and let these teach us as well.

Philip's Astounding Example

Sometimes unusual or extreme examples teach us best by bringing the point to be learned forcibly to us. Such is the profoundly eloquent example of extreme use of self-power as revealed in the case of Philip, a thirty-five-year-old Vietnam army veteran who was forced to call upon his innate self-power to assist him through a devastating health problem. I met Philip in the intensive care unit of the hospital, where he was being treated for Guillain-Barré syndrome, a fairly rare and unusual illness that attacks the peripheral nerves that control muscles and often temporarily renders people paralyzed. In my capacity as a psychiatrist, I was called to consult with him by his primary care physician, and I found Philip in a state of partial paralysis but also experiencing an extreme sense of powerlessness and helplessness.

Typically, Guillain-Barré syndrome starts with a cold-like illness but quickly worsens. For Philip, who had been healthy and active, Guillain-Barré first caused paralysis of his feet and legs, then his lower trunk, and finally his upper trunk. He was hospitalized after developing breathing difficulties associated with the muscles controlling breathing, and he was placed on a respirator to save his life. Thankfully, this strange condition usually totally clears up in several days to a few weeks and is rarely fatal.

I was called in to talk with Philip because he was experiencing a high degree of distress and agitation, fighting with nurses and being unable or unwilling to settle down. His doctor hoped I might be able to help him. Philip could not talk to me because he was intubated and using a respirator, a medical procedure where a tube is placed down the throat into the lungs through the larynx. He could swallow neither food nor water and needed intravenous feeding.

We devised a fairly simple and straightforward communication technique on the spot. When I asked him questions, he would answer yes or no by shaking his head. While not perfect, this means of communication proved more than adequate and actually allowed us to communicate on a complex level. When I needed more detail, I posed questions as a chess player might, asking questions several moves ahead. This way Philip could answer with a series of head shakes leading to the detailed information I needed.

Philip was in a state of panic, a condition of near irrationality caused by his emotions of fear, anxiety, uncertainty, and helplessness, all of which were associated with a very rapid heart rate. He was thought to be hallucinating by the nurses who cared for him, and he acknowledged this to be true. According to them, he was seeing something outside his hospital window. I thought it might be people. He also let me know this had never happened to him before. I wondered if he was not experiencing delirium, a condition of apprehension, disorientation, and distortion of reality that was often accompanied by visual hallucinations, caused by altered brain metabolism from illness or drugs or alcohol. I searched his medical records and asked him questions and could find no cause. His drug screens were clear; he did not use illicit or prescription drugs or alcohol. This condition would not be caused by the Guillain-Barré, so I had to look elsewhere.

The nurses gave me a clue. He was fighting the respirator, more than most patients, so I followed this lead. When I queried him about it, he let me know he was panicked by the sense of helplessness he felt imposed by his illness and magnified by the respirator and intubation tube. Curiously, he was less bothered by the hallucinations. He also understood that it was very unlikely that he would die from this illness. His condition had less to do with fear of death but was a direct result of the sudden and extreme powerlessness and helplessness imposed on him.

The solution to Phillip's state of panic would require him to not feel so powerless and accept the medical treatment. A useful thought came to me, and we devised a strategy. I suggested that he consciously agree to give his power to the doctors, to the respirator, to the nurses, for the purpose of getting him well. He could use this agreement as a form of self-power, a power from his own mind, to apply to his situation. That way, I told him, he was not powerless. He quickly seized the opportunity, nodded his head yes, and agreed that he had to have the treatments until his own body healed and took over.

The results were dramatic. Philip no longer fought his respirator and was calmer. The nurses and attending physician were relieved and reported him as more accepting of treatment. I continued to see him in the intensive care unit until he could transfer out.

When Philip was off the intubater and the respirator, recovering, he told me the people he had seen in his hallucinations (which were now fading in intensity and frequency) were the wives, children, and parents of the Viet Cong he had killed in Vietnam as a machine gunner on the front lines. Many of his buddies had been killed when the enemy almost overran their position, but he held them off, killing several during the firefight. We discussed his war experiences and their aftermath, and we analyzed his feelings. As a soldier, Philip was put in a tough spot in the battle situation—kill or be killed—and he responded appropriately, carrying the day though losing friends and killing enemies. He felt badly for the men he had to kill, and empathy because they had loved ones too, just like his dead comrades. He felt relief but some guilt that he had survived when his comrades had not.

With the unwelcome, severe helplessness and powerlessness imposed by his illness, his old terror and unresolved guilt from his prior battlefield situation—which he had solved then by fighting and killing—had returned, but this time he was rendered absolutely powerless and was unable to act against the causative conditions. Payback from his slain enemies' families arose in his mind, and he hallucinated them menacing him during his stay in the intensive care unit. He knew they were not real, but his feelings were. Now, through understanding that these feelings were from the war, he removed his guilt, and by using his power to give agreement to the medical treatments, he removed the terrible helplessness and powerlessness imposed by the illness.

It all made sense to him. He got better and we parted. He was grateful and so was I. I was grateful for his recovery but also for another reason, too: I had learned from Philip the power and the capability of the self deliberately giving power—in this instance, the power of agreement. The implications were very clear: we never have to perceive ourselves as totally helpless or powerless as long as we have the ability to give or apply our self-power to whatever we choose.

When we apply our will, our decision making, and our persistence in a process, we are exercising our self-power. We are all in possession of self-power and use it every day, employing it to live well and to develop as individuals. We utilize our self-power to improve ourselves as we perceive the value of doing so.

Susan's Self-Power Put to Good Use

Susan, a medical student, put her self-power to use by choosing to develop her caring and communication skills, ultimately becoming a compassionate and understanding physician beloved by her patients. She had such a good bedside manner, giving time to really listen to her patients. One of them was Mary, a sixty-two-year-old with a chronic cardiac condition, and she told everyone, "You are in very good hands with Dr. Susan. I trust what she tells me to do, and she cares so much." Mary sent all of her friends to Dr. Susan; many others did as well.

While a medical student, Susan was praised for her good caring manner. She was rewarded and reinforced for her good patient-care skills, and as a physician she always performed professionally in this manner. She consciously applied herself (and her self-power) to doing so. In other words, she decided consciously to apply her caring and sensitivity to each of her patients. After developing a successful and large practice, Susan had to use her self-power again, this time in a way that might seem contrary to her caring manner with patients. As her practice grew, taking more and more of her time and energy, Susan the individual had less time for her growing family and her rewarding personal life. She needed to make adjustments, to find a more equitable balance between the personal and professional, the public and private aspects of her life. Again, Susan employed her self-power and made wise self-decisions to manage her life in a way to keep this important balance. She hired others to work for her and share her patient load, and she joined with other physicians to share weekends and nights on call so she could be free for family and self-concerns after office hours at least three-fourths of the time. Also, she took a full afternoon per week off from work. This new balance paid dividends to her quality of life.

The Exercise of Self-Will (the Self-Power to Choose)—Results When You Don't, Results When You Do

In contrast to Dr. Susan, I have witnessed people who do not know, or who act as if they do not know, that they have self-power. They rarely exercise their power to choose, to manage their affairs or life; they do not see themselves as having options and the freedom to use them. As a result, they can develop a certain kind of depression.

Jean, a fifty-five-year-old married woman with four grown children and an aging but still fairly independent eighty-year-old mother, felt totally de-energized and found it difficult to get out of bed and face the day. Before seeing me, antidepressants and anti-anxiety medicines had not been helpful, and she had been feeling poorly for several months. After a physical examination and laboratory studies, Jean was deemed normal and healthy; the answer to her problem was not to be found in her brain or body.

During our first two meetings, she told me of the many demands to which she was forced to respond. These included her mother's request to be taken to the store, her daughter's constant need for a babysitter for her two children, an ill neighbor needing lunch every day, many daily household duties, and worst of all, the cooking and cleaning for a big dinner scheduled that weekend. She felt overwhelmed and imprisoned by her chores; there was simply no time for a break to see a movie, have a visit with friends, or read a book. Even when she did take a break, she was constantly reminded of all she had to do. She was like a reflex, forced to respond to each duty and each request without self-choice, as if everything were an obligation performed in a lockstep manner.

Jean was suffering from a chronic, long-term pattern of not treating her inner self and mind in a healthy manner, and she was depressed as a result. I told her that I believed she needed a break, that she needed to consider treating herself better, and that a change was as good as a rest. It is important to understand we all require breaks and leisure time to be healthy, and without them we simply shut down. I counseled that until she put herself on a good care schedule, she could expect to continue to be exhausted and depressed, and she would shut down occasionally.

A good care schedule includes time for adequate sleep and pleasurable activities, such as vacations with freedom from duties, time with friends, listening to good music, reading, watching movies, going out to dinner, and any other number of things that feel good.

I also learned that Jean's self-credo was, "Always provide service to others." Unfortunately, she had taken this admirable quality too far, leaving her overworked, guilty, and without an outlet for self-relief. In essence, she became a slave to her credo; a machine with no expression of her own self-choice, no exercise of her self-power. She had so empowered her service credo, without empowering good self-care, that she no longer exercised any control over her life.

A dramatic turnaround came in our third session. As Jean went on and on about all she was doing and requested to do, I tried to interject with conclusions I had come to about her situation. She paused, let me speak, and then went right back to talking about her many obligations as if she hadn't heard me. Surprised that she didn't respond to my input, I interrupted her again. "I just pointed out your pattern, its cause, and the fact that you do not seem to be able to make a choice for pleasure, for taking a break," I said. "I advised you to tell people you will consider their request and get back to them later, but you acted as if you hadn't heard me. You kept right on talking. Why?"

She stopped and quickly said, "I heard you, but I don't know what else to do. Thinking of doing something else scares me." I described to her how she acted as if she possessed no self-will, no self-power, to manage her life or act in her own behalf. I was aware of Jean's religious beliefs that emphasized service to others, but it also was based on the principle of agency, the responsibility to discern, choose, or decide. I suggested she followed the "service" belief to the exclusion of exercising her agency to discern, decide, or choose and thereby give herself some freedom and relief. I said, "The old adages and biblical scriptures to 'love thy neighbor as thyself' and 'charity begins at home' are being ignored by you." I figured that if I pointed out her lack of following her own religious beliefs, I might convince her to change. This made immediate good sense to her, but she acknowledged she had some fear that she could not change her pattern.

During our next session, Jean told me she felt a little better, though a little guilty at not immediately saying yes to all the requests made of her. (Remember the definition of guilt? Guilt is an elastic stretch signal that arises when one stretches an old agreement with a person, principle, or pattern.) "To realistically and wisely use guilt," I told her after defining it, "decide whether to reaffirm the old agreement or make a new one with yourself that changes the old one when it is no longer useful or worth it."

By our fifth session she felt even more relief; she had said no a few times, put some pleasure into her life, and actually felt like getting up in the morning and facing the day. Jean had been awakened to using her self-power through discerning and deciding rather than defaulting her choice and reflexively obeying requests. She now was using it to feel better about herself and to improve and change her life.

Jean continued exercising her newfound self-power and self-choice, improving in her ability to do so over the next two months. Even though she still had some vulnerability to others' requests, she was taking much better care of herself. Her depression cleared, and she ended therapy. I still get yearly letters of thanks.

Anytime we feel enslaved or not free, too burdened, or too quickly in agreement with others' points of view, we would be wise to question whether we are thinking and deciding for ourselves, or blindly going along. Stop, analyze, and reaffirm by choice or change to get back in charge of yourself. That gets us back into using our self-power more wisely and well.

A Common Power Giveaway That Causes Dejection and Brief Depression

During my work on this book, I saw two good examples of how bright, capable, and responsible achievers inadvertently gave power away and created pain for themselves.

The first was Bill, a writer, who told me how disappointed he was with himself, and how down he felt because he failed to reach some rewriting goals he'd set for his new book. He had written the first draft much faster than expected. Feeling enthused and excited about this productive episode, Bill believed he could do the rewrite in two months and be ready for publication. To his dismay, though, it was more complicated than he had anticipated. After five months, he was only halfway finished. It was serious work, he told me; he had not been wasting time and was progressing, but nonetheless, it was taking much longer than he'd hoped.

I noticed his furrowed brow and downcast countenance as he spoke, and how he shook his head slowly to demonstrate how burdened he felt by this unexpected unraveling of events. I could empathize. I had felt that way at times and often heard people say similar things when asked how their day was going. "I'm not getting anything accomplished," they would tell me, or "I do not get anything done," yet they were going hard at it all day long.

Chelsea, a young woman who manages a section in the publication department of her company, told me a similar story less than a week later. She sometimes got depressed for not accomplishing all she set out to do at work. On this particular Saturday, she was down about the lack of accomplishment she had made over the previous five days. "It seems like I don't get anything done," she told me. "It happens a lot."

When I asked her why she had not met her goals, I learned that she placed a fairly high expectation on what she planned to accomplish each day. Inevitably, though, personnel problems, interruptions from upper management, or any number of things she hadn't planned on came up. The problems and interruptions were important and frequent enough that they prevented her from accomplishing all she'd set out to do.

Both Chelsea and Bill had created their disappointment and depression by setting their expectations so high. Though they knew on some level why they could not accomplish all they had planned, and neither had been lazy or complacent, they still felt inadequate or down when unable to meet their goals. For Chelsea, interruptions and personnel problems stopped her; for Bill, the rewrite's complexity slowed him.

Feigning seriousness for effect, I asked each the ludicrous question, "How often have you been able to do more than you were really able to do?"

They responded similarly. After a surprised laugh, both smiled as they realized the fruitlessness of holding on to their initial expectations. They both also saw how illogical and pain-producing this was. Reality had turned out differently than their original expectations.

Both Bill and Chelsea had been empowering their old expectations, not the reality of experience. They had transformed their expectations into necessity beliefs and were being crucial and absolute about them. In essence, they were unknowingly fighting against a critical truth: whenever reality and preference (expectation) clash or collide, reality always wins.

We know this intuitively, but we need to recall and empower this logical truth at times to protect ourselves from producing the pain of failed expectations. We need to learn how to hold our expectations less tightly, perhaps view them as options, and allow for some flexibility to change. By doing this, Bill and Chelsea were both able to let go of the burdensome feelings of depression they were experiencing.

If a boss tells you that you aren't meeting job requirements and you believe too many other important things get in the way, ask your boss for suggestions on which requirements are the most important to fulfill first. If you think your job requirements can't be fulfilled without added help, ask if you can be given more help or resources.

Another Power Giveaway: Parent to Child

A frequent power giveaway often happens between a parent and child, with the parent giving parental power away to a child who shouldn't have it. We see this in the example of Lillian, an accomplished businesswoman and financial consultant with a particularly demanding eight-year-old daughter. Lillian was working one evening, presenting recommendations to a small group of investors about their interest in a project. I watched as she expertly analyzed an investment opportunity carefully and gave such a good case for not going ahead that the investors declined that particular opportunity. It was easy to see that Lillian was capable and competent, possessing a brilliant eye for business analysis. However, in her relationship with her child, I witnessed a crack, a power leak in her otherwise formidable self-presentation.

During a break, Lillian telephoned her daughter Krista, and I inadvertently overheard Lillian's part of the conversation. Lillian was apparently concerned about Krista possibly being upset at her absence, and I listened as Lillian explained what she was doing and how long she might be. Her tone and manner carried a twinge of guilt. Lillian told

Krista that she would be home at 9:15 p.m., and she would see her then. Lillian sounded firm, setting the expectation and controlling the situation fairly well after having given a little power away by feeling guilty. But then Lillian stopped being firm, and in a little girl's voice beseeched her daughter, "I'll be home at 9:15, okay?" Obviously, Lillian was seeking Krista's agreement. Krista's response, audible from several feet away, was a wailing, "No!" Lillian re-explained the situation, and then she again asked in a vulnerable and pleading voice, "Okay?"

This exchange went back and forth a few more times, until Lillian blurted out that she had to go, but she followed it with another "Okay?" Each time, Krista strengthened her refusal to agree. Finally, Lillian hung up in desperation after saying, "I'm sorry, I'll see you in a while. I have to go." Lillian appeared flustered and slightly embarrassed and, knowing I was a psychiatrist, commented to me, "I need to come see you." Her comment is one people frequently make to me, though most are not really serious about it.

Lillian the composed, logical financial expert had just given her power away to her daughter. She handed it to her on a silver platter, seeking agreement from Krista with the question, "Okay?" The omnipotent Krista was not about to agree. In their interaction, Krista ruled and Lillian had a power leak. She wanted her daughter to agree, wanted it to be all right with Krista so that she would not feel guilty about causing some temporary pain and displeasure for her.

Lillian would have to learn to set expectations and show Krista that she was the mother in charge. Lillian would have to say, "I'll be home later, as planned. Good-bye." She needed to quit giving her power away by asking if it was okay. Besides, Lillian was going to stay, get the job done, and not go home prematurely just to satisfy Krista's demand; why not speak the truth and let it be? It is far more effective. Realistically, Lillian had many other important things in her life besides her daughter, so as long as she took adequate time for her daughter during the week, she need not feel guilty. Additionally, Krista needed to learn that she could not so easily manipulate her mother through guilt, and that putting up with the frustration of not always having her demands met was good for her. Otherwise she might become a spoiled and somewhat monstrous child.

This problem is very common. We have all seen examples of this with parents and children in public. The child acts up or demands something. The parent, perhaps out of fear of public embarrassment or fear that his or her competence as a parent will be seen as lacking, inadvertently asks their child to please mind. Children can become little tyrants quickly when they sense they have the power and will usually act even worse.

Trying for agreement is a commonly attempted strategy when we feel guilty or fear the displeasure of others. Instead of mastering the problem in ourselves and becoming more self-capable and powerful, we give it away, trying for agreement to remove the feared displeasure. Even if we get agreement, those who "agree" with us see our weakness and may decide to halfway agree, minimizing or patronizing us, losing some respect for us, and seeing us as weak. Later they might use this to take advantage of us in a situation that benefits them but may be to our disadvantage.

Passive Longings, a Power Giveaway That Makes Us Weak and Often Disappointed

In a culture that frowns on self-promoters, people who always seem to be pushing their agenda (bragging about accomplishments and generally taking center stage) appear distasteful to us. As a result, many of us remain silent, harboring passive longings about getting recognition, without doing anything to occasionally bring some acknowledgement or recognition to ourselves.

Each of us longs to be recognized for our value and for who we are as friends, companions, valued employees, and family members. We harbor passive longings and want the important people in our lives to recognize our accomplishment or value without us touting them. We see these unsolicited acknowledgments as proof or substantiation of our true value; we like compliments if they are sincere and well founded.

Unfortunately, these passive longings usually remain unresolved and unfulfilled and result in power giveaways. Our passive longings leave us disappointed, unfulfilled, and sometimes angry about other people's lack of consideration for us. Take for example Peggy, who every year hoped her friends would do something big on her birthday. She longed for unsolicited interest and recognition on her special day. She empowered that longing, held onto it, waited and hoped they would surprise her with some special event. Every year she failed to inform anyone that her birthday was approaching—she neurotically reasoned that she would feel more valued if they thought of it on their own, if she did not have to tell them. So she remained passive and quiet, never revealing her desire to her friends, and once when her birthday came and went unacknowledged, she was crestfallen and more than a little resentful.

Why did her friends not think of her? Peggy had given power to her unspoken passive longings, which could not act or inform on their own. How could her friends be expected to know if she did not somehow mention her birthday? None of her friends were so passive; none of them waited long for another to mention the hidden hope, as Peggy did. Instead, each usually gave a hint or brought the subject up as a matter of course. By not saying her birthday was coming up and that she wanted the whole group to go to lunch at her favorite restaurant, Peggy slighted herself.

Jim had been painfully self-conscious and lacked confidence in many situations. Though he was a part of the group in the others' eyes, he didn't feel that way. Instead, Jim often left himself out of peer-group activities, waiting and hoping to be invited by the gang for a matinee movie, a short trip to the sporting goods store, or an overnight getaway at a cabin. His fear of unacceptability undermined his ability to easily feel he belonged with the group. Everyone else assumed they were part of the gang and automatically included themselves, making statements like, "Where are we going?" or "Whose car are we going in?" Jim, on the other hand, was painfully self-conscious and unsure of himself, and he never spoke up on his own behalf. He gave his power away to his passive longings and then wished and hoped the others would say, "C'mon, Jim, let's go." Because of this, Jim left himself out a lot of times when he wanted to participate, and he unwittingly created troubling misperceptions in doing so. His friends often misread his holding back, not realizing he wanted to be coaxed or asked (which would have become tiresome to them). They concluded he was disinterested or even snobbish. If Jim had conquered his fear and dared to be direct and assumed he was part of the group and included himself as the others had, the misperceptions of him and his personal disappointments would have never occurred. Instead he gave his power to his fear and insecurity. It weakened him, interfered with his opportunities, and inadvertently robbed his group of friends of his potential contributions.

When you discover passive longings in yourself, question what they might truly mean. Try to put your goals or desires into focus, and although at first it might be difficult, actively pursue them, informing others verbally of what you would like. In most cases, you will be pleasantly surprised at the response you receive. The key is to turn the object of your passive longings into a goal to actively seek or achieve by directly stating it or doing it, taking the responsibility for doing so. You will be looked upon more favorably as able, confident, willing, active, and a leader. You will be admired.

Spouses often hold passive longings too, wanting to have their unspoken desires agreed to, hoping for fulfillment from their partner. It can be the wishes for compliments or praise, romance and making love, special surprises of going out to eat, or fixing favorite dishes. Maybe it is the wish for a surprising little gift or endearment that goes unexpressed. Whatever it is, there will be far less disappointment and confusion if such things are brought out and mentioned. Couples do better if they talk out, ahead of time, a way to let each other know what they desire. They can agree to let each other know such things as "I would like to go out to dinner tonight, how about you?" or "How about a movie tonight?" or "I'm up for some romance tonight. How about you?" Also, if one desires an endearing hug or compliment, he or she can give such to the partner, and it will usually be reciprocated.

The Vulnerability Mechanism That Gives Our Power Away and Wastes Our Energy

Closely related to passive longings is the human vulnerability mechanism. It is easy to slip into when we begin to feel a little bit helpless about upcoming situations that are important to us. We can start wishing for the result we want to happen—and fearing that instead, the unwanted result will happen. Continuous wishing and fearing keeps us feeling vulnerable and not in very good control, whether or not we truly are. A very brief episode of wishing and fearing, thinking it only once or twice, then letting go is all right. However, when we repeatedly wish for the desirable outcome and repeatedly fear the negative result, we put ourselves mentally into a position of uncomfortable helplessness and vulnerability to the possible result. When we too strongly depend on that possible future result, we create mental pressure and waste our energy, and we set ourselves up for greater disappointment if our hope doesn't materialize the way we wanted. We can do this to ourselves about myriads of things: taking a test, an athletic event, or bidding on a desired item, such as a house, a car, or an art object. We can also do it about medical diagnostics that are important to the status of our health.

Anything we wish or fear in unrelenting fashion tends to convince us we are vulnerable and not in control. It is a self or mental position to avoid by not wishing and fearing so much. The point is that putting our self-power too strongly and repeatedly upon wishing and fearing, and remaining in that stance, does not do us any good and does not influence the outcome. It just makes us more intensely helpless, pressured, and vulnerable, wasting our self-power and energy. The cure? Stop your passivity and take action; pull your self-power back from the wishing and fearing, and do something else more useful and less wasteful. Acknowledge that you desire a certain outcome and fear another, and then say something like, "I'll deal with it when the results are in," or "I can live with whatever happens. C'mon, self, let's go do something else while we are waiting."

Negative Self-Assumptions—The Greatest Weakeners

One of the great weakeners and power giveaways is what I call automatic, negative self-assumptions. Most of us indulge in this power giveaway when interacting with people, and a special set of circumstances (usually containing past feelings of inadequacy) triggers a sudden feeling of nervous self-consciousness, followed by an automatic assumption that we are deficient, unliked, do not measure up, or are not acceptable.

Automatic, negative self-assumptions usually occur when we are talking with someone who does not respond with the usual give and take of friendly conversation. Take for instance when Sally talked to an authority figure (her professor, Dr. Jones) who did not respond to her at first and then seemed to be staring at her or questioning her rather than conversing in a friendly manner. She immediately froze with self-consciousness and felt silly, on display, embarrassed, and flustered. She struggled to not stammer and tried her best to cover this response, but she came away from the experience feeling there was something wrong with her and that her professor thought she was an inadequate, bumbling female student who would never amount to much.

Tragically and unbeknownst to her, Dr. Jones was nearly deaf, and in trying to hide this fact, he focused intently on her, attempting to understand by reading her lips. Both Sally and Dr. Jones were my patients at the time, and I heard each one's distorted account with negative self-assumptions. Sally mistook his staring as criticizing, his slow response as a sign she was a bumbler, and his asking questions (in his attempt to clarify and understand) as judging her harshly and dismissing her views. Sally, like many of us, is vulnerable to certain visual or conversational cues, which result in the feeling of self-consciousness. In the absence of really knowing what was going on, she felt uncertain and inadequate. Why did she do this? Why do we do this?

When Sally recounted this and other similar experiences during therapy, I discovered that her specific vulnerability to automatic, negative self-assumptions first arose in childhood, growing up with three older brothers. They would put her down with mean, teasing comments, and at times they displaced their own anger or frustration with their mother onto their little sister, a much easier target. Sally became sensitive and vulnerable to feeling she was inadequate or deficient, particularly around her brothers. She learned to feel uncertain about her value until they invited her to join them. When her brothers hesitated to include her or didn't specifically ask her to join them, she automatically felt put down. Sensing her weakness, her brothers sometimes used her vulnerability against her.

It should be noted that Sally's brothers were often kind and inclusive. They were protective, and as adults they are warm, loving, and proud of their little sister's academic accomplishments. In spite of this, Sally's old wounds could be evoked in situations with others, such as the hard-of-hearing Professor Jones.

In situations such as with Dr. Jones, Sally gave her power away and relived the remnants of unresolved childhood fears of inadequacy, exclusion, and its pains. In what could be termed tragic comedy, I'd wager poor Professor Jones, feeling self-consciousness from his growing deafness, saw a momentary look of befuddlement on Sally's face and assumed she observed his defect and thought less of him. Both accounts illustrate the waste of energy and pain from the self-esteem weakening power giveaway of negative self-assumptions. We are all vulnerable to these until we expose them and learn to do differently.

Exposing Negative Self-Assumptions

Dr. Dan Hughes, a neurologist, shared with me a great example of exposing such vulnerabilities. He had a high school and college acquaintance named Andy, whom he had frequently felt self-conscious around, so he avoided him unless they were in a group together. Andy had the ability to appear confident and at times showed a sharp and sarcastic tongue that he used on Dan and others. He seemed as if he thought he was too good for Dan, and because Andy was a sharp dresser and more social, Dan felt like he could not have his respect.

Years later, Dan and Andy worked on a hospital project together and became good friends. In a particularly comfortable moment, Dan told Andy of his former self-conscious times—and to his utter surprise, Andy responded by telling Dan he had actually felt threatened by *him*. Dan had done so well in school, Andy told him, and was so cocky and confident (totally different from how Dan perceived himself) that Andy worked very hard over the years to be less threatened by Dan and others. It was a moment worthy of consideration. What a waste of power both had experienced by giving away their power to self-conscious, negative assumptions. What a freeing feeling they both had in finding out what had created those painful feelings within them and then being able to let the feelings go. The actual truth of the situation freed them both.

To help overcome these times of automatic, negative self-assumptions, scan your memory for times you experienced painful self-consciousness, embarrassed feelings, or the sense of not being good enough in someone else's eyes. It might take some time and energy, but it is worth it. Go back to your earliest painful memories, and you may get a clue to their origins. Even if you cannot recall their exact origins, realize that they are distortions from old hurts and protections, and they have no current value or purpose; instead, they will hurt you.

If you strongly believe these assumptions are accurate, it would be wise to use them as a signal about what to improve in yourself. Even so, be careful not to give too much of your power away to others' perceptions of you. Take them under advisement and ponder them; find out more by asking others how they perceive you in those situations to determine whether your self-assessment matches their assessment of you.

Let these memories remind you not to give your power away. Let them help you take back and command the power you once lost. Dare instead to view yourself as worthy, perhaps witty and certainly fun to be around. View yourself as someone always able to contribute usefully to others, and then proceed on these positive self-assumptions. Self-power and confidence will increase, and you will be continuously stronger and more capable psychologically if you choose to do this.

The Power of Embarrassment

We all know the feeling of embarrassment; it comes with the shock of suddenly being the center of unwanted attention or the butt of a joke, or from making an obvious mistake in front of others. The red hot cheeks, the feeling of foolishness, the desire to get away—these reactions are familiar to us all. The truth is that embarrassment happens to all of us, but it is how we deal with it that determines if it has a lasting, painful impact or if it disappears after we learn from it.

It is probably safe to say that no one likes to be embarrassed. In fact, many tend to avoid people they have been embarrassed in front of and go to great lengths to make certain it doesn't happen again. The power of embarrassment (and the closely related feelings of shame and humiliation) are considerable and can create significant problems when allowed to persist. I have seen it destroy the lives of people who continuously fear embarrassment and allow it to control many of their actions; they give it great power, usually because it happened often early in life when they were helpless to counter it with better self-views and less a sense of helplessness.

I like to put the overreacting enemy within embarrassment, shame, and humiliation in its place by taking away its enduring or long-term power. Its short-term power is fine because it helps us make corrections and improvements, but its long-term power can debilitate and create the risk of suicide.

Donna was just such a person, suffering years of giving power to the fear of embarrassment and of being an easy target, first from teasing by her older siblings and then later from friends and coworkers. The result was predictable: she developed a negative self-view, believed she was worthless, and became a social recluse. She was desperate for friends and acceptance, but at the same time her attempts to make friends were often unsuccessful because of her fear of unacceptability, leaving her ever more fearful and self-doubting. Ultimately she gave up trying to meet new people.

Around people she already knew, Donna felt she was an object of scorn and derision. This belief prevented her from connecting in a warm and meaningful way and kept her from receiving what she needed most: friendship with people. This pernicious and eventually pathological fear hit its zenith the night she tried to commit suicide. According to her, "Life had become a painful monstrosity." The weed of despair and fear was choking off the flowering of her life. She thought suicide would give her a relief and get her out of her pain. Longing to belong, she gained a momentary sense of harmony and belonging with something—the idea of death by suicide. The suicide urge beckoned stronger. "Oh to be free of the fear, out of the pain, and finally be at peace," she thought. She tried it.

Months later, with therapy and new awareness, she saw the truth. In reality she was a sensitive, caring person who had desires, longings, and skills like anyone else. She learned to understand that she mattered and had value, and most important, that she had inadvertently developed her problem. She accomplished this by understanding why and how it happened. The understanding she acquired helped reduce her fear of embarrassment and her pervasive sense of humiliation.

She began to develop some of her new acquaintances into new friendships, putting her self-power into positive assumptions about herself and into expanding her life experiences. She more accurately and realistically assessed happenings and situations with people, rather than automatically becoming embarrassed and feeling "no good." Weeks and then months passed, and Donna became stronger and more able to feel positive. Occasionally she reverted to the fear of embarrassment, but it was neither as severe nor as long lasting. She was able to see it as it was, a brief signal, and made corrections because of it. As she progressively gave it less power, it had less power over her. Her life was no longer narrowing, it was expanding. No longer riddled with pain, she found more pleasure.

Donna's situation is not unique. Millions of people suffer from feelings of self-negativity created by embarrassment or humiliation. Donna's recovery was facilitated by not giving power to embarrassment or humiliation. She learned that by simply not turning away, by facing these experiences as they happen, she could remove the power they possessed. By forcing yourself to do this, to not turn away, you neutralize any long-term negative effect.

When people have done something that causes initial humiliation, shame, and embarrassment to them and their families—a politician's affair, an employee's embezzlement, a public figure arrested for sexual encounters with call girls—the obvious best strategy is for them to take their punishment, acknowledge their guilt, and then correct their vulnerability through therapy or some other means. They should face it, acknowledge it, and choose the wisest future course, perhaps one recommended by trusted advisors.

Ask yourself this simple question: How long can I remain acutely or immediately embarrassed? Most people respond, "For a long time." If you face embarrassment as it happens and do not look away, if you feel the hot sensation in your cheeks and successfully fight the urge to turn and run away, its negative power will dissipate within a few seconds. You will return to the state of calmness or neutrality that you were in before the embarrassment. By facing embarrassment, you rob it from creating any long-term negative impacts. It is the ongoing *fear of embarrassment* that gives it the continuing negative, restricting power in our lives.

The Strength and Great Value of Conscious Self-Agreement

Earlier, we saw how Philip, the Vietnam veteran, self-agreed to medical treatments that saved his life. After experiencing the feeling of being helpless and powerless, Philip consciously agreed to allow the respirator to assist him. Although physically unable to assist himself, he still possessed the power to apply himself mentally and to make the decision to calm himself. Almost immediately his fear and terror began to dissipate.

Although self-agreement has great power, it remains untapped in most of us. When we are surprised by an unfamiliar or uncertain fear-laden event, we easily give our self-agreement power away. It happens when panhandlers ask for money; when car salespeople use powerful, high-pressure tactics to close the deal; or when phone solicitors employ guilt or tragedy to shame us into making a donation. We are taken aback, and instead of asking ourselves, "What is this? How will I handle it? What should I do?" we acquiesce and simply go along, giving our power away and letting these situations possess power over us. It can also happen with bad news: the office alarm went off, a frozen water pipe burst, your child cut his lip at school and needs stitches. We panic instead of keeping cool and being fully effective at solving the problem.

When we panic, we initially are overwhelmed and think or say such things as, "Oh no! What will we do? How bad is it? We have to get help! Hurry!" Usually the initial panic subsides as we decide what to do to fix or help fix the problem. These little crises happen to all of us. To handle them efficiently and not give away our power to the crisis, we first need to remain calm, be patient, and not become overly alarmed. Next we do an important maneuver: we consciously and deliberately decide to self-agree with ourselves, taking all the components of the matter at hand and organizing them. We have an open dialogue with ourselves, agreeing to first analyze the situation and then proceed wisely, always staying in good self-control. So if the office alarm goes off, call the alarm company and let the police investigate. If a frozen pipe bursts, get the water shut off as soon as possible, call the plumber, and then contact your insurance company. Accept the reality. If your child cut his or her lip, take him or her to the hospital, or authorize the school to do so if you are not in the area. The general rule is to say to yourself, "I'll study the situation and then decide."

By doing this, by agreeing to explore, discover, and sift through the data before deciding what to do about it, we disarm any initial surprise or pressure we have encountered and remain unified and bound to a wise, strong stance of self-agreement. This approach is also very useful both before a negotiation and later, when we enter into the actual process. To repeat, we can agree with ourselves to not make a rash decision, to not decide immediately but instead to take the time to think it over. It is a way of being prepared in advance, of being unified within ourselves before a situation arises so we do not give our power away automatically to the other side's desires. The self-agreement with the self is a good technique that allows us to handle whatever occurs in the best way possible.

Useful Agreements and Power Giveaways

When we agree to have an operation, we have talked to the surgeon and perhaps relied on a trusted primary care physician who recommended that particular surgeon, which helps us trust the surgeon more. If we get a second or third opinion that backs up the first opinion, we will feel better at giving our power away to the surgeon and the anesthesiologist to operate on us. As this example shows society runs on a multitude of useful agreements and power giveaways, though of course they are not infallible at all times.

Implied or Passive Agreement and Acquiescence

There is a form of agreement that goes on most of the time in human interactions. It is not the conscious form of agreement that I have been describing, as when you agree with yourself or another person about a course of action or what you both observed. No, it is an implied or unchallenged agreement, an agreement that occurs through default, or passive acquiescence, or not realizing one should agree or not. It happens with all of us when we initially tend to trust and follow instructions given by a teacher, nurse, or emergency room clerk. In new situations we look to the guide or leader, who asserts an idea or gives a "rule" or guideline as if that is the way it has to be. We automatically give them power and passively accept what they tell us. If we agree with ourselves that it is wise to follow their lead, that is okay. Sometimes, however, we may not have communicated the gravity of a situation, such as with a more severe medical problem requiring immediate attention. Make sure the nurse or emergency room clerk understands; demand to be initially evaluated if you think they do not fully understand.

Much of life for all of us is lived through our implied agreements. However, here is a note of caution: if we are not careful, we will give too much of our power away through these implied agreements. Instead we will function far more strongly, capably, and confidently, more in charge of our lives, if we consciously give a moment of thought to each of these experiences. During that moment we can unify our energy of self-power by agreeing within ourselves to agree, to not agree, or to continue to evaluate. It is wise to give your power to others when it is for your benefit—to the surgeon during your operation or to a pilot who flies the plane you are using for travel.

The Majestic Power of Self-Agreement with the Truth, and Truth Acknowledgment

Actual reality is the strongest force we have. When reality and our preference collide, reality always wins. As we saw in chapter 2, when we fight the unwanted reality, the truth of what occurred, we recreate the original pain. To function at our best, we must be in line with reality and truth. Agreement with the truth of reality settles our mind, stops the power giveaway, and sets or reinforces a precedent for self-analysis and making decisions.

When we find it hard to accept unwanted realities or truths, we often continue to fight against them, and we somehow ultimately blame reality and truth. A good strategy when this happens is to say, "I do not like this situation, but I acknowledge and agree that it really did occur." It is still the truth, and by using this self-agreement strategy, you rob the disliking it of any negative power it possesses. This extra step of acknowledging the truth—even the truth that you do not like—binds your mental self-energy with the full truth of reality. It frees us and does not allow us to recreate pain. Stop fighting the truth of actual reality. Accepting and acknowledging the truth is the greatest source of peace and self-unification that we possess.

Chapter Summary

1. You are never completely helpless. You always have your self–power, which you can apply for giving permission or for allowing things to occur with you.

2. The self-agreement with the self means you say or think, "I agree with myself, before this negotiation or transaction, that I will take it under advisement and will not decide until later, when I am away from the situation." That welds your self-power to your self-interest and keeps you from being vulnerable to others' plans or desires for you, which may not be in your best interest.

3. The self-agreement with the truth surrounds and circumscribes all other thoughts and patterns. You can actually hate something without feeling the upsetting feelings of hate by saying, "The truth is I wanted a different outcome. I hate the result, but the truth is that it happened the way it did, even though I hate it." The mind remains pain-free and calm, as opposed to when you say, "I hate it!" which gives an unpleasant

experience of the feelings of hate. The truth element, which is accepted in the first statement, keeps the pain of hate from developing. The truth is stronger than the hate. Here again, how you say these things to yourself and how you phrase them really counts.

4. Do not passively give your self-power away. Know when you are giving your power away and for what purpose—a purpose that works for you.

5. When you do not feel free and in charge, see to what or whom you are giving your power. Then make a decision with yourself whether or not to affirm the agreement consciously, or attempt to change it to one more beneficial to yourself.

6. Even when you feel relatively helpless, you can retain a sense of self-power and remove the helplessness by giving agreement with yourself to allow the circumstances.

7. Only give your power to others over yourself when it is to your potential benefit.

8. You can remove the pain of disliking or hating something by acknowledging the truth of that and empowering the truth: "I do hate it, but it is the truth nonetheless." The truth is more powerful than the feeling or hating or disliking, so the pain of those feelings disappears and you will be free, not stuck in the pain of hating.

9. Almost all human interactions are done by implied (automatic, unstated) agreement, by default (passive acquiescence), or by conscious agreement. Conscious agreement is by far the strongest self-position to take.

SECTION 2

Use Psychological Truths to Remove Barriers and Increase Your Abilities

CHAPTER 4

———◆◈◆———

Our Mastery Mechanism: The Accomplisher

Your natural mastery mechanism has a formula, a psychological truth that you can use to accomplish ever more. It is a great tool of your increase force.

We all have an inherent mastery mechanism that produces our accomplishments. This mastery mechanism is a major component of our increase force; it is how we accomplish tasks such as learning to ride a bicycle, drive a car, or any complex skill for use in a technical job. You can use it deliberately to accomplish greater things throughout your life than you naturally would. Our mastery mechanism works for us anytime we attempt something new. Although we may be clumsy initially, as in the first attempt at playing golf, we get better with repetition, practice, and play. Good instruction hastens the learning process. When we deem ourselves good enough, we have learned to play golf. If you resist this psychological process and psychological truth, you will experience dissatisfaction, poor functioning, and lack of success. Use it well, and you will continuously accomplish and continuously increase your abilities.

Childhood Mastery Tasks and Adult Mastery Processes

In child development, the term *mastery task* refers to the large number of physical, thinking, emotional, and social skills that normally develop in humans from infancy through adolescence, during the so-called immature years; learning to crawl, stand, and then walk are examples. We learn to talk and play. Later, we read and then develop math skills. As teenagers, we learn more complex and sophisticated social skills. We also learn how to drive. We work toward our own independence.

From childhood on, we develop far greater and more complex mastery skills, and the process of mastery continues throughout life. The sum total of our mastery skills depends, to an extent, on our ability to identify and embrace increase. When we learn to use our mastery mechanism with skill and precision, applying its processes more efficiently and effectively, the better we can identify and remove our personal barriers, opening up new and limitless horizons.

The Motivations of the Mastery Mechanism: Desire and Fear

This process of mastery begins with a goal, the accomplishment we want to attain. Our goals are usually motivated by one of two main conditions, desire or fear. We either seek something because of the desire of a pleasurable outcome, the allure of it, or because we are threatened, fearful, and at risk if we do not accomplish the task.

Sculpting and painting are examples of a pleasurable outcome, as is trying out for a school play or an athletic team. It could be entering any contest with the hope of winning. It may be learning how to plan a successful family vacation so that all members' interests are well served, or it could be a new hobby. The object that lures is desirable; we want it so we set out to obtain it.

Fear is the motivating force when we are in undesirable places or dangerous situations. We need to create better or safer circumstances to be free of the undesirability or danger. One example is how to complete a confusing tax form so that we can file taxes and avoid penalties; another is taking tests. Even if we have unpleasant experiences, we do it to obtain the privileges earned and granted. The goal of surviving life-threatening situations in military combat comes from learning the best combat skills. Fear is a big motivator in the mastery of new skills.

As you may have guessed, there is more to mastery and accomplishment than a goal or motivation. In all situations before the new accomplishment is obtained, uncertainty exists in various forms. There is the uncertainty of what to do first, and then there is the uncertainty of how to do each step along the way, each part of the process. Additionally there are the uncertainties of whether the tasks can be accomplished, and to what degree. We all start an accomplishment process with the certainty of a goal and a general path, but because we have never done it before, we have many degrees of uncertainty to deal with as we go forward.

When our goals are desirable, the lure is pleasurable, and the anticipation (uncertainty) is positive and usually not too difficult to overcome. Both beckon, and we become more pleasurably excited the closer we get to the goal. Many of us love cooking, and the first time we make an apple pie, we must go through the many processes and stages to get it right. With an apple pie, the crust is the most important element. When we place our pie in the oven to bake, our anticipation is mostly positive; we know in advance that the crust must be light and flakey, with just the right texture and taste. When we achieve this goal, our crust golden and perfect, we obtain the accomplishment, the pleasurable triumph, the certainty of completion and accomplishment.

When fear shadows us as we go up the accomplishment trail, we feel harried, tense, and worried we will not make it. When we finally do succeed, passing the test and obtaining the privilege or license despite our fears and woes, we feel relief and often need a rest. Fear-induced motivation uses a lot of energy.

The way around the fear is to be willing to accept the fact that not every attempt at accomplishment is going to work out. However, we can learn why or why not and increase our ability. By doing so, we increase our confidence and reduce our fear.

As we go about growing our mastery by accomplishing one goal after another, we go from the certainty of the goal into the uncertainty of the processes, and finally to the new certainty of the accomplishment. Each time we accomplish a goal, we obtain a new platform of certainty; the foundation we stand on becomes wider and more solid, and we are able to take on more and lose our balance less often.

So throughout our lives, we repeatedly go from accomplishment to accomplishment, from certainty through uncertainty to newly obtained certainty.

The Mastery Force and the Mastery Mechanism

Life is replete with problems and tasks we have never faced before and do not understand. When we attempt to find solutions, we gain new understanding. During this process we often discover new, related ideas or explanations about how things work. By solving problems, we increase our expertise and improve our ability to obtain answers; we add to our repertoire of solutions and ways to approach problems or situations.

In medical school we practiced a tongue-in-cheek, three-step road to mastery when learning to do new procedures such as a spinal tap. "Watch one, do one, teach one." Though this is an oversimplification, it offers an understandable process to follow. When you finally get to teach one, you are not only proficient at doing it, but you understand the process sufficiently enough to teach it well.

By utilizing our sense of certainty and uncertainty, we accumulate skills and master more tasks. Once we turn a problem into a solved certainty, the new know-how can become automatic through some repetition and will be available for future use. When life introduces new uncertainties, we can learn to no longer fear them and shrink away; instead, we can more readily move forward, finding solutions and growing.

We can either be lured by the positive uncertainty of the new desirable opportunity to master, or we can be challenged, perhaps frightened, by a new uncertainty. Either way, the onslaught of challenges continues. We can choose to master them, but we cannot choose to avoid them without peril. If we do not confront new uncertainties, our life will narrow and we will cower in fear. Our natural psychological growth pattern will be restricted.

The Physical World and the Psychological World: Differences and Similarities

When we are confronted by a danger or a physical threat, the prudent choice is to avoid it if at all possible; "Be or get safe" is the rule. However, in the psychological world sometimes growth includes frightening uncertainty— that is, danger or threat to our sense of well-being. Whatever the threat is, be it anxiety or fear of not accomplishing a desired goal, the only way to master it is to overcome its difficulty by understanding and eventually solving it. In a phrase, stand firm and master it. If we do not do so, these frightening uncertainties will constantly pop up and get in our way. It prompts a saying: "Those things you have significant uncertainty about, and that you do not master and understand, will chase you and narrow your life." By that I mean your mind will always hold onto that which is uncertain about what you are facing. Uncertainty is one of the calls to mastery, to handle, to attain beyond.

Here are two examples. Bob, a thirty-six-year-old salesman, had succeeded at a variety of sales jobs, but he was never was able to advance further in a company. To do so, he would have to become a sales manager; after that, he might advance further. He didn't know why, but he feared the responsibility of handling other salespeople; he felt guilty and inhibited at critiquing, criticizing, or mentoring others in sales positions. His inhibitions stopped his career path, reduced his income possibilities, and left him feeling vulnerable. "I can only do sales," he told me at the beginning of therapy. We uncovered, and he solved, the reason for his inhibitions: an overcritical father put Bob down, causing painful and humiliating feelings. At all costs, Bob avoided being seen as similar. He had to learn that constructive criticism could be gently delivered and genuinely helpful before he could give such to those he might manage. He was able to do this eventually and obtained a sales manager's position.

Some people are anxious in public and don't like to venture out of their houses. They miss out on a great deal of what community life has to offer if they don't learn to overcome this, missing entertainment, festivals, art shows, concerts, and the like. Some have this problem so pathologically that they have agoraphobia (fear of the marketplace) and chain themselves to their homes, living a life of fearful anticipation. These people require actual clinical treatment to break their reclusive patterns. The fear and uncertainty compounds ever greater, and their lives become ever more painful until they master the problem and remove it.

In the physical world, get safe and preserve life; avoid the dangerous uncertainty. In the psychological world, stand firm, analyze, and master the problem. Too often I have seen people try to flee and avoid psychological uncertainties, much to their dismay. Alas, we cannot flee—the uncertainties are inside our minds, and we cannot get away from them. We can only settle the uncertainties by solving them.

Our built-in mastery mechanism works even when we become overly content or slothful. It alerts us when we are not progressing and offers us a diet of boredom, the feeling of restlessness, the gnawing sense of a need to do something, or a fear that we are being passed by and are not keeping up. It happens with young adults or kids who have been pampered or overindulged. Some parents dote and are uncomfortable seeing their offspring discomforted. Unfortunately, when these overprotected individuals face their own life directly, they feel pain as they compare their life with those who achieved more. That results in the pain of shame or the ongoing discomfort of low self-esteem. Sometimes enough of this pain will get them moving and start handling life.

There is yet another difference between the physical and the mental or psychological self. When we become injured physically, we need medical attention and then healing before our full function, our range of physical motion, returns. But with the mind and a big new uncertainty, it is initially similar but ultimately different. We are vexed and stopped for the moment because it becomes difficult to proceed when we feel so uncertain. Our mind's range of motion is focused on confronting the problem and its uncertainty—and not much else. When we discover the answer to the problem and see how to handle it, the uncertainty goes away, and our mind returns to normal. However, there is one huge difference between the mind and body. Both return to full function with the problem solved, but the mind now has new capability, a greater know-how. It has both mastered and increased.

Occasionally our new solution is only partially correct and does not fully work. We then must go back through the process, making refinements or further discoveries before we can successfully work it out.

By growing your own mind and life-handling capability, you will encounter discovery after discovery. You will comprehend and understand what you have learned, and you will realize your gain in workable know-how. You will have mastered.

Certainty, Uncertainty, and Mastery Early in Life

One Sunday in the 1970s on national public television, I watched a child-development study exploring differences among infants. It focused on their levels of curiosity, daring, and hesitancy. I interpreted the study as showing the relationship between certainty, uncertainty, and mastery in the very young.

The researcher demonstrated the differences infants show in becoming curious and interested in new objects placed in front of them on a table. All the infants eventually explored the new objects, but some showed much quicker interest and less fear (a stronger exploratory drive) than others.

The infants were about six months old and sat in the lap of their mothers next to a table. A colored small object was placed on the table in front of the infant, and after a timed duration, each infant either vigorously or cautiously picked up the object, placed it in his or her mouth, and eventually set it back on the table, sometimes with the mother's help. The infants then usually repeated the sequence.

After an infant was comfortable with the first object, a new object was introduced a few inches away from the original one. Some infants immediately reached for the new object; others shied away and reached for the familiar object. Some looked back to the mother, presumably seeking direction or approval that it was safe. Eventually each child picked up the new object, but many had to get secure with the old object first. The sequence of introducing a new object was repeated several times, and the individual patterns each infant demonstrated remained consistent throughout the experiment.

My interpretation was that the familiar object and the use of the mouth to explore it, as well as sitting in the lap of the mother, provided familiarity and some sense of certainty. Most infants stayed with this process for a while, getting a sense of security, safety, and familiarity—in other words, a feeling of certainty—before venturing further to the newly introduced object. A few brave infants (or reckless; you choose the interpretation) immediately sought the new and discarded the old. All of the infants went from new uncertainty (the first object) to making it a newly won certainty, and then eventually to the next new uncertainty.

In a similar manner, toddlers increase their physical ability. First they stand, then walk while leaning, then eventually walk unassisted, having gained the skill through trial and error. Like infants and toddlers, we all keep moving forward to our next new challenge, our next new uncertainty, while retaining our previous certainties. We keep turning the uncertainty into a new capability, a new certainty, new expertise. With each gain, we increase in skill and knowledge. This fascinating process is hardwired within us. The mastery process is both a psychological truth and a true psychological process.

Two Types of Mastery: Mastery by Understanding and Mastery by Doing

Theories and even facts we understand serve as tools for contemplation, problem solving, and research. This is mastery by understanding or comprehending. In a system of thoughts, concepts, truths, and facts about a given subject, comprehending is the mastery form. Once we possess this type of mastery, we can apply new comprehensions to gain even greater awareness. We can also apply this mastery process to prior problems and reinterpret them in the light of our new knowledge. The "Ah ha!" of discovery and new understanding herald the arrival of this kind of mastery.

However, no matter how much we intellectually understand certain processes and how they work, we must actually do them to master them. It is not enough to understand the engineering of a racing bicycle if we are to repair or modify it; we also need hands-on experience. For a child to learn how to ride a bicycle and overcome the fear and uncertainty about succeeding, the child must actually ride the bicycle to gain the skill. Unless the skill is physically accomplished (learned), the fear, self-doubt, and lack of confidence will not go away. Giving a speech in front of an audience can be frightening, so the way to gain confidence and minimize the fear is to give speeches—a lot of them. This eventually reduces the performance anxiety and its element of fear. Mastering a psychological fear or overcoming a phobia requires success at doing it. Although the understanding, preparation, and forethought are important, only by doing it will we accomplish the mastering.

Learning physical skills, such as a sport, dance, or playing a musical instrument, requires the correct moves and repetition. By doing something again and again, we gain a desired level of skill. All of the intellectual energy, and the observation of others doing it, will not and cannot substitute for the actual activity of learning to do it.

The Metaphor of the Horse and Rider: Encouragement

For some, learning to observe, understand, and then manage the power of their mind and all it produces can be overwhelming and disconcerting at first. In the following mastery process metaphor, the horse is the raw energy and power of your natural untrained mind; the rider is the comprehending, deciding, and managing part of your self. The metaphor gives both an overview and encouragement to make the effort to gain the rewards.

You, the rider, desire to domesticate and learn to ride a previously unridden and powerful horse. You study the horse and its characteristics as it trots inside a corral. One morning you decide you will attempt to ride it. You have the ranch hands hold and saddle it, and then you climb on. The horse bucks, runs, crow hops, and tries to throw you. It bangs your leg against the corral wall and finally throws you. After dusting off, you try again and again. Discouraged, you have the horse taken back to its stall. The next day and for several days afterward, you try again.

Finally, one week later you succeed in riding the horse. You soon develop a trusted partnership with this proud steed. Now you can open the corral gate and ride your horse into the open range, exploring new vistas; you can tether it and have a picnic while enjoying the great outdoors. Compared to walking, by learning to ride the horse, you have greatly increased your range of options and levels of freedom, capability, and power.

Our life, mind, and consciously aware self are like the metaphor. The rider is our desire to master and gain new ability. The powerful horse is the potential we currently have, both unused and untrained; it also represents the vast signaling system of our mind and our automatic capabilities that have served us so far. The rider becomes the strong leader, the conductor who coordinates all of the aspects of our mind and self to increase our capability, opportunity, and range of options. There can be effort and struggle along the way, but there are many rewards to keep going. Once we have developed this valuable partnership sufficiently, we are well on our way to a life of ever-increasing capability.

Mastery Failures

Giving up too quickly and easily, when the going gets tough, is a common cause of mastery failures; you do not learn or accomplish the tasks before you. This type of failure stops your forward progress and limits your horizons.

These failures may also set into motion the wheels of poor self-actions like being stuck in envy or jealousy instead of learning from it. Being stuck and always blaming others, instead of accepting responsibility, is also a poor self-action. Yet another unsuccessful way to compensate for a lack of success and an unwillingness to attempt accomplishing goals is by always having to be right. It is a way of being stubborn or unprogressive, never modifying or learning a new view.

To master envy or jealousy, we must consciously make note of the problem, give it up, and attempt to obtain through self-accomplishment what is being envied or what we are jealous about. For the mastery failure problem of always having to be right or always blaming others (which are very restricting), the right course is honestly asking ourselves, "What is my role here? What can I do differently? What can I do to improve or master this situation? What is the real truth?" These simple, heartfelt questions put us on the right track to stop the maladaptive behavior and instead move toward a good solution.

Still another common psychological mastery failure is avoidance. Although avoidance works in dangerous physical situations—the "let's get out of here fast to be safe" reflex—it does not work in situations that require problem-solving thought, effort, and the discovery of new methods. Only by solving the specific situation or mastering it can we progress. The best strategy is always to face problems and dilemmas.

Limiting Out—A Mastery Failure

Limiting out is a pervasive and unfortunate failure at mastery or best effort; I see it all too often in the medical profession and in parenting. Limiting out is the act of stopping short of finding an adequate solution to a problem on the part of the person who is vested with the responsibility for solving the problem. If you find yourself limiting out, it means you are not accepting the fact that there are unsolved uncertainties still operating. When you limit out, you stop exploring and dogmatically stop the opportunity for discovering the truth; this is a failure of mastery. Instead, suggest help elsewhere, through consultation with someone more expert.

Limiting out is also a failure to inquire further when a result different than the one expected occurs. I have seen it when physicians were consulted by me or other family members for a proper diagnosis. In my case, I am fortunate to be able to quickly identify when a complete diagnostic study and successful treatment has not been done. Unfortunately, this has happened several times to both my family and me. Admittedly, we all had complex and difficult diagnostic problems. Fortunately I have colleagues I can ask who are masters at their medical specialties, and they have guided me on these frustrating occasions of poor diagnosis to seek consultation from other trusted medical experts. When one of my daughters received an inadequate diagnosis from several specialists and wasn't getting any better, the late Dr. Sherman Coleman, a much-revered professor and head of the Department of Orthopedics at the University of Utah, candidly said it sounded like she "had seen a lot of doctors but had not seen any physicians."

I see this daily during my consultation service at a general hospital. Occasionally an internist or surgeon will chide a patient because the treatment is not working or the surgical result was different than expected. The physician may say to the patient, "This should not be. It should be different." Needless to say, the patient reacts with confusion and frustration. At that point, I get called in to see the patient as a psychiatric consultant. To be sure, there are often associated psychiatric (psychological) elements, but often the physician who makes the shortsighted comment has failed to accept the troubling and confounding new uncertainty, and has not looked further for solutions. For best medical practice, it is necessary for the physician to accept the unusual result as a truth that requires further study, a mystery to solve. Limiting out does not help the patient, and the doctor comes off looking foolish, short-tempered, easily frustrated, and inadequate to the task. The way to stop limiting out is to be intellectually honest and speak frankly and truthfully to the patient. "You've had an unexpected and confusing result. I do not understand why, but I'll pursue it with the assistance of consultants if necessary, so we can find the most that medical science knows about this." That is what a good physician does.

I see limiting out with parents who get frustrated with their children for rules' infractions or episodes of frequent, pestering questioning. For example, take the situation when a child fails to do an assigned chore or duty, such as cleaning up his or her room. The child asks, "Why do I have to do this?" The limiting-out parent counters, "Because I said so!" rather than carefully and thoughtfully explaining the reasons why to the child. We have all limited out on occasions, but by being aware of its existence, we can stop doing it and instead find a mastery way of solving the problem.

Children often do not see the value in picking up toys. It is easy to show how someone could trip and fall from stepping on one, or how easy it would be to break a favorite plastic toy if someone inadvertently stepped on it. These explanations and demonstrations help. If the child continues to resist, leaving toys on the floor, ask the child to walk on the floor barefoot. The child will protest, "No, I'll hurt my feet if I do." The wiser parent then responds, "Now you know a good reason for picking up your toys after you use them."

Studies in child development show that when children know the purpose for a restriction or punishment, they will accept and learn from it. A good explanation is that they are to pay an energy price, a punishment, for obstructing the family or creating problems for others. Then a creative punishment (doing a useful chore, for instance) is meted out. When interviewed later, sometimes many years later, the offspring view their parents as fair, respectful, and understanding. They believe they were taught lessons wisely and well. Most parents appreciate being viewed this way; it is far better than being viewed as irritable, ill tempered, or limiting out.

Chapter Summary

1. The mastery mechanism, the mastery process, is instilled within us from birth and serves us well.
2. Desire and fear are the primary conditions that motivate us toward our goals.
3. In all situations before a new accomplishment is obtained, uncertainty exists in various forms.
4. We all start an accomplishment process with the certainty of a goal and a general path, but because we have never done it before, we have many degrees of uncertainty to deal with as we go forward.
5. The way around the fear is to be willing to accept the fact that not every attempt at accomplishment is going to work out. However, we can learn why or why not and increase our ability.
6. Once we make a problem into a solved certainty, the new know-how can become automatic through some repetition and will be available for future use. When life introduces new uncertainties, we can learn to no longer fear them and shrink away. Instead, we can more readily move forward, finding solutions and growing.

7. No matter how much we intellectually understand certain processes and how they work, we must actually do them to master them. For a child to learn how to ride a bicycle and overcome the fear and uncertainty about succeeding, he or she must actually ride the bicycle to gain the skill. Unless the skill is physically accomplished (learned), the fear, the self-doubt, and the lack of confidence will not go away.

8. Giving up too quickly and easily when the going gets tough is a common cause of mastery failures; you do not learn or accomplish the tasks before you. This type of failure stops your forward progress and limits your horizons.

9. Another unsuccessful way to compensate for a lack of success and an unwillingness to attempt *accomplishing goals is by always having to be right.* It is a way of being stubborn or unprogressive, never modifying or learning a new view.

10. Avoidance is helpful for dangerous physical situations, but it doesn't help solve problems. Face and master your issues in order to grow and progress.

11. If you find yourself limiting out, it means you are not accepting the fact that there are unsolved uncertainties still operating. When you limit out, you stop exploring and eliminate the opportunity for discovering the truth. This is a failure of mastery. Instead, look for help elsewhere if needed.

CHAPTER 5

--- ◆◆◆◆◆ ---

The Flow of Certainty and Uncertainty in Our Minds

Your natural information categorizers (certain or uncertain) operate continuously to guide you as you process incoming information. You can deliberately use this psychological truth for greater clarity and efficiency.

The processes of certainty and uncertainty work naturally, subconsciously, and constantly for us. Certainty and uncertainty are the great guideposts of our mind's fundamental information-organizing ability, and learning techniques for setting them can help you return to paths of clear thinking when you become confused.

Let me acquaint you with how constantly they operate with this example scenario. We'll take a hypothetical drive through a neighborhood, paying attention to our thought processes. While driving along, we notice a "For Sale" sign on an attractive house, and we slow to look it over. There are information sheets on the sign post, so we stop and take one. We note the sales price, square footage, number of rooms, and other details. If we are interested, we jot down the realtor's number for a later call. We have been lured by a positive element of uncertainty—something attractive. We start again, looking side to side at the neighborhood as we move through it, assessing its attractiveness. If it looks good, we get a sense of pleasurable certainty. If it does not look good, we say no to the neighborhood and the house—this time it is in the negative.

A moving object suddenly comes into view from a yard on the left. Startled, we think, "What is it?" (uncertainty). We identify it as a soccer ball (certainty), and because of prior learning (prior certainties), we quickly realize a child might dash out into the street, so we hit the brakes to be safe (a known certainty). No child darts out, and we look around. No one is coming yet, so we drive cautiously for a brief time, then drive onward. We see an intersection a few houses ahead, but just then a car backs down a driveway on our right. We slow down, uncertain if the other driver sees us. The car finally slows and stops near the street, so we assume that we have been seen and that it will not back into us (assumed certainty). We drive on, watching carefully. Seeing that it is okay (certainty), we pass the car. When we arrive at the intersection, the light is red, the certainty signal to stop until we get the green to go.

Our minds often alert us to new uncertainties. We encounter and make assessments, seeking a level of certainty. We apply known techniques or recognize familiar, old certainties as we go through our lives. We respond and categorize in terms of uncertainty or certainty, giving us the ability to handle the copious amounts of data and situations we face daily. We do this automatically, mostly unconsciously. These are natural gifts of our mind, perhaps our most basic and useful processes. They help keep us safe by identifying what is dangerous or what is benign in our environment. They help keep us clear-minded by categorizing our incoming information, which gives us security and an adventuresome attitude to seek and explore new experiences and unknowns. As we shall see, they are components of our danger signals and our anxieties, integral parts of our mastery mechanism and our overall greater increase (knowledge-accumulation) process.

Our certainty and uncertainty senses are the great information and truth organizers of our minds, whether something is a known or an unknown. There is a psychological truth about them: Minds seek certainty and uncertainty at all times. In order to make something certain, it must have been uncertain first; in order to seek, there must be uncertainty that is sought into, to eventually make it a new certainty. Certainty is an aspect of our repertoire to handle life, our abilities, and our knowledge up until now. But we cannot grow and gain (increase), which we continue to do lifelong, unless we seek new experience, knowledge, and discovery. I call our continuously operating certainty-uncertainty sequence our continuously operating mental pulse. It comes about in response to our physical movements and observations and our constant mental movements, our thoughts.

True and helpful as our certainty and uncertainty organizing mental process is, it is most beneficial within a certain range where the amount of uncertainty is neither too great (overwhelmed or confused by so much uncertainty) or too little (flat, bored, not progressing, clinging to old certainties while avoiding new learning or opportunities).

When we monitor our processes in handling life, we discover we deal constantly with the known and unknown; past, present, and future; certain and uncertain. Some outer events, such as the seasons, elections, holidays, and athletic events, are known and certain to the extent that we plan for their expected or scheduled occurrence. Some external complex forces, such as the state of the economy, earthquakes, and any unforeseen things in the future, remain uncertainties until more information is available.

As a psychiatrist, I have seen that those who handle uncertainty less well generally experience more difficulties, more problems, and greater impairment in their quality of life. Conversely, those who handle the uncertainties well tend to solve problems more easily, have less pain and inefficiency, and have a better quality of life; they are realistic thinkers.

The certainty and uncertainty senses not only categorize information but also organize it. When we are certain about something, our mind stores it as handled and lets it go. If uncertain, we continue to explore it until we have the fullest understanding we can obtain. If the subject or issue is not very important, we quickly decide to not deal with it and let it pass from our mind; if it is important, we keep working on it. It is this decisiveness that keeps us clear minded and less confused or overloaded. At the most basic level these senses support survival, determining friend or foe, benefit or danger, unimportant or valuable.

These marvelous internal senses are great guides. When we choose to learn about them consciously, applying them by choice and design, we benefit from their powerful clarifying effect. When we add this consciously learned dimension to our lives, we move from doing haphazardly well to always doing well, without as much effort.

The Many Faces of Certainty

The purpose of uncertainty is to attempt to handle a situation about which we are uncertain, so we can successfully complete it. In essence, we change uncertainty to certainty. When something is certain, we know it for sure; certainty is definite, and there is no question about it. We have clarity as to what it is and how it works. Certainty is also a statement about reality—it is a truth. Further, it is a psychological truth for each individual.

The Foundations of Certainty

Our repository of certainties is like our own personal mental library, which contains the learning, knowledge, and skills we have acquired and now possess. We utilize these certainties and capabilities every day. A skilled craftsman says, "Yes, I can make an attractive and functional cabinet for you in this small space. I know how; I've done it before." An electrical engineer willingly takes on a large and complex project because he or she knows how to do it.

The Settling Effect of Certainty

Certainty has a powerful settling effect. I recall a medical experience while working as a young psychiatrist for the air force many years ago. I became ill with daily headaches and a constant fever, and it became increasingly difficult to work. I discussed my symptoms with a neurologist colleague. He thought I might have a viral infection stimulating some migraine headaches. Two days later, I sought further consultation with a very good internist and infectious disease specialist. When I described my symptoms, including a constant burning under my skin, he told me he knew I had encephalitis (a serious brain infection).

Astounded, I asked, "Why are you certain?"

"Because I have just seen six other cases of confirmed encephalitis today, with exactly the same symptoms."

His explanation was exactly what I needed. He knew what my illness was: I had encephalitis. I immediately felt relief; there was an answer to my fears and worries, to my medical uncertainty. Just knowing what my illness was settled me down quickly, even though I had a potentially dangerous disease. Now we could proceed with treatment. How powerful the sense of certainty is!

Using Former Certainties to Deal with Future Situations

Even painful situations can offer valuable experience and later serve as warnings. Painful memories are invaluable when we deal with similar situations in the future. When we compare new situations with our older certainties—what we have experienced before—we can call upon established strategies for dealing with them. Recognizing prior successes gives us confidence to proceed into new uncertainties. These new challenges are our new opportunities; sometimes they are even new dangers.

Relying on True Certainty

I live by this credo: I will never say I am absolutely certain unless I truly am. If I have a slight bit of uncertainty, I want to say so openly, both to myself and to others who may be involved. I want to know and speak the truth. I have found far too often that people indulge in flights of opinion, conjecture, and theory, which they then attempt to pass off as truth or certainty. I suspect we all know someone who does this, and we have done it occasionally ourselves. This practice lacks credibility and is wrong—it is false certainty. Conversely, real certainty provides an excellent foundation from which to venture forward, because it is solid and true. When we use true certainty regardless of whether our new ventures prove successful, they will not fail because they were based on a faulty structure that is claimed to be certainty. Try this out for yourself: Say aloud, "I will never say I am absolutely certain unless I truly am." If you do this, you will be able to trust your sense of certainty.

We merely need to look at early childhood to see just how strong the inherent process of seeking certainty is. Notice children or toddlers and how frequently they are drawn to nearby objects. They want to touch and possess everything they see, constantly grabbing items. They like the familiar—their bottle, teddy bear, and blanket—but they incessantly seek out and pick up everything new. They like to acquire, creating an ever-widening circle of accumulated certainties (familiarities). Of course, at the center of their circle is the special certainty of mommy, daddy, or a sibling. They accumulate new certainties while clinging to the safe and familiar.

Potential Problems from a Dominating Need for Certainty

As nice as the sense of certainty can be, there can be problems from a too dominating need for it. A common pitfall is the premature rush to certainty, usually because uncertainty feels too uncomfortable, foreign, or blockading. I have seen people give up a useful stance or position in an important negotiation (one with significant consequences for the future) because the uncertainty and infighting becomes so unpleasant; they just want to get it over and find relief. This is a common situation during property settlements at painful times of divorce.

Ann gave up a large portion of her economic future because she became tired and harried during legal battles with Ned, her divorcing husband. She had been a stay-at-home mom, raising the children while Ned benefited from her father's financial assistance during his professional schooling. Realistically, alimony plus the agreed-upon child support were warranted. She needed the money to further her education, obtain a better job, and have some potential future investments. By now Ned had a handsome income, and their standard of living had risen. Divorce laws at the time allowed for an equitable settlement, but mediation and relative standardization of property settlement values had not yet come into vogue, so these were negotiable. Ned's tough attorney wore Ann down with requests and interrogatories. Her mediocre and passive attorney let her do the deciding without much advice. She finally gave up, letting Ned have the lion's share just to get the process over, to stop the uncertainty and be at peace. A few months later, Ann woke up to the painful reality of too little money. She was not so at peace and realized she had done the wrong thing in going for certainty too soon.

Ann came for therapy, and we worked on her certainty need. This need caused her to close off options prematurely, not only in the divorce negotiations but in other areas of life. She chose to get educated in a field with limited chance for growth or expansion, both economically and intellectually. This pattern to pick certainty quickly began as a child, when she had passively agreed and submitted, like her mother, to a dominating and strong-willed father. Her father had done well economically and had taken care of everyone in the family; in doing so, he had generally made wise decisions. Ann identified with her mother's patterns and liked the ease of not having to think through the uncertainties and make tough decisions.

Unfortunately, when Ned divorced her, she again chose the passive and easy route rather than identify with her deceased father's tougher negotiating stance. Though her father had taken care of both her and her mother earlier in life, Ned was not going to do the same for her. Her dependency on certainty clouded her logic about her own future. After a year of therapy she could tolerate uncertainty better, even relish it at times, and she eventually went back to court and obtained a better settlement.

Other Vulnerabilities to a Certainty Need

Super salespeople throw us off guard, making us uncertain if we are not prepared for them and wearing us out. I used to be this way when I'd buy a car. Instead of shopping around for better prices, I'd succumb to "I'll make you such a great deal that you'll buy now!" Friends have told me the same thing. Now I am much more comfortable and in charge of myself, so I am no longer vulnerable. When we say yes to get certainty, we are easily victimized. Most of us may have bitten once or twice. We want to stop the whirling uncertainty and get people off our back. We want to feel certain and settled, and we are more vulnerable and uncertain if what they are selling has some actual appeal. Our certainty need takes over, and we say yes just to end the encounter. After a few experiences, we learn to avoid these pressure strategies and say, "No thanks, not interested."

The Many Faces of Uncertainty

To varying degrees, uncertainty is an ever-present, general condition. It is a guiding force keeping us aware that the unknown and the uncertain needs our attention and has considerable influence. Tomorrow's result is uncertain because it has not happened yet. Though astronomers tell us the sun will burn out in a few billion years, it concerns us little, being so distant. The weather, later in the day, is uncertain though there is a prediction, and we may have to use that information for our planning.

Although everything in the future is uncertain because it has not happened, there are patterns we can rely on, such as the sun coming up each new morning. On the other hand, that same predictable certainty will end sometime in the next few billion years.

There are external, unwanted uncertainties as well: ever-changing economic conditions, disasters, power outages, droughts, crimes, accidents, acts of terror, and changes in law. When we go about our daily lives and venture out into the world, though we tend to think we know what will occur, we do not know for sure how the day will turn out until the results are in. Only then, at day's end, do we see all of the new, unplanned, uncertain situations that occurred during the day.

By and large, the greater the number of uncertainties that influence an outcome, the greater the risk or likelihood of not getting the desired result. New circumstances interrupt and interfere with our plans and outcomes, but so do new opportunities. Ultimately the end result of uncertainty is growth, new certainties, experience, and skill development if we respond to it well.

Uncertainties That Pose Formidable Threats and Challenges

A number of uncertainties fall into the category of threats and pose formidable challenges, requiring great attention on our part. In fact, a large portion of our waking mental life is spent considering and being influenced by these kinds of uncertainties. The simple truth is that we cannot escape them, so it's important for us to first recognize and deal with each in a timely and skillful manner.

"My child is ill with a fever of 104.5! What should I do?" one frantic parent asks the on-call pediatrician. "I do not feel good and my chest hurts. What is it?" a forty-five-year-old inquires at the emergency room, fearful he might be having a heart attack. When we sense danger, we experience frightening uncertainty. We go on alert to better protect or save ourselves. Anxiety or panic can create frightening uncertainty too. Though these uncertainties are painful and difficult, they also have considerable value.

When uncertainties about new situations come our way, particularly new opportunities, many of us suffer from terrifying blockades: "I can't try that. I'm afraid I won't succeed." Or, "What will people think of me?" Or, "I've never done that before; I've always been afraid of the unknown."

Some dangerous uncertainties can even kill us, such as the panic and hysteria of desperate people clogging a nightclub exit and fleeing a fire. Terrorists' actions are dangerous and unpredictable; they play on our sense of frightening uncertainty, evoking and dangling its power before us.

Overload Uncertainty

Overload, a product of recent times, is an addition to the list of uncertainties we encounter. There is little argument that our modern, fast-paced, information- and technology-based environment creates pain and can make us cast about anxiously, searching for relief. Overload uncertainty occurs when we perceive we have more to deal with than we can possibly accomplish: there is too little available time, not enough energy, or too few resources. The examples are legion: a mother harried by demands of her children, husband, career, and endless deadlines. The result is we can become bewildered, overwhelmed, angry, irritable, and frustrated. Although overload is not welcome, it can be managed.

Mark is a one-time patient who devised a useful way of handling it. "Overload happens," he told me, "when you have more to do than time to do it in." When there are far too many tasks, he concluded, the logical options are to add more time, prioritize each task, or delegate the work to others. When Mark felt overloaded, before he decided how to proceed, he put all the tasks he needed to accomplish on a list or calendar, including the deadlines. Starting with the most important, the list allowed him to visualize each task and realistically estimate the time and work required to accomplish it. Not surprisingly, once Mark created and analyzed his master list, he felt relieved. By committing the factors of his overload to paper, he neutralized the confusion and anxiety, and the overload lost its power.

Uncertainty tends to multiply when we try to manage or balance too many things simultaneously. The simple act of listing allows us to put overload issues into a more realistic venue, where perspective thrives and we can eliminate the fear of forgetting something and the confusion of keeping everything straight. Next, Mark made decisions: he prioritized, dropping some tasks on the list and delegating others, and then he set a schedule he liked to call "Do when due."

Occasionally a project is so large and has so many diverse and conflicting elements that we feel overwhelmed by the amount of work required to do it. When this happens, divide it up into smaller chunks and do these more easily handled amounts. As long as we occasionally look at the total project in overview and then get back to doing the smaller sections, we will eventually complete the project in a more comfortable and efficient way. Also, if we find a big problem with a task or one without a solution, we need not let it dead-end us. Simply turn to another task and return to the problem area later. Rest assured that many times problems will solve themselves as projects progress, or they are more easily solved when we return to them at a later date, knowing more.

Confusion Uncertainty

A simple but powerful technique for dealing with confusion caused by too much uncertainty is to create a certainty and uncertainty evaluation of everything involved. Frank, a busy media executive, managed the great volume of information and deadlines associated with his work by making a list with only two headings, certain and uncertain. Once Frank finished the list, he only dealt with the items listed under "uncertain," because he already knew the certain items. We can get so caught up in the uncertainties that we even start being uncertain about what we already know or have accomplished. Somehow the uncertainties are contagious, attacking and invading every aspect of our thinking. When we seek clarification by creating a certain and uncertain list, and then we only deal with the uncertain, the confusion and anxiety disappear and everything becomes more manageable; our mind settles. I've provided an example below.

Frank's List

Certain, Done:
- Cost of the original Jones advertising project
- Deadline date for printout of company's new brochure is number one
- Cost of seven of eight items to complete the Armstrong project
- I have already let Mr. Armstrong know the cost of the seven known items
- Three other projects 50 percent completed
- A 4:00 p.m. Thursday doctor appointment

Uncertain, To Do:
- Cost of the two requested changes in the Jones project
- Find out second and third brochure possible completion dates
- Get bids from two sources for the cost of item eight in Armstrong, to discuss overall costs when bid on item eight is in
- When can we start two new projects?
- Call dentist, make appointment

Worrying Uncertainty

Worrying is another condition of uncertainty. When it is employed briefly, it can be of great usefulness because it gets our attention and concern, allowing us to double-check all aspects of an issue or concern and making sure we are prepared for unforeseen events in the future. This includes such things as preparation for a job interview, or enough study to handle the questions of a school examination. Worry arises when we concern ourselves with all the instructions for an upcoming surgery, or when practicing for a music recital. "Have I done enough? What's going to happen when I get on stage?" We can worry a great deal when we consider all of our concerns about our teenager or elderly parent.

The list of things we worry about is endless and becomes a problem when the number reaches a point of excess and feeds on itself, doing no further good. Worry becomes a wildfire of uncertainty, burning with concerns and not letting us be at peace. My patient Jill was a constant worrier. "I worry about things ahead of time, over and over again. I have trouble letting worry go, until something is over, and then I can be at peace," she told me. We correctly identified that she was doing more than occasional useful checking ahead of time, to make sure she had done everything she possibly could and that some factor in the upcoming situation had not changed from before. By worrying, she was excessively engaging in what I call "substitutive action," grinding her mind, thinking and rethinking ahead of time, because she did not like to accept that she was helpless to do anything further to influence the outcome of an upcoming event. She was impatient and strongly felt the need to "make sure." She had overdeveloped her belief that worry helped, to the point of superstition. To be free of excessive worrying, she needed to acknowledge and empower the truth that there was no more she could realistically do, and to then let go with her mind. By becoming consciously aware of what she had been doing and changing to what realistically worked better for her, she broke her worry habit and freed herself. Her case was classic as to what worriers do.

Frightening Uncertainty

Fear of the unknown is another uncertainty; it is a natural condition, known to exist within all of the animal kingdom. This fear falls into the category of frightening uncertainty. Initially, fear helps us by protecting us from venturing into areas we are not well equipped to negotiate. It fences unknown areas off-limits until we develop greater capacity to understand or comprehend, giving us time to develop the skills to proceed. There is an inverse relationship between amount of capability and amount of fear with uncertainty. Generally, the greater the fear is, the smaller the capability is in comparison. Said another way, the greater the capability is, the less the level of fear is in frightening uncertainty; enough capability will overcome frightening uncertainty.

Fear of the Unknown Problems

For some, the frightening uncertainty (fear of the unknown) can become pervasive. When this happens, self-growth and range of exploration are severely limited, which can cause us to seek havens of security when a better approach might be to cautiously explore. If we do not ever venture out, never attempting anything new, our mental and personal growth becomes stunted, and then a new fear—the fear of being left behind—invades and paralyzes us. If we're not careful, each of us can fall prey to frightening uncertainty, increase it out of all proportion, and then find ourselves clinging too tightly to our prior "secure" certainties. Then we become less adventurous, feel stale, get bored easily, and yet constantly have a slightly unsettling feeling. We lack zest for life, missing out on the excitement that new discovery or new learning can bring. We live half-lives that are too certain and unfulfilling.

We do not need to be a daring adventurer or an extreme risk taker. But if we do not learn to venture out and deal with new life situations, or if we do not attempt our increase our abilities and knowledge, we pay a price of not having sufficient capacity to deal with new circumstances. When this happens, it becomes painfully apparent that we must act, or our fear will worsen and our capacity will become even more insufficient.

After all, lives, societies, and technologies evolve, and to some extent we need to keep up. This bears repeating. Those things we are uncertain about, that we do not master but would rather avoid, will chase us and narrow our lives.

Succumbing to Alarming Uncertainty

There is a potentially contagious form of frightening uncertainty that alarmists create when they experience immediate concern or fear about something that might happen in the future. They express it this way: "Oh my gosh, what if ...?" Some examples are, "What if we arrive late? What will happen?" Or, "Oh my gosh, what if the predicted storm hits sooner than expected and spoils our party?" For a family trying to buy a house, it could be, "What if the seller doesn't accept our offer? What will we do?" These types of questions, generated by the overreaction of fear, can stimulate fear and uncertainty in others who hear it.

I had a patient, Jennifer, whose father walked anxiously around the house, wringing his hands and exclaiming, "Oh my gosh, all will be lost! All will be lost!" He even did this with small concerns and worries. Moments later, the entire family followed suit, feeling alarmed, scared, overwhelmed, and unsure of what to do. It took this patient some years after growing up, and some therapy, to see the negative effect her father's alarmist attitude imposed on her. She did it herself until she developed a calmer, more analytic approach.

It started with a question I asked during a psychotherapy session, in response to one of her alarmist questions of "Oh my gosh, what if ...?" "Well," I asked, "what if it *did* happen the way you feared? What then? What would happen to you, and what would you do?"

She stopped, stunned. After a moment of silence, she answered, "Well, I'd pick up the pieces and go on. That option would be closed off, so I'd do something else."

"Then all was not lost, and life didn't end?" I asked.

"Of course not," she replied, smiling and relaxing. She saw the ludicrous nature of her father's approach and her identification with it.

The technique for solving this overexpression of frightening uncertainty is to answer the fearful question with the feared result and then ask, "What then?" It points to the realistic fact that life goes on, in spite of disappointment or adversity. There are always new options and new strategies.

Evolving in the Face of Frightening Uncertainty

When we decide to evolve, to grow or develop by conscious design, we are introduced to new but masterable frightening uncertainties. We experience these when we perceive, rightly or wrongly, that our capacity is inadequate to handle the new growth task. Our old instinctual or learned fear of the unknown resurfaces to protect us. With experience, confidence, and courage we can talk ourselves past the fear and proceed.

To help along this path, ask the following questions. "What causes me to act or feel this way? What is a better way? Why am I vulnerable to this type of situation? How can I strengthen myself? Whom might I consult to assist me? Why do I keep making that same interpersonal mistake over and over? Even though it causes me some grief and difficulty, why do I keep doing it? It must have served a need; what need? What would work better instead?"

As you gradually discover answers to these questions, your psychological strength and capacity increase. You will have greater self-knowledge, self-direction, and more life-managing tools. You will develop greater ability to handle uncertainty.

Severe Frightening Uncertainty in Both the Danger and the Anxiety Signal

An exploration about frightening uncertainty wouldn't be complete without pointing out this important signal's pivotal role in two of our very critical life-management signals: our danger signal and our anxiety signal. These signals alert and ready us to evaluate threats to both our safety and our quality of life. Recall these were previously discussed in the "Emotional Alphabet" chapter. They will be further elaborated in the "Anxiety" chapter.

Frightening Uncertainty in the Very Young: An Example

Frightening uncertainty affects everybody, even the very young. One morning my one-year-old nephew taught me some valuable lessons about certainty and uncertainty. Kirby had been bouncing and crawling around on a king-sized bed in the adjoining hotel suite, giggling and playing with his aunt. Their play was interrupted when she was called to the phone. She kept her eye on him as he continued to romp around the bed. At a point he got too close to the edge and tumbled to the floor before someone could reach him.

Just as his aunt picked him up, Kirby expressed his first response, surprise, with its attendant loud cry, and I think a brief moment of incredulity and slight confusion: "Where did the bed go? What happened? I was so safe a moment ago." His sudden loss of the platform of certainty was very upsetting. His cry changed to fear: "How could this happen? What has happened to me?" Then came both emotional hurt and the awareness of some physical hurt. He felt a sense of danger that it had happened to him—he was hurt and did not like it.

As he went through this progression of awareness and emotions, his cry changed in pitch, inflection, and intensity. It conveyed the sequence of responses I was privy to hear. Young children often live in what I call the kingdom of childhood certainty. Every need and situation is responded to by caretakers, and children rely on this, much as they physically rely on always being caught when thrown playfully in the air. Recall also how often an infant, secure in your arms, will throw him or herself backward, to be caught and safely held by your encircling arms; he or she expects and relies upon this, assuming the encircling certainty will always be there. When it is not, they have a rude and shocking awakening, just as Kirby had in his experience of "certainty lost." Kirby became more cautious around edges and drop-offs from that moment onward.

Welcome to the real world and the need for agility in handling the variable loss of smaller certainties and the constant barrage of new uncertainties.

The General Rules for Handling Uncertainty

Knowing how to identify and categorize the individual varieties of uncertainty gives us significant power in handling our lives. We have seen ten different types of uncertainty that can cause us problems, as well as a different but successful strategy for handling each. We can categorize them, and then we can use the appropriate general strategy for solving the type of uncertainty problem. It will fall into one of ten possible scenarios described in this chapter. This makes our task far easier and much more manageable; in turn we become more efficient and capable in handling our lives.

Positive Uncertainty
The Lure of Positive Uncertainty

Uncertainty can cause concern, but it has an equal ability to be positive. Positive uncertainty (the promise of reward or the allure of a good gain) makes life exciting and rewarding. Positive uncertainty is a great motivator because it gives us the zest to obtain the objects of our desire. It is the main ingredient of pleasurable anticipation, and it is often nearly as much fun as the gain we obtain later. If we could not imagine what a trip to a new or favorite place would be like, we would not be excited to go there or be lured by the prospects of the fun and enjoyable time we might experience. Positive uncertainty feeds us with pleasure ahead of time, keeping us moving forward toward desirable goals. It gives us enough of a taste to keep us wanting more, the final and bigger rewarding pleasure of accomplishment or attainment.

Remember as a child how excited you were on Christmas Eve? I could hardly sleep. My brother and I got up at five and asked our sleepy parents if it was time to see what Santa brought us. That is one of the heights of positive uncertainty during childhood.

Thrills

Years ago I asked my eight-year-old daughter what her favorite amusement park ride was and why. She immediately informed me, "The Wild Mouse, because it feels like you will fall off, but you know you won't!" Her description of the thrill of a scary roller-coaster ride is one reason people flock to amusement parks. We enjoy the daring, the thrilling risk, and the excitement. Often when the ride is over, we dash back to the entrance to have another go. Playful positive uncertainty can be a lot of fun.

Anticipation in Games and Competitive Sports

We like to play competitive games and test ourselves. We are also enthusiastic spectators, watching our favorite sports teams. One thing we like is that the game's outcome is uncertain, and we are excited and anxious to see if our team wins—again, positive uncertainty. We like it and give it to ourselves frequently. Perhaps this kind of positive uncertainty serves as a hedge against the greater, more serious uncertainties we face in daily life.

Have Enough Positive Certainty in Your Life

Modern life can sometimes seem flat or dull, or it can be continuously busy with no opportunity for pleasure. When this happens, take a moment to reflect. We may not be having enough positive uncertainty in our lives. If this is the case, we can set up some enjoyable anticipations: plan a vacation, find some entertainment, or take some time away. Doing this is part of good self-care.

The Dangers of Positive Uncertainty
Addiction to the Chase

There are potential dangers to positive uncertainty. It is possible to get so addicted to the chase, the challenge, and the excitement that we do not take time to enjoy the results. If we are not careful, we may get to the point that we find little fulfillment from our successes; people who constantly fall in and out of love and need frequent new infatuations may have this problem. It is also possible to become so driven to seek accomplishment that we never stop to enjoy the actual accomplishment; instead we seek more and more, pushing ourselves continuously. Eventually it becomes all we know and defines us.

The way to break this cycle is first to become aware of it. In the infatuation, the one experiencing frustration may need therapy, but he or she must dare to go deeper, to learn more about the other person, to develop greater trust and ongoing mutuality. People too driven to accomplishments must become aware of the pattern and hear the inner voice saying, "I must do this, then this, before I ...." They need to dare to smell the roses, take a vacation, spend more time encouraging others' hobbies or pursuits, and so on. It will be hard at first and may seem unexciting, and it will take some months to develop and enjoy a more rounded life habit.

Pie in the Sky, Too Good to Be True, "I Have to Have It!"

There is another vulnerability related to positive uncertainty that can hurt us if we fall prey to it. Enthusiasm, excitement about a goal, the strong desire to move forward, and even greed can override our good judgment. We may fall prey to "pie in the sky" investment schemes or spend over our heads for a house or car, leaving us further in debt. We might fall for a flimflam man's line, lured by a "once in a lifetime" opportunity whose outcome seems too good to be true. Another example is gambling, the positive uncertainty propelling us on and on until we have lost everything. We have probably all had a painful lesson or two.

Certainty and Uncertainty Working Together, the Adventure of Life

The great answer to uncertainty, even frightening uncertainty, is capability. In general the greater our capability, the less concern our uncertainty becomes. By growing capability over time, former frightening uncertainties become merely uncertainties, then certainties.

Uncertainty Yields to Capability

When frightening uncertainty is not truly physically dangerous, the knowledge of the inverse relationship between it and capability can help us dare to face the frightening uncertainty. We can learn to understand it and develop methods to handle it, and as we do, we gain improved mastery, greater strength, and new capability. Rest assured that uncertainty yields to the certainty of capability. With victories over frightening uncertainty, both our confidence and willingness to evolve will increase. We *can* transform frightening uncertainty into the spirit of discovery. When we accomplish this, we can say with conviction, "Excitement exists at the edge of the new unknown." It is an exhilarating, confident, and adventurous way to live.

Certainty and uncertainty work together as the vital mental pulse of our evaluating and accumulating processes. We are always seeking certainty to make things known and clear. We are always seeking into uncertainty to bring in new data, to gain new awareness, new certainties, and greater experience with more capability. We go from uncertainty to new certainty, to the next uncertainty, making it the next certainty. Both are basic to the functioning of our mastery mechanisms and to our increase drives and their continuous accumulations. We could not survive without this inherent pulse of certainty and uncertainty.

Chapter Summary

1. Know consciously what you are certain about and uncertain about when you begin to analyze a situation.
2. Know the kinds of certainty and their value.
    a. The certainty of medical diagnosis has a settling effect. It gives a foundation for treatment and what to expect.
    b. True certainty is true clarity, the new foundation for further venturing and exploring.
    c. Certainty is the known; uncertainty is the unknown. The known settles us.

d. Prior successes and accomplished certainties can give us confidence for dealing with new situations.

3. Problems with certainty:

   a. A dominating need for certainty can cause poor decisions based solely on seeking relief from uncertainty.

   b. A need for certainty can create vulnerability to salespeople's pitches, causing us to agree in order to reduce the perceived chaos created by the sales techniques.

4. Ways to handle uncertainties:

   a. For overload uncertainty, add more time or people, create lists, prioritize, and delegate.

   b. For confusion uncertainty, commit to creating a list of the certain and uncertain, and then deal only with the uncertainty.

   c. For frightening uncertainty or the fear of the unknown, venture forth carefully and increase capability as you go.

   d. For alarming uncertainty, the solution is to answer the alarm question with a question, "Well, what if it did, then what?" The alarm and fear will quickly dissipate.

   e. For evolving and frightening uncertainty, ask questions of yourself and others, such as, "How can I handle this? What can I do to prepare? Why does this give me fear? How can I reduce the fear?" Question the fear, dare to decide, and proceed.

   f. Severe frightening uncertainty is the main ingredient of anxiety, fear, and uncertainty that your quality of life is at risk. The answer is to assess the situation, make the best decisions and preparations, go through the experience, and accept the result.

   g. For severe frightening uncertainty, the human physical danger signal, get safe from the danger; remove it or remove yourself.

   h. For the positive uncertainties:

      1) The anticipation of a pleasurable outcome or rewarding result is a great motivator. Most of us need a good supply of positive uncertainty to feel good about our existence.

2) Thrills, games, and competitions give us brief feelings of positive uncertainty followed by a certainty outcome. These serve as hedges against the greater uncertainties in life.

3) The dangers of positive uncertainty:

    a) Addiction to the chase, infatuations, and continuous accomplishments to the exclusion of a more fulfilling life that contains other elements, such as deeper love and non-vocational fulfillments (family or travel) and avocational interests.

    b) Succumbing to "pie in the sky" promises through believing and hoping too strongly in a desired outcome. To overcome this danger, evaluate thoroughly, get expert advice, and proceed carefully.

5. The truths of certainty and uncertainty

    a. Certainty and uncertainty give us value in yet another way. We can categorize virtually everything we have in our mind and anything we are dealing with as certain or uncertain.

    b. The mere act of taking inventory will give us a feeling of manageability and peacefulness about our lives from time to time.

CHAPTER 6

—◆═✕═◆—

Mind Functions and How Best to Use Them

You would not know anything without the valuable psychological truth of contrast, the natural process that gives us awareness. Put it to use to expand your knowledge.

When considering buying a new desk, we might compare the surface of one desktop to another, then colors, textures and shapes. We compare the variety and grain of the wood of each, employing the element of contrast to decide which we like most. When this process is complete, we conclude which we prefer and why. Part of this process employs our memory: prior comparisons, contrasts, and knowing—that is, our stored certainties. These strongly add to the basis for the preferences from our current comparisons. The process of comparing current perceptions with our prior knowing (our stored certainties) is the basis of forming new likes and dislikes.

By comparing and contrasting, a basic element to conscious awareness, we arrive at conclusions; we know.

All of our senses offer the opportunity to compare and contrast. We taste sweet versus sour, slight bitter versus more bitter. Our eyesight compares and contrasts objects best, and we often size things up using our vision. The English language provides another excellent example:

countless adjectives add distinguishing and more highly defined or subtle contrasts to our descriptions. Our knowing and distinguishing depends on the contrast of present with past or prior knowledge. For instance, with ideas or theories, the new contrasting elements produce the impetus for comparison with prior knowledge. After some pondering, a new awareness or even a totally new concept or theory may come.

All of this seems obvious, but the basic element—that contrast gives us awareness—is a psychological truth and can be deliberately applied when we do not know how to proceed or what to do next. In this case, the answer is, "Obtain more contrast." Perhaps you ask a management consultant to assist your struggling business, or you consult a physician because you don't feel well and don't know why. The doctor considers your symptoms and medical history, comparing the findings you give as you contrast them to what you feel is normal for you. The doctor then compares those to known medical patterns of illness. Physical examination leads to other contrasts and comparisons, as do lab studies and other diagnostic tests. Then a diagnosis is made and recommendations are given. From contrast springs an awareness—in this instance, a medical diagnosis.

When we do not know enough and need more contrast, I say, "Move past more contrast points." For example, Annette, a forty-two-year-old mother of four, was sure she wanted a divorce, yet something in her voice, the lack of definite and no-nonsense certainty, made me wonder. Sure enough, at our next session she was wavering and more uncertain. Could she make it on her own? Did she really want to go through the turmoil? What would the future be like? She went back and forth over the next few weeks. Twice she claimed she knew for sure, only to change her mind again. I suggested she was telling herself she was certain because she was tired of the uncertainty; she was trying to force certainty too soon. "The truth is clear, you are still uncertain," I suggested. "You don't know enough yet to make a decision. You really need to know more first."

Eventually Annette got a divorce, but not before she learned some valuable lessons about herself. She needed more contrasts, more knowledge and experience, before she could really know for sure. Further, she discovered a tendency to form a false sense of certainty too soon because of her discomfort with uncertainty.

The later teenage years and early twenties, the identity-seeking years, hold many uncertainties about life choices, including mate, career, and philosophy of life; these uncertainties may continue beyond the twenties. Consider the college freshman who announced to me, "I've found the religion that is true for me: Buddhism." Two weeks later, he sheepishly yet enthusiastically informed me, "Fundamentalist sects have all the answers." After trying out four religions in an eight-month period, he concluded he still had a lot to learn; he was not really so sure anymore. He was able to quit announcing the latest new find when he became wise enough to give up his impulsive certainty need. He needed more contrast and more experience before he could really know what religion worked for him.

After the identity years come further changes and transitions that carry enough uncertainty to periodically put us in turmoil; such things as job changes, parenting issues, health problems, and marital problems can do this. Occasionally the uncertainty element can prevail and upend tentative certainties and decisions. In these cases, more needs to be known, more experience needs to be gained, and more information from contrast and comparison needs to be garnered before a full and committed future direction is chosen. How can you really know before you know? You cannot, of course. You do not know until you have experienced enough contrast. Then, you know that you know.

The Process of Bringing an Awareness into Being

When we analyze and search for an answer, a new awareness, there are five steps that bring it into being. First, we look at or think about the situation or circumstance. Next, we compare it with what we know from before, our memory of similar situations or circumstances. Third, we get distance from the comparison points, either historical distance (that was then, this is now) or physical distance (standing back and affording us an additional perspective). Fourth, we analyze: "What do I now see, or see differently than before?" Last, most of us turn or cock our head to one side and let our eyes scan upward and away from any of the comparison points. We pause and wait. Usually, the discovery or the new awareness comes to us accompanied by a pleasurable, "Ah, that's it!"

As the new awareness arrives, most of us turn our head and gaze forward as we continue to think about this fresh, new discovery. Turning our head up and away seems to allow us to look at our thought process from a distance; it is the final maneuver that brings the new awareness. Turning our head when we are thinking and pondering, comparing and contrasting, attempting to make new conclusions, is universal. When we watch people do this, we can see how engrossed they are in this process of thinking. Perhaps one reason for looking up and away is to prevent interferences from our immediate environment. At any rate, this series of maneuvers facilitates the discovery and helps bring it home.

Most of the awareness-producing process happens automatically. However, when we consciously employ these steps to facilitate the process, we gain more frequent and fuller awareness, and we gain it sooner.

The Mind Function of Time Sense: Its Wise Use and Misuse

When time sense is violated or misused, pain results. Using time sense correctly removes the pain. The past has been the subject of poets and philosophers for thousands of years; it is the vast storehouse of all that has happened to us, all that we have learned. The past is the receptacle of all our knowledge and certainties, and the source of many of the answers we possess today. Our cherished memories feed our souls, and our painful ones remain on vigil, ready to help, assist, and advise. At a moment's notice, we can access the past for the truth regarding the vast array of experiences and the lessons we have learned throughout our lives. The past is one of the great resources from which we extract prior learning to predict consequences and grow our wisdom or attain that elusive state, peace of mind.

Fortunately our past allows us to review prior successes and former solutions. When we want to define new things, we use our past experience to compare with the new, and this comparison gives us the ability to contrast what we are considering with all the other similar experiences from the past. The comparison usually offers us a new understanding and a new definition. By comparing and contrasting, we gain new awareness. We cannot really know what something is without comparing it with past experiences and then noting the difference. Through this process, we gain understanding and a better realization of what we are dealing with. We can predict the consequences of future actions from stances and actions taken in the past, thereby adding to our wisdom.

Though the past is indispensable, many people misuse it, assigning guilt to themselves for the way they've handled things in the past, even though they didn't have the information they have today. A fascinating question is: Why should they have regrets? The answer is complex. Their regret is really a magical wish to undo history. Of course, none of us can do this. The unreality of this wish to undo history is a painful waste of energy and only increases self-deception. This error is common and plagues many people. Because it is a misuse of the truth of time, it has no ongoing good use and causes pain. If we discover ourselves indulging in this behavior, we can use it as a signal that we are making a logical error and correct it, releasing the illogical regret, joining with the truth, and removing regret's pain.

If we ask, "Based on your knowledge and awareness at the time, did you make a good and right decision?" and the answer is, "No, I did not spend the time and energy I should have, and I knew it then," we then have reason for some minor regret. Use this regret as the impetus for doing things differently today and in the future. Learn from the experience and make it your goal that it won't happen again. Most important, from this moment on, query yourself: "Have I done the very best I can? Have I done enough? Have I used my best judgment?" If you ask these questions and answer them truthfully, you will have no cause for regrets in the future.

You will honestly be able to say, "Given the same circumstances, and my same level of knowledge at the time, I would have done it exactly the way I did. Now, with more information, I would do it differently. That truly was then, this really is now."

The Great Changer Force of the Mind

A simple, powerful force operates when we choose to change direction in life. As obvious as it is, most people frequently don't use it well and don't face it squarely. When you use it with certainty, your life actions are much more decisive and efficient.

When we ask, "Is it really worth it?" we set into motion the question of whether or not something is truly worth the time, energy, and commitment to do it. It is a simple question but is one that offers a great opportunity to clear our heads and answer directly and honestly. When you are uncertain about starting or continuing an endeavor, ask yourself, "Is it worth it?" Answer honestly with the truth of what your mind tells you. It will be one of the four answers below.

Answers	Result
A. "Yes, it is worth it."	You will stay with it.
B. "No, it is not worth it."	You will stop your participation.
C. "I do not know for sure."	You will stay with it until you are certain.
D. "If a certain condition or factor happens or is present, I will (or will not) stay."	The decision depends upon certain conditions or happenings being present.

Sally, a forty-four-year-old hospital volunteer, said, "No, it isn't worth it, not anymore. The time spent for the return isn't worth it anymore." She wasn't getting the satisfaction she wanted because she didn't see her efforts making much of a difference with patients. "Giving comfort doesn't do much. The patients are too sick to respond to my care," she thought. Until that moment, Sally had mixed feelings. Her ambivalence and indecisiveness kept her involved, even when she didn't think she wanted to remain any longer in her volunteer position. When she posed the question, "Is it worth it?" she could put all her thoughts and her uncertainty out on the table, take a look, and make a decision: "No, it isn't worth it." She ended her participation and went on to other things she valued more.

John, a director of nursing at a community hospital, had been thinking at times that his job wasn't worth his efforts. When the factors were clearly laid out and he could see the ramifications, he pondered giving it up or staying with it. At that point, he could sense it was still of significant value to him. He liked working with all the people and didn't want to leave. He didn't want to lose all this, especially his pleasurable personal associations. "No, I will stay with it. It's worth it," he concluded. He knew the why or how it was of value to him and could see it clearly now. The worth-it-ness question pulled it together for him. In review, he realized that his busy life and frequent bouts of sleep deprivation kept him unclear. Now he knew and agreed with himself; he reaffirmed his commitment to running the organization.

Worth-it-ness captures the essence of whether to hold, stay, or change. It is the boiled-down compilation, the amalgam, of all the factors that influence whether or not we change. It simplifies our understanding of the value of what we are attached to or holding on to, so we can decide whether to stay with something or truly give it up. Worth-it-ness is the great decider and changer of our conscious mind. Although we are not always aware of it, we use it constantly. When we consciously and deliberately pose the question to ourselves, even saying it out loud and then answering truthfully, we give ourselves clarity and truth. On occasion we will not know the answer at the moment. When this happens, it's important to suspend judgment until we have enough new knowledge or further experience to decide.

Chapter Summary

1. We all use contrast to create our various awareness and to identify the many things we encounter in our daily living without really thinking about it. We can use this process knowingly and deliberately, to identify more complex things or puzzling or mysterious things. We

do this by comparing what is similar to or different from the subject we are studying.

2. The more contrast and comparison situations we set up, the greater will be our awareness about things.

3. Continue to research a subject until you have enough awareness to know what it is. This can be a brief episode or can take a long time, depending on how much you already know about the subject.

4. Compare the present circumstance or feeling to a prior time by asking, "When have I felt or seen something like this?" Your answer will help.

5. Keep your time sense straight. "This is now, and this is how I feel about a former circumstance. That was then, and that was how I felt about it then." Do not regret a past thing you did if you wanted it then, just because it turned out poorly. Blaming a past action that was once desired from a past perspective by using a future vantage point (the present, which of course because of experience now sees differently) is illogical and will give you pain. Correct the situation and stop the pain by saying something truthful, such as, "If I knew then what I know now, I would have done differently. But I did not, so I did it the way I did, and I accept that." The pain of regret disappears.

6. When you are uncertain about starting or continuing an endeavor, ask yourself, "Is it worth it?" Answer honestly with the truth of what your mind tells you.

CHAPTER 7

———◆◆◆◆———

Our Greatest Forces: Actual Reality and Truth

Truth and psychological truth work in coordination with the force of actuality reality, which is the strongest force that exists. You will function at your best when you understand the similarities, differences, and powers of each of these basic entities.

Here is where the strength, and therefore the beauty, of a psychological truth fits in. A psychological truth is a pattern of functioning, past, present, or future, that uses the forces of actual reality and truth to cause the best functioning possible for a given situation. You have seen, and will continue to see, the term *psychological truth* in this book, describing various patterns of best functioning.

When we are healthy and our minds are working normally, we automatically understand reality and depend on it as we go about our daily lives. It is the foundation of what we sense and know; we accept it and go along without question, even the dispassionate and mundane happenings.

We tend to like truth as well, often seeking it out on subjects like math, philosophy, or history. Builders, engineers, and scientists use its principles to construct buildings, airplanes, automobiles, and space shuttles. Certain laws and principles govern our physical universe. Even so, we occasionally discover new ones as our science evolves. We understand they are dynamic and have relativity and exceptions—they are not absolute and unchanging. This is all part of the reality we know.

Actual Reality

Have you ever wondered what the differences and similarities are between reality and truth? Let us use the term *actual reality* as our foundation to better understand these two concepts. I define actual reality as all that has ever happened or is currently happening. It includes everything we know about, plus all the things we do not know about but that nonetheless have happened. Actual reality is very broad and inclusive, perhaps even infinite. For our purposes, the practical element of actual reality is the set of occurrences and forces that affect us: a thunderstorm, an increase in property tax, the death or birth of a family member.

Actual reality is the strongest force with which we deal and includes all other forces. It is the combination of all that exists or has existed. When we use it well—that is, go along with it or create new things that succeed—it is our strongest force. When we create something that succeeds, we have created a successful reality.

The Nature of Truth

Closely allied to actual reality is the quality of truth. When something in actual reality has happened, it has truly happened. Truth is used as the verifying aspect of a reality that has occurred. Even if someone tells a lie, an untruth, that lie was truly said in actuality, even though its content is false. When the lie is verified as false, it can be said to truly be false. Truth's quality of verifiability is about the exactness and correctness of the actuality.

Truth has other qualities too. It can be used about the future, which actual reality cannot. One can say, "It is true that if I fly at thirty thousand feet, I will need oxygen." Or, "If we go hiking and get hit by a rainstorm, we will get soaked unless we take rain gear." The accurate predictive quality of a truth is based on the truth of actual prior experience. We use aspects of truth for our planning.

The Peril of Ignoring or Fighting Reality

At first glance it is obvious that something must fit with actual reality to work; it then is a successful reality. We all know this. But in myriads of real-life situations, it isn't so simple. We all sometimes choose to ignore reality briefly when things do not work out the way we wanted them to. Instead we hang onto our belief and hope, even if only for a moment, wishing the results were what we desired, not what they are. Bill, a novice writer, was sure his article would be published in his favorite magazine. It wasn't accepted. He was incredulous and hurt, thinking there must have been a mistake, and he took a painful week to accept the news and stop fighting it. This happens less often in real-life business situations, inventions, or product development: if those aren't working out, the money flow to support them stops fast, and the results are obvious. However, when it comes to personal hopes and beliefs about such things as relationships, creative projects, employment opportunities, financial investments, and even the weather, we tend to hang onto our wishes and hopes, our preferences, longer than is realistic. We may later unrealistically place blame or rationalize reasons, rather than finding out the real truth (the actual reality) as to why things went as they did. Realistic appraisal is the great teacher because it tells us the real reasons for a result, giving us what we need to learn. That is why I like to say actual reality is our strongest force. In the example above, Bill had experienced authors and writing teachers critique his writings. They found many things he needed to improve upon if he was to be a successful writer. Now, at least, he had realistic direction. Nothing works out unless it conforms to and is actual reality. That is a truth that is too often ignored at the price of emotional pain and waste of energy—inefficient living—until corrected.

Our Highest Organizer, the Mind's Supreme Force

The human mind's highest organizer, its supreme force, is truth, so the more we know truth and use truth, the better we will function, the more efficiently we will use our energy, and the closer to actual reality we will tend to function. Fortunately we are able to recognize truths when we see them, probably because our brains and minds (if intact and not diseased or severely impaired) have an open path of recognition, with years of experience, to these strongest forces of truth and actual reality.

Some Examples of Psychological Truth

The psychological truth of the logic of causation was the first one discussed in the chapter on mental pressure. It depends upon probability and capability, not future forcing by making crucial, absolutely necessary statements while motivating yourself to cause a result. If we use the logic of causation well, there is no mental pressure. We instead violate this truth with the subtle and illogical, crucial thought patterns that create the pain of mental pressure. If you say to yourself, "I must make this happen. I have to," the pain and confusion of mental pressure is created.

Further, we previously had seen how emotional pains are pointers to truths undiscovered or not used if known, or abilities not yet developed. Recall the pain of frustration when you are unable to proceed with your well-thought-out plans. There is usually something true you had not known. This valuable psychological truth points us in the right direction and tells us, like a general formula, what to do to progress, master the situation, and develop greater capability. Recall in the emotions chapter that each of our emotions arise from a specific life-negotiating, situational truth pattern as long as our perception of the circumstance is accurate. Think of how many of these situational truths (emotions) we experience daily. When we extract these underlying truths, we can use them to live life better. For instance, remember that the emotion of anger arises automatically when our current flow pattern, movement, plan, or expectations are interrupted and obstructed. We can use that truth to reset or change our strategy to understand and accommodate the interruptive obstruction, to learn, and to move on without the anger

Use Your Psychological Truths

We have many psychological truths within us that we have used off and on, without knowing what they were. Much of the power available to you in this book comes from the multiple ways the various psychological truths can create best functioning for you. They can become part of your conscious knowledge and life-handling repertoire; then you will be able to live continuously well.

Chapter Summary

1. Actual reality is the strongest force we have, so do not fight it; go with it.
2. If you create something that works, it is a successful, workable actual reality.
3. If something doesn't work in actual reality, it needs something different or something more to work.
4. When reality and preference (desired outcome) collide, reality always wins. We create pain by continuing to mentally fight against what has already occurred.
5. Truth is the validation element that something really did happen or is now happening.
6. A psychological truth is a pattern that we think or do that always creates painless best functioning.
7. A psychological truth is supreme in the area of its influence.
8. A psychological truth, inherent or created, can be recognized, learned, and intentionally used in all human minds.
9. Psychological truths create our internal truth-discerning system.

CHAPTER 8

The Remarkable Force of Increase: The Growth and Wisdom It Gives

By nature, we are designed for increase. When we realize this, we can maximize our ability to increase in the learning and mastery of new skills. We can use it to provide our preferred forms of increase throughout our lives. For the common good we can derive an ethical guide for increase.

A great and unrelenting force courses through our lives, constantly exerting its supportive and life-enhancing influence. It is so ever present that we often fail to notice it. This marvelous force is underappreciated—it makes us what we are and makes us what we will become, taking each of us up the long trail of life, from infancy to adult understanding and attainment. Increase is the force of learning, skill development, and more. It always operates within us, even when we are passive. If we relax, absorbing scenes and stories from television, we will increase a little, accumulating new memories and visual experiences. When we see the psychological truth that we are organized for increase by nature, then we harness this great force and maximize our capacity for increase.

When we ponder, remember, or wonder, we are increasing subtly. As we choose areas to direct our energies in our areas of preference—to learn how, to improve, to become expert—we increase and progress rapidly. When we make discoveries that unify and simplify fields of knowledge we have been exploring, we increase even more, perhaps exponentially.

We can all look back and acknowledge how far we have come. If we compare our childhood to our teen years, we can see increase. If we look back five years or one year or even to last month, we can identify our increase. We continue to become more than we were. We increase in knowledge, experience, decision making, and even wisdom. Starting at birth, *we are set up for gain*. There is no way not to increase. No matter who we are or what we do increase is the dominate force in our personal evolution and psychological life-handling composition. Increase is a psychological truth.

Gain we can and gain we must, to some extent, or we will have some pain. This pain comes when we do not answer the call of increase. It speaks to us consciously and even subconsciously. Our conscious aware system alerts us to grow and increase. If we do not heed its messages, we experience the pain of boredom, feeling stale or even flat. It can be a feeling of falling behind others. It eventually becomes the fear of being bypassed or left.

When we are not increasing well—when we feel depressed, unmotivated, and without meaningful purpose—our increase slows but never stops. When we are bored, feel flat, or fear being passed by, we are not increasing well. We are always proceeding (and remembering) from uncertainty to certainty, to new uncertainty. The pulse of our mind is an accumulator, a pump for producing new knowledge and new experience, further increasing us.

On subjects that are important to us, such as purpose, meaningfulness, or areas of discovery, if we are not expanding, aiming, or accomplishing, then we may feel a painful, disquieting loss of meaningful purpose. If our life-handling tools and abilities have not grown to meet our current life circumstances, we may even feel despair. We are best served if we understand and learn to use our increase force well.

We are born with a highly developed organ of increase: our brain, or perhaps more accurately, our cerebral cortex. We feed it information and it responds. We inadvertently do this all of the time as we go through our day, noticing, listening, tasting, and comparing and contrasting. When we choose to learn something or develop a skill, we intentionally put it to work so we can acquire new knowledge or new coordinated movements for our skill development. When we choose to master something, such as to become an accomplished musician, we practice long and hard. We learn under the direction of a more skilled musician or teacher. We increase.

Look at the great and respected performers in society: visual artists, writers, musicians, gymnasts, actors, and professional athletes. They have all intentionally pursued their passion or career with a burning desire to become the best they can be. They have used the inherent force of increase within them to move forward in the paths of natural talent they chose to amplify. Other than their distinctive talents, they are not so different than the rest of us. We all have used our ability to increase in order to become good in areas we pursue, particularly those where we have a natural inclination. We can count on the value our increase force gives.

Generally, knowing about increase and its resulting gain should give us some measure of confidence. As we come to know and use the process of increase more intimately, precisely, and exquisitely, we can accomplish great things and profit in significant ways.

The Need to Increase Can Be Forced upon Us

Life is filled with an endless litany of circumstances that, wanted or unwanted, force us to increase as we learn to handle them. No matter where new awareness and experiences originate, we increase with each new stimulus. As we have seen, however, we increase faster and farther when we actually seek to learn, discover, and master in our chosen ways. Learning the best ways to identify and utilize opportunities to increase will help us to handle life and all it brings. Some increase through continuing education. Others learn by repetition of a method, getting better all of the time.

Becoming Better at Increase

As we get better increasing, our abilities become more focused, polished, and accomplished. We gain expertise and embrace new challenges and do more with them. We venture into new territory and discover what we have not seen before. The process is ongoing. We increase further, and all the while we are expanding our ability to increase. This happens with astronomers and astrophysicists in their work exploring new galaxies and planets with Earth-like features that might support life. When they come upon mysteries and unexplained phenomena, they create new theories to prove or disprove, and their knowledge and capability continuously expands. Creative photographers increase in the range and complexity of their subject matter, all the while increasing their ability to discover and see more. A medical director keeps learning to increase knowledge and skills. Teachers take seminars and learn new methods to improve their skills and teaching abilities, as well as their own innovative methods and skills, which they continue to develop.

Young mothers read and talk to pediatricians to increase their knowledge and abilities to take care of their infants and toddlers. Workers go to school to increase abilities at specialty areas in their work. Management holds seminars. Therapists study unique patterns and read of others' experiences with patients, then ponder new approaches and try them out, increasing their knowledge learning all the way.

This book is a product of my own desire to increase. As I looked for answers and ways to understand the things my patients told me they were confused by, I asked them questions that soon led to clarity for both them and me. I pondered the vast number of answers I received over the years, saw similarities, and made connections and correlations that eventually created the psychological truths that compose this book. My therapeutic abilities increased accordingly: I could more quickly spot which psychological truths my patients were violating, as well as which truths could cure the problems.

On the personal front, I discovered that new uncertainties would frequently come up in my mind. There was a pattern of increasing variety to the new uncertainties, as well as to the number. My mind became full of interesting questions. As I worked out the answers that converted the uncertainties to new certainties, I felt excited and even joyous. I loved the process and looked forward to it. It taught me a great deal about living life and the processes of discovery and creativity. It truly evolved me. I have continued to intentionally increase my self-knowledge and my abilities throughout my life; the process has become self-perpetuating.

The Pains of Resisting Increase

What happens if we attempt to resist increase? We will feel its force, and it can pain us, twist us up, and create fear and cowardice. We may feel boredom. When unwanted things happen—and they always do—and we feel the initial pain response, then we are faced with a choice. If we resist increase by avoiding mastering the situation, we will experience even more pain; we will be blocked or stopped. Our increase energy will press on us, wanting a good solution. In a way, all persistent psychological and emotional pains of the psyche are failures at increase and mastery. When we feel this pressure, it is important to first acknowledge it and then to act upon it. Next, we should join forces with this natural process to analyze and understand the problem and then handle it. The result is that the pain will disappear and we will have a new ability. That is increase.

Inadvertently avoiding or restricting the increase force of the human psyche by voluntarily chosen illnesses, such as drug addiction or eating disorders, will create great psychological pain and disability. People with these disorders devote nearly all of their thinking time to their addiction; by doing so, they subvert and tether the inherent increase force. Of course, this process creates both psychological and emotional pain. Their natural increase force is not allowed to release and carry them to new accomplishments. It is understandable why these individuals become depressed and filled with despair. How can the severe, life-restricting actions of drug addiction, or eating disorder's constant compulsion, be a vehicle for handling all that life is or can become? It cannot.

Self-Enlargement through Increase

I like to look at the increase force as a diagram. Imagine many arrows radiating from a circle outward. You are at the center, and each arrow is a separate subject, growing and developing outward, enlarging the sphere of yourself in an ever-increasing way. Illustrated this way, increase is an all-inclusive directional force; the direction of increase points all ways on any subject and at all times. We are always increasing, learning, and gaining.

If we compare ourselves to who we were as children, we can see the tremendous increase that has occurred. Remember second or third grade? How about junior high, or even five years ago? Look at the tremendous change, the huge increase in knowledge, abilities, experiences, and self-power.

The Mandate of Increase and Mastery

The physical health of our bodies is kept safe and intact by generally avoiding pain-producing phenomena. But when it comes to the mind, those inner thoughts or emotions we view as dangerous, uncertain, or frightening require mastery to clear them—avoidance does not work. When we avoid, we create greater and greater pain or psychological pressure and dysfunction. Why? Because increase is continuously operating. When you avoid increasing, avoid mastery of something that is in your mind and vexing you, you will eventually feel fear that life is passing you by, and you will become ever more timid. You will lose zest for life, have a little if any joy, and feel flat and often bored. You will miss out on the experience of discovery and that feeling of excitement existing at the edge of the new unknown. You may begin to feel that your life is in stasis, that you are paralyzed. You may find that you can't keep up with others' conversations or understand parts of them because you haven't been keeping up on news, world developments, or current topics. You will miss out on the pleasures of accomplishments and new understandings. Mastery and increase will provide you much, much more. We must stand and master the uncertainty. If we try to avoid and get safe from it, it will chase us and narrow our lives.

Unfortunately, many of us try to avoid facing our uncertainty, fear, or other psychological pains. We try to not think about them. For example, some people shut off their feelings and avoid the painful memories and emotions that are part of grieving the untimely death of a loved one. They do this at their peril, because this can later create a severe depression known as pathological grief. It is far better to face and deal with the pain of grief as it arises.

When any bad happening or uncertainty affects us enough to cause emotions of upset, hurt, fear, anger, or devastation, and we do not deal with it, understand it, and further obtain some mastery over it, it will negatively affect the quality of our life. The increase force must be allowed to continue unimpeded, otherwise the force will psychologically jerk us around. Mastery, ongoing and growing, is the best answer.

Signals, Possibilities, and Potentials for Increase

There is a simple maneuver we can deliberately do to greatly increase our personal knowledge and capability. We can attach signal meaning to everything we can perceive about ourselves. These self-perceptions include our thoughts, fantasies, dreams and daydreams, emotions (we saw how to understand our emotions as signals already), behaviors and actions, physical sensing data, and intuitions. We can look at each individual element as information about something, a signal.

When we see each thing as an alerting signal about something and then learn what that something's information is about, we have a message of new and useful information. For instance, when we have a thought that solves a problem, we can add thoughts of potentials and possibilities to it: "Where else can I use this? What can I apply it toward? What are five possible uses for it?" Or when we want to try out a physical skill—the serve in tennis, the chip shot in golf, playing a musical instrument, or painting a scene—we can observe ourselves, improve our actions, and even take lessons. These all result in an increase in capability.

Here is a useful example of a daydream being a signal. Your daydreams lately have been about pleasant scenes in nature, with rivers, lakes, mountains, wildflowers, and forests. The signal could mean it is time to take some time out in nature; your mind is hungering for it. You might have a daydream that has you fighting with someone, making angry statements to him or her. Take the daydreams as a signal that you are feeling obstructed, and see if it is from the relationship in your daydream. If not, then consider by whom you feel obstructed and for what reason. Then, make a decision about the best way to handle the situation in actual reality.

When you find yourself thinking about quitting work and doing something else, it may mean you are overworked, not having enough new variety of situations (work only), and so it is time to take a vacation. You will usually find that the break refreshes you, and you don't need to change jobs.

We have enormous amounts of information coming to and through us daily (signals, messages, all our perceptions) that we can apply to our own increase. We have to select what to use, of course, because we have far more signals coming through us than we can possibly handle consciously.

Deriving a Psychological Sound Ethic to Guide Increase

By itself, increase is just a process and has no morality, no good or bad. Murderers learn to get better at murder. Dictators and despots learn to increase the ways they use their political power to oppress. Those who do harmful things to others can most surely increase in their ability. Actions either harmful or beneficial can increase as capability and scope increases. We see increase as good or bad, beneficial or evil, only when we attach ethics, morality, or values of a particular culture or belief system to it.

With regard to handling our personal increase and the collective increases in our own society with its ideals of liberty, equality, and individual rights, some self-governing and societal governing needs to occur when increases collide. I have seen a comprehensive, useful ethic derive from the fascinating interplay of three components. First is a consideration ethic based on empathy for the experiences and rights of others. Second is enlightened self-interest that world societies have learned over the centuries, realizing that our assistance and exchange with other societies, plus their opportunity and productivity, adds to our opportunity and productivity because of our interdependence. Third is an embedded life purpose in all individuals that contains the elements of survival and obtaining, maintaining, and improving quality of life. All motivations contain the purposive element of perceived benefit. This life purpose is a more comprehensive form of perceived benefits. When we weave these three components together, we come up with a psychologically sound ethical guide that states, "Those who allow or encourage the increase of others do good and provide or allow the value of opportunity, as long as the increase does not have deleterious effect on the common good, now or in the future. Those who prevent the opportunity of others' increase without their agreement do harm."

This consideration ethic psychologically defines good versus bad, help versus harm, or good versus evil. It seems to fit any or all situations, including individual or social situations, governing situations, and even religious situations. It is a workable guide, an ideal to be sure, yet comprehensive and practical for evaluating actions or intended actions.

Increases in Wisdom

A simple definition of wisdom might be this: the understanding of the great truths of excellent long-term workability. In ways, humankind values wisdom above all other things. Those who possess it are revered and have great insight both on the human condition and how culture and society work. When we name individuals who have possessed wisdom, we think of Plato, Socrates, Christ, Mohammed, Sir Isaac Newton, George Washington, Abraham Lincoln, Madame Curie, Albert Einstein, Thomas Edison, and Mahatma Gandhi.

The real question about wisdom seems to be, how do we obtain it? The truth is, each of us at one time or another has exhibited wisdom, yet few of us have a working understanding of where it comes from or how to grow it. The timeworn conventional idea that wisdom somehow arrives with age and experience is true in part, but not enough.

Wisdom's Knowledge of Causes and Effects

For me, wisdom and great comprehension of truths are inseparable. This principle operates through life, societies, history, and every environment. Those who possess wisdom have learned the cause and effect of important happenings, then use this information to teach and guide the human family. Knowing about cause and effect influences the direction of such important ideas and functions as societal decision making and program creating, as well as functions of government. Wise people provide the ideas and stimulus for the development of useful organizations; they innovate and often invent. Integrated elements of wisdom include the possession of good judgment, discernment, and the ability to read trends and then forecast accurate outcomes. Those who possess wisdom have a greater sense of continuity and peace; they view the world and what happens as part of a larger whole, and they react in positive and productive ways—even to things that are out of control.

Wisdom of Learning from the Past

The wise learn from past experiences through analyzing and discovering the factors that created them. They can then project that knowledge into new or current varieties of experience. Further, they are able to then govern or advise about the various consequences, good or bad, of projected actions. They can use this accumulated knowledge to guide present and future explorations, steering away from future disasters or perversions of well-intended but ill-fated, faulty aims.

Abraham Lincoln knew the value of abolishing slavery for both the present and future of human rights, personal dignity, and liberty. Teddy Roosevelt established the National Park System to preserve natural wilderness and provide sanctuaries from ill-conceived progress that exhausts our natural lands and resources. Albert Einstein discovered the theory of relativity, and his studies and results gave strong impetus and direction to the nature of the universe and to the use of atomic energy. Edison invented the incandescent light and gave us many of our modern conveniences. These people all influenced the direction of civilization's future by using far-reaching wisdom.

The Role of Judgment

Good judgment develops from experience. We can look at things we've tried, both successes and failures, to find out what went right or wrong. After a while, we begin to understand the reality of the consequences of our actions. This helps us to wisely guide new endeavors.

Wisdom's Components

To obtain and nurture wisdom, we must master many uncertainties and gain knowledge and truth of good certainties or best functioning. Wisdom arrives when we obtain enough useful, productive, and safe psychological resources for life-handling capability. In essence, to use something well, we need to have knowledge and perspective of what that something is, what it does, the nature of its functioning purpose, and what it creates. After the attainment of such full understanding and utility, it becomes part of our wisdom and a tool at our command.

Earlier we saw the example of Ann's too-dominant need for certainty and her inability to understand and use uncertainty; she displayed this pattern lifelong but particularly during her divorce proceedings with Ned. When she later developed enough knowledge and perspective about uncertainty, she could tolerate it better. She was able to shed her dependency on her ex-husband and stop closing off options prematurely. Ann not only won a better settlement later, but she also learned the value of uncertainty and the opportunity it could bring for exploring any number of possibilities for making better decisions.

Many people have now mastered how to motivate themselves without any mental pressure, from fully understanding the results of logical truth thought versus crucial and absolute illogical thought. The freedom from mental pressure and personal stress has made their lives far more peaceful. They have saved enormous amounts of energy through mastering this one thing. Abundant and wise life-handling capability develops when we come to know and understand our many psychological truths, as well as the best functioning and outcomes they provide.

Chapter Summary

1. The force of increase is always operating within us.

2. We can increase by intention best, but we increase some through simply experiencing life.

3. Physical maturation and psychological growth and development happen automatically and help us increase.

4. Think back on all you have gained, how much more knowledge you have now than one year ago, five years ago, ten years ago, since age fifteen, and so on. This is the force and process of increase working within you.

5. If we resist its force, we can feel bored, flat, and even fearful of being bypassed, and we can be bypassed.

6. Ask yourself the questions:
   a) Am I increasing enough?
   b) Do I have some special areas I would like to increase in? If so, which ones?
   c) What wisdom have I developed? When and how did I develop it?
   d) When are instances that I have used wisdom and been glad?

7. To increase wisdom, analyze causative effects of completed situations and the present effects, and then attempt predictions about future results from influences you currently know. Later, compare those completed effects with what you predicted. Learn from the similarities and differences.

8. When in doubt about whether something is ethical, apply this guide: "Those who allow or encourage the increase of others do good and provide or allow the value of opportunity, as long as the increase does not have deleterious effect on the common good, now or in the future. Those who prevent the opportunity of others increase without their agreement do harm."

9. The more we know of the psychological truths that create greater increase, the more we can consciously guide and maximize our increases in knowledge, wisdom, understanding, skill, and ability.

CHAPTER 9

---◆◈◆---

The Clear and Beautiful Truths about Motivation

You can discover the real truths about motivation, both yours and others'. This will help you learn to inspire others and obtain their agreement so that you can become a better leader. You can overcome resistance to desired motivations.

Motivation is the major moving force in all living things. It causes organisms to outwardly interact, affect, and respond to their environment. In humans, this inherent force is a basic psychological truth. It continuously operates, even at times of low or seemingly absent motivation. Motivation is the position, form, and direction your mental and physical energies take, the intent of your self-power to impel you to operate in a certain way for a particular reason. Motivation has long been a somewhat mysterious subject as to what it is and what causes it. It stimulates discussion and questions. Sometimes the answer is obvious, as when we know exactly what our motivation is. Other times, our intent is obscure and seems to escape our understanding. When it comes to the actions of other people, the first thing we want to know is what motivated them to act. Why did the mother drown her children? What motivated the employee to steal? Why did the billionaire give all his money to an environmental group? What were the motivations?

Motivation is composed of an organizing purpose and an assessment of worth-it-ness, the value judgment about whether or not to attempt to fulfill the purpose. Is it worth the energy output to attempt it? How likely will success be? How important is it to others or us? How fraught with difficulty or complications could it be? Does it need to be done to be safe? We assess worth-it-ness factors constantly while focusing on and organizing purpose. Worth-it-ness assessments happen so quickly that we often do not even know it has occurred. Everything we do, without exception, starts with a motive or purpose.

The following fascinating examples show us how mysterious and obscure motivations can be. These two people taught me an enormous amount about motivation in a most astounding way.

The Mystery of Motivations, Revealed

Mont's motivation was a mystery. Mont was a patient in an adolescent residential facility where I serve as medical director. His actions perplexed the professional staff. He was a large fourteen-year-old sent to us by a family services agency to work on his out-of-control behavior. He was aggressive and angry, and he frequently required special procedures to calm and control him so that he wouldn't hurt himself, other patients, or the staff. When discussions and medications aimed at calming him were unsuccessful, and he continued his aggressive behaviors, we needed a solution. We scheduled a special meeting with Mont and the entire staff who worked with him.

Before he arrived, the staff described his behavior as oppositional, defiant, angry, aggressive, and noncompliant. They were discouraged and doubted he could make progress. When he came in, I explained that we wanted to understand him better, to help his stay with us to be successful, something it had not been thus far. He agreed it had not been and stated that he did not want to be here—he missed home. I explained that everyone was concerned about him and asked why he was behaving as he was.

He lowered his head, paused, and replied, "I don't know." This is a typical response of adolescents in these circumstances.

"Mont," I told him, "you do not even go to the bathroom or eat unless you have a purpose for doing it. With food you want to fill a hunger, and with the bathroom you want to relieve yourself. We're all the same. None of us do anything unless we have a purpose, and we believe it's worth it or we wouldn't try. So, what's your purpose in doing these things? I want to know."

To everyone's surprise, he stated, "I figure if I was bad enough, you guys would send me home to my mother."

We all looked at each other with a surprising new understanding. So that was it! "But Mont," I told him, "you can't go back to your mother. She's in a long-term alcohol rehabilitation program. The state has taken custody of you. I'm sorry for your upset and lonely feelings, but currently we can't send you back. The state requires that you be here."

He nodded and sighed, "Yeah."

After a few quiet moments, he agreed to improve his behavior. He would accept that he was here for treatment and would participate in the program.

When he left, the staff had been edified. He wasn't "just oppositional"— he had a purpose that made his behavior understandable.

Three weeks later, the staff reported that Mont was acting up again. He had provoked staff into using calming "take downs" and mandt holds, special physical maneuvers to safely calm and control aggressive behaviors. This was occurring with increasing frequency. I recalled him smiling as he told me of needing a mandt hold; he was almost proud, unable to conceal his grin. *What was this behavior about?* I wondered.

I called another meeting, similar to the first. I introduced it with the purpose and worth-it-ness factors as reminders, and I asked Mont if he could please share or reveal his purpose.

Mont smiled and gladly offered an explanation. "Well," he started, "you know Simi and Tumau?" I nodded. Simi and Tumau are two very large and strong staff members, both ex-college football linemen weighing more than 350 pounds apiece. They were the ones he provoked to use mandt holds, a modified big bear hug, when other measures did not calm him or modify his aggressive behaviors.

"Well," Mont went on, "I have two older, bigger brothers, and I just love to wrestle and play-fight with them. So, getting Simi and Tumau to take me down and put holds on me is like wrestling with my brothers. It reminds me of home."

We were astonished at this revelation, even more surprised at this than from his first disclosure. After a few moments reflection, I sympathized once again with his missing family and home. I told him logically he would get home sooner to his brothers and mother if his behavior improved and he completed treatment with us. He would also be better equipped to handle his life.

He now understood the longer-term view and purpose of treatment. Over the next three months, Mont changed his motivation, made progress in treatment, and was able to return to his hometown to live in a group home that allowed him to have visits with his mother.

Although Mont's motive and purpose surprised and even shocked us, his reasoning and his actions displayed classic motivational or purposeful intent. Each of us, no matter what we do, are moved to act or are directed by purpose. So, what is purpose?

The Organizing Key

Generally, purpose is an organizing goal for obtaining something of benefit. This benefit can be for us, for a group or organization we are affiliated with, or for others who are the object of the benefit. Purposes can be carefully thought out, discussed, and refined; conversely, they can be immediately reactive, like quickly ducking to avoid being hit by a flying object. Purpose can also be reactive but then carefully thought out, as when crafting a response to a disaster. Purpose comes in many sizes, shapes, time scales, and levels of importance; it can be individual, community-oriented, national, and even international as in organizations such as NATO, the United Nations, and the World Bank.

A More Obscure Motivation

Sometimes purpose seems logical and well thought out, but many times purpose is complex and confusing and can actually work against our initial intent and long-term best interest. Consider Ruth's situation.

A college senior, Ruth was referred to me because she was failing her classes when she had always been an A student. She was having trouble motivating herself to study or complete assignments; for some reason she seemed to have stalled out. She did not appear to be in great distress and did not have significant depression, though she did have some anxiety. Through the initial explorations over several psychotherapeutic sessions, I could not see evidence of any of the more classical complexes such as guilt at succeeding as an oedipal competitive victory, or separation anxiety—in this case, the fear of leaving the dependency on the safety of school with its structured and predictable life.

In the oedipal competitive victory, a child, now grown up, surpasses in accomplishment the parent of the same sex, and having done so she experiences guilt. The guilt then causes the surpasser to inhibit her success as punishment for the surpassing. In the unconscious mind, this is the same as symbolically killing one's competitor. The original story comes from the ancient Greek myth about Oedipus, who kills the king to marry the queen, not knowing they are his parents because he had been away from them since childhood. When he discovers the truth, in great guilt and agony he blinds himself as punishment.

This complex was not operative as a cause for Ruth's recent class failures. She didn't need to fail to assuage guilt over going further in school than her mother. This was different. I decided to ask her a question that I have named the law of adaptive value. This question attempts to discover the causes of unwanted behaviors that some individuals persist in, even though they do not want to.

I asked, "Ruth, even though failing classes in your biology major is puzzling and creates a problem, and appears to be of no value to you, take the view that it is your mind's way of trying to do something positive for you, doing something to help you. Though it might seem ridiculous, what could it be trying to do for you?"

She listened thoughtfully and after a few minutes came up with an answer that astounded both of us. Ruth told me that she and her younger brother had been very close growing up. Though he was a grade behind her, they had taken classes together and often studied together. They talked about both becoming biologists, and indeed, she had chosen biology as her major. Then devastating news shocked the family: her brother was diagnosed with bone cancer in one leg. Though surgery was successful and he was cured, he was forced to stay out of his junior year in high school. Eventually, he got back to school but had not started college until this year.

Ruth told me, "His cancer cheated us out of all that time together. He's just now into college, and I'm in my final year! I've just realized I've stalled out so I can be in school longer, so we can be together in biology and continue being close like it used to be." What a surprise for both of us. I had never run into a clinical situation exactly like it before.

Ruth was practical enough to realize she could find other ways to enjoy and be close to her brother, and that she did not need to fail or slow her graduation to accomplish this. When her purpose was brought to light by my question, she gained control of herself and then was able to create a better solution than what her unconscious mind had given her. The truth and logic of both the unconscious purpose and the better conscious alternatives were now available to her.

The psychotherapy had succeeded sooner than expected. The power of the question from the law of adaptive value brought about the rapid resolution. We explored further the notion of survivor guilt that can often pertain in tragedies. In this instance, she was the survivor and her brother was the person who was ill. He had the cancer, and she could have felt guilty about being unscathed, so she had to punish or hold herself back, assuaging her survivor guilt. This notion never seemed to fit her situation, and we dropped it. Ruth succeeded in bringing her grade point average up and graduated.

The Power of the Law of Adaptive Value

The law of adaptive value is a good tool for those trying to figure out a strange, seemingly illogical motivation or behavior in themselves or in others around them. At the time I formulated this question, I had become convinced that our minds are our friends. Generally speaking, our minds work hard to make life go successfully and well. I had convincing and overwhelming evidence that these behaviors, which did not seem understandable, were still trying to help in some way and subsequently got in the way of the best current solution.

The question is, how can we address these confusing or annoying patterns and find their underlying, positive purpose and motivation?

By consciously asking ourselves what these behaviors are trying to do for us in a positive sense, we will have our answer. When we do this, we can then decide consciously what is the best way to proceed to accomplish our aim. When we understand the underlying, formerly positive purpose for the annoying behavior, we can extract and use the purpose but drop the annoying behavior. Remember that there is logic, motive, and purpose in all we do. Most important, remember that our mind is our friend.

To be sure, purpose and motive are not always so obscure or dramatic; they are usually not difficult to understand or identify. In fact, most of us know exactly what our purposes and motives are the vast majority of time, and we usually select our purposes and attempt to bring them about. It is only when we do something we do not quite understand, usually occurring from a former way of doing things, from an older layer of the mind that gives us a prior way of handling things, that we are vexed and confused as to why. The law of adaptive value reveals that older yet true prior purpose.

Examples from Nature

Nature offers unvarnished lessons in motive and purpose. For an example, take the clutch of quail outside my office window on an early autumn day. I heard the rapid staccato of clucking coming from the garden. I saw a male quail sitting atop a solitary rock, slightly above the vegetation. He was clearly on the alert, clucking continuously and looking around in all directions. Below, I saw a female moving slowly, head down, pecking at seeds. With her were twelve chicks scurrying about, feeding, exploring, and playing. Two chicks seemed more adventurous than the others; they investigated the perimeter but returned often to the safety of their mother. Except for the male, they were all scratching and feeding; he remained on alert, watching for danger. When they crossed a sidewalk and disappeared into the garden, he followed at the edge, ever alert. The male never ate, though the rest did continuously.

I had witnessed purpose on the part of the male quail. He was on guard so the others could safely eat. He understood his distinctive role and served a definite purpose. Within the entire animal kingdom, purpose is widespread.

This experience reminded me of a similar example years earlier. I was at my cabin on the Henry's Fork of the Snake River in Idaho. I arose just before sunrise, feeling excited to experience the magic of this treasured place. In the predawn light, I stepped out on the porch and noticed a dark form moving near the riverbank. I stood quietly and waited. A moment or two later, I realized it was a Canadian goose when it flapped its enormous wings and lumbered into flight. Once airborne, it began honking loudly as it flew down river. Suddenly I heard more honking and wings flapping, and I saw the silhouette of a large gaggle of geese rise off the river and fly into formation. They flew higher, their dark bodies contrasting against the pastels of the early dawn sky. They moved majestically on until they disappeared to both sight and sound.

Several minutes later as I stood marveling, two goose hunters carrying shotguns exited a neighboring cabin. They had missed their chance to bag one of these majestic birds because I startled the solitary sentinel goose whose purpose was to signal the flock. I marveled at the sentinel's bravery and wisdom: this one goose positioned himself at the edge of the cabins so he could best alert the flock, allowing their escape before danger could approach. The sentinel goose had a valued purpose: protect the flock. Purpose is present in all of nature's animals.

Motivation, with its purpose and worth-it-ness assessment, is a natural psychological truth. Humans, as distinct from other members of the animal world, can project into the future, consider consequences, and plan accordingly. These elements influence our choice of purposes and assessment of worth-it-ness.

Preference

Whether you know it or not, you already have preferences about many things. Preference is an ever present force and creates desire. Preference starts early in life and is about what our likes and dislikes are, about what our tastes and predilections are. We learn or discover our preferences two ways: from our own experiences and from the experiences of others who are important to us. Through this process we learn what works for us and what doesn't. We learn what proved to be good or useful as well as what was a waste of time and energy. We also learn what we really get excited about and what we do not like. These explorations into preference shape us by helping us to discover what we truly like. To a large extent, preference is what makes us choose to become a writer, a lawyer, a librarian, a professional athlete, or whatever else. Preference is also a way of discovering what leisure activities we like, or whether to do a task now or later. Without preference we might not start a family, go to college, or consider starting a business. Preference shapes our life.

Where does preference originate? Preference is partly genetic and partly a unique blend of our experiences, development, evolving choices, and opportunities. Some of our experiences become preferences quickly, and others take more time. We may not enjoy exercise workouts initially, but over time they become an enjoyable habit. The same is true for acquiring tastes for certain foods and drinks.

Preference also fuels desire, which is the activating urge that pushes us to re-experience a preference. Desire gives us a predictable pleasure we have known before. It arises for its moment from a host of preferences we have developed. It might be a favorite dessert, revisiting a preferred beach, or playing a favorite golf course.

A difference between preference and desire is that desire has an element of positive uncertainty, the anticipation of a pleasurable experience and outcome. Preferences, on the other hand, are our pleasurable certainties; we know we like them. The positive uncertainty contained in desires motivates us to have new experiences or try out new things. We do not know if they will turn out to be a preference or not. Still, we have the desire to attempt something unknown. Curiosity and the process of satisfying it is often enough to desire to try it. Who knows, we might hit the jackpot and discover a great new preference—that's part of the gamble. It could be said that we even have a preference for seeking novelty, for seeing what new experiences bring. In this sense, the desire to seek into the unknown and make discoveries springs from the occasional novelty-seeking preference within us.

Volition

A phrase we have all heard or used one time or another is, "Of my own volition." When we add context, it goes like this, "I joined the army of my own volition" or, "I decided to take a year off college of my own volition." Volition is the power to choose and to direct ourselves in the ways we want. Volition is the force that organizes and focuses our self-powers—things such as talents, abilities, energies, and responses to stimuli.

The process of utilizing our volition is an integral part of each of the many decisions we make over time. It is part of our personal history. In concert with our genetic makeup, it shapes the direction of our lives and creates the ongoing and growing identity of who we are—and further, who we become.

Each of us has an exquisite sense of our ability to choose. We perform these acts of choice all day long: what to eat, where to go, what to do, what to buy, and what to agree to. The list of choices goes on and on. Because we do it so often, our choosing and deciding becomes almost automatic. Smaller choices we make into habit, such as getting up in the morning, grooming, and eating breakfast. While these examples require some thought and awareness of conscious choice, it is not nearly as extensive as the effort of choosing what clothes to wear, or even choosing the right course of action to solve a business problem.

Problems arise when we give away our self-choice and instead follow or agree with what others want us to do when it is not in our best interest. An example is when we fall prey to a dubious sales pitch or investment scheme. We, and no one else, should be the owners of what is of value for us. When we can agree or conclude it is worthwhile to agree with someone else's ideas, it is because after careful evaluation we see it to be of enough value to be for our own good. This type of agreement is not a problem; it's when we agree or automatically go along with things that are *not* in our best interest that we have problems.

To a large extent, purposes are products of our volition, always intended for our benefit. With time, the wisdom of our choices will become evident. If the choice is a good one, it will bring the value we hoped for or something similar. If the choice is a poor one, it will bring less than we hoped for or, in some cases, new problems. Remember the example of Mont? His purpose for fighting with the staff did not work, but when he accepted the better strategy and participated in his treatment program, he was able to get home with new skills, understandings, and successes, which would sustain him better in the future.

With luck, fulfilling our purposes will come close to what we intended and wanted. We gain both during the process and from its completion. On the way to creating the new value, we can make the process fun and efficient. The image we project, the object of our desire, and the value we seek give us an alluring picture to spur us on, giving us positive uncertainty as we get closer to completion. This happens, for instance, when we get close to completing a piece of creative writing. For a long-distance runner, seeing the finish line coming closer on the way to completing a personal best time is exciting and satisfying.

We use these purposes and the ideas of their fulfillments as overviews and guides to see how we are proceeding. Throughout the process, we get little satisfactions of moving well as we accomplish each step. When we complete the process and obtain our goal, we get the satisfying feeling of fulfillment and accomplishment. We have newly won certainties; we have the gained value and the freeing feeling of release after completion.

Purpose Problems

When our purposes tend to be short term, and we do not fully consider their long-term effect or consequences, we eventually create problems. An example is credit card debt. Although the short-term purpose of obtaining a luxury is fulfilled, the long-term accumulated debt can be devastating. Not curbing the desire for instant gratification has significant negative repercussions. One educated and successful couple told me, "We were living in a plastic paradise, and it caught up to us. We learned the hard way." Not planning for retirement or having health insurance are good examples as well. In the final analysis, not having long-term, purposeful goals makes us less able to guide our future to a positive outcome.

The truth is, if you do not have some important and significant purposes, life is flat. Short-term purposes will not suffice either; they cannot sustain for long. We all need to feel we have value and some ongoing, useful purpose. Some excellent but unheralded purposes include being a good mother or father, son or daughter, friend or neighbor. A worthy purpose is taking care of a disabled or elderly grandparent. The giving of ourselves benefits others and brings us satisfying purpose. Not neglecting ourselves and learning to live life well is a noble purpose.

A good mix and balance of short- and long-term purposes goes a long way to help us to live well. Purpose and value are unique to each person, but in general the goal of purpose is to focus our motive force toward obtaining benefit from gaining a desired value.

Low Desire

Too little desire happens in situations of depression, demoralization, health problems, or chronic and repeated defeats, especially when there seems to be no way to change outcomes. These situations can create a sense of hopelessness, of it not being worth trying again.

With depression we find little or no pleasure (anhedonia), and our energy levels are so low that it almost feels as if gravity is pushing us down. There is no motivation to move forward, and the pervading sense that there is nothing desirable about the future leaves us without the alluring images of desire. We feel stuck with no way out. Many search for relief through mind-altering drugs that may seem to offer temporary relief, but they only compound and prolong the problem. At a certain point, despair creeps in and causes severe anguish. The need for relief becomes paramount and makes us consider dying by suicide or accident.

In depression, low desire is a product of the illness. Appropriate psychiatric care, either psychotherapy or medication (antidepressants), may be required to restore and increase energy levels.

Many physical illnesses require appropriate medical diagnosis and treatment to restore energy levels so that desire and purpose can return. Chronic pain can also sap energy and affect desire and pleasure. Frequent sleep deprivation, so common in our modern life, is notorious for diminishing desire and purpose. The cure is obvious, but many people are slow to make the fundamental adjustment. Our fast-paced world constantly tells us to go, go, go if we want to get ahead in life; this view can come at the high price of impaired performance, less sustaining power, and lowered desire and purpose. This may go unnoticed at first, but eventually the consequence can be severe. A basic physical and psychological truth is our need for adequate sleep. If we do not get enough, we can't do enough.

When we experience a string of disappointments or perceived defeats, we may become demoralized and feel hopeless, simply wanting to give up. "Why should I try anymore? It's futile." We may begin to think of ourselves as victims and even believe that God is against us or that we are being punished. People vexed by these situations usually require interventions by friends, extended family, spiritual leaders, or psychotherapists, who can provide a new perspective and rearrangement of their thinking. The new perspective of "Keep on trying because, you've had an unusual run of things that didn't work out," helps boost the person's morale. "It can't always be that way. Learn why each situation didn't work. You can use those lessons to be more successful next time," I'll say to them. People can be shown that a defeatist view is a product of a downward spiral of thinking. The more you down yourself, the less able you feel. The more you feel less able, the more defeated and down you feel. Eventually you believe you can't do anything, which of course is erroneous. Further, people can be shown that these painful episodes can be brief episodes over a lifetime of future possibilities, with successes and near successes. If they progress to the point of seeing themselves as victims, or that they are being punished,

I will tell them, "I don't think so. I don't think you're so bad, so important in the negative that God or anyone else would feel the need to punish you. That makes you too terribly important. That's a distortion, so give it up." This unburdening process—along with moral support, care, and love—work to assist in getting back on track again.

Many of us are able to pull ourselves out of a funk or even a brief brush with despair by making a choice to take a new risk, to view the pile-up of demoralizing events as an unusual run of bad luck, something that will not last forever. How one can accomplish this is described later in the book. Rest assured, there are strategies for pulling oneself out of the mire of demoralization and self-defeat (chapter 16), or the terrible anguish of despair (chapter 21).

Excess Desire

Unchecked or out-of-control desire is the opposite of low desire and can cause serious, even disastrous problems. Take overeating, for example. Giving in to our desires for certain tastes or experiences satisfies short-term cravings but ultimately creates significant long-term problems. For instance, if we do not apply self-control, we may receive momentary pleasure at the cost of long-term health problems. Some of us overeat at mealtime and compound the problem by eating frequently during the day. This satisfies taste desires and offers the momentary soothing effect of the food, but we eventually gain more and more weight. The cycle creates increased physical mobility problems and causes us to feel embarrassment and shame. Some joke about themselves in an attempt at humor yet often suffer low self-esteem. We all are aware of the long-term consequences of overeating, including heart disease, diabetes, high blood pressure, joint problems, and early death. But even though we know this, we deny its inevitability to justify gratifying an immediate desire. We are not truly helpless at resisting but want the particular food so much that we rationalize, "I could stop, and someday I will." But we really do not want to.

Before major health problems from obesity develop, we tend to believe we will eventually stop overeating and lose weight. Not surprisingly, it usually takes some painful physical ailment or the onset of a more serious health problem before we force ourselves to make the decision to change. Not until a potentially dangerous situation occurs do we honestly and openly consider the consequences. Oftentimes, instead of facing our situation and stating with certainty that we intend to lose weight, or stating that we intend to remain obese and accept it, we put this process off to some vague or undefined future. Conversely, some overweight people admit to themselves that they do not like how they look or feel, physically or psychologically, and they successfully take action before they develop major health problems. They are motivated and honest with themselves.

Some put on weight and keep it on to help avoid what they view as unwanted or risky situations. Intimate emotional relationships are often avoided by those who have been hurt in childhood either by sexual abuse or emotional abuse. Obesity is used as a barrier to anyone developing a romantic or close friendship interest in him or her. These people are afraid relationships will evoke overwhelming feelings from the past and will end up abusive. Those recently divorced may use weight gain to give them space and time to heal. They experience a feeling of freedom, unencumbered by new people becoming romantically interested in them. Often they are afraid they cannot control their own impulses or are unable to say no, so they use weight to control the nature and pace of new relationships, particularly romantic ones. Some do not know how to discourage uninteresting people, so they use the unattractive weight to substitute for the lack of capability at handling relationships.

For these people, psychotherapy is usually required to solve the problems of avoiding interpersonal dilemmas. Reportedly, 35.5 percent of American men and 38.8 percent of American women are obese.[4] Certainly most overweight or obese people are not using their weight to attempt to solve interpersonal problems—their problem is that the *desire* has become excessive. They submit and it dictates; they develop a dependency on their desire and empower it as the master. When their desire takes over their lives, they no longer see with honesty and clarity. While each of us possesses the willpower necessary to subordinate the desire's power, these people instead see themselves as powerless. They do not want to stop. The real truth is that we decide where we use our power. Will we submit and bow to a strong desire, or will we assert our will and manage our life well? That is the question.

If someone is to overcome not wanting so stop, they have to make the choice for good health (and for stopping or cutting down the overeating) stronger than the choice for not wanting to stop. Only when they see that something is their choice—to overeat and not want to stop and become obese, or to stop overeating even though they don't want to and thus be healthier—will they own the result. To say, "Well, I'll cut down tomorrow," or "I won't always overeat" is a self-trick for continuing the behavior. They need to face the future certainty, the long-term result. "If I continue, I will become (or stay) obese. If I cut down in spite of the desire to not want to stop, I will become more slender." Truth thinking can be powerful here. The bigger surrounding truth is, "If I eat too much, over time I will gain weight and become obese. The other truth is that I want to eat; I don't want to stop. Further, I hate it that I can't easily control my desires. But the bigger truth, the ultimate consequence of not eating less, is that I am choosing to be obese in the long run." If obesity is the choice, so be it. If being healthier and thinner is the choice, there will be self-power to modify the eating behavior. The difficult factor, as in so many things about health, is that the big problem result is far off, many years in the future, and the momentary desire is right now. That is part of the real truth, and it is the great seducer to continue the short-term momentary behavior thousands of times, for many years. The incremental results pile up to create the health problem. The process creates the result.

Other Addictive Substances

Even before alcohol becomes an addiction, it can be used too much to avoid, soothe, calm stress, or change the way we feel. This abuse destroys clarity and robs us of energy needed for social and family quality time. Two teenage patients of mine, Jamie and Bob, sister and brother, told me about their mother often drinking in the late afternoon and evenings when their father was away on business trips. They told me if they wanted serious help with a problem, they would have to ask their mom in the morning, when she was thinking clearly. However, if they wanted to do something questionable or risky—staying out late, going to a party with kids their mother didn't know—they'd wait to ask permission in the evening, and it was usually granted. They said their mother did not usually want to be bothered with thinking much, so she usually said yes at those times. Her best thinking wasn't available to her teenagers because of the drinking. Fortunately over time, family therapy and therapy with the parents corrected this and other issues.

Jill, a mother of four, ages seven to eighteen, told me in therapy that her husband, Ron, would either stop at a tavern for a beer on the way home from work or have a drink before dinner to "unwind" from the workday. He couldn't be bothered during his unwinding period, a time that could have been spent more productively with his children while his wife was fixing dinner. Often after dinner, because of many activities like homework, there was little time for family or individual discussions with the kids that included their dad. When we gradually confronted Ron in couples therapy and family therapy, plus some individual therapy, we got at the problems that Ron was avoiding. His parents were distant when he was growing up. He didn't know how to be available to his children. He learned and gave up his "unwinding drink," replacing it with enjoyable interactions with all of the members of his family, and everybody benefited.

There are those who drink martinis at lunch. I have often asked professionals or business people who do this whether they would seek my professional help at two or three in the afternoon if I drank one or two martinis at lunch? They all get my point; there is no hiding place at that moment of clarity.

Some like the stimulating effects of nicotine. They also enjoy the ritual of opening a pack of cigarettes, lighting up, inhaling, and then exhaling with a big sigh to reduce the feelings of pressure. We all sigh occasionally to release pressure and relax, but cigarette smokers do it more ritualistically. Of course, if they persist they pay a terrible price. In 2010 there were 443,000 smoking-related deaths according to the CDC.[5] But like those who overeat because of desire, the ill effects are a long way off, and the disastrous future is rationalized away in favor of the momentary pleasure, the object of desire. Nicotine addiction shows a brain action so strong that not even nicotine patches can modify it.[6] No wonder smoking is so hard to give up. Yet people have been able to do so, by the millions.

Pornography

Pornography addicts and sexual addicts—those who excessively, continuously seek sexual or pornography experiences, with little or no resistance—have used their naturally strong sexual drive with its desires compulsively. The momentarily gratifying pleasures that these out-of-control and overemphasized or perverted desires bring lures them to continue, again and again. Pornography or the sexual addiction becomes the master, and the individual a voluntary slave who seeks this powerful pleasure at almost all costs. Psychotherapy is usually required to once again become in charge and create more practical and useful ways to live life. We will see below what can happen to the brain when pornography, overeating, alcohol, and drugs (including nicotine) take over and become addictions.

Excess Desire Gone Awry

Some new research shows ominous findings of brain changes in obese people and pornography addicts.[7] The changes are in the brain's natural rewards systems and its pleasure centers, which are being disrupted[8] in ways that appear to be similar to the brain changes in the following drugs of addiction: heroin, methamphetamine cocaine, alcohol, and nicotine.[9] Chronic use of these drugs of addiction hijacks the reward circuitry of the brain. Each brain circuit spans several brain regions and includes nerve cells, junctions between these cells, and the chemicals that carry messages from one nerve cell to the next; together they make up various organized pathways in the brain. The reward circuit of the brain relies heavily on the chemical dopamine. It gets used up and reorganized (the hijacking) to more exclusively support the addictive process, be it food, sex, or the drugs mentioned above. The dopamine reward brain circuit demands feeding of the particular addicting entity. This means that in order to give up the addicting habit, an obese person, someone addicted to pornography, or a drug or alcohol addict person will have to fight both a mental or psychological hunger and a brain with a biologically heightened desire. That can be very difficult.

The addiction and brain circuitry research that I have cited reveals many of the particular brain changes that occur in addictions. Nora D. Volkow, MD, Director of the National Institutes on Drug Abuse, and her colleagues have produced a great body of work on these subjects. Donald L. Hilton Jr., MD, recently summarized a large number of studies and references them in the helpful review article "Can Pornography Use Become an Actual Brain Addiction?" These articles provide further detail and direction for those who want a more in-depth discussion of addiction and brain changes.

Marijuana acts somewhat differently but can cause brain damage in important functional areas and affect mental health in heavy users. Long-term heavy cannabis use (five joints daily for ten years or more) in males causes harmful effects on brain tissue and mental health.[10]

In the study cited below, the hippocampus and the amygdala showed the structural damage of reduced volume (tissue loss), subthreshold psychotic symptoms, and decreased verbal learning. The hippocampus is a very important brain structure through which many important brain pathways pass. It has, among others, the functions of long-term memory and evaluating the significance of episodic memory of personal events and related emotions and spatial navigation. The amygdala deals with our emotions, helps process memories, and manages our response to fear and stress. Obviously you wouldn't purposely want to damage these important structures, but long-term marijuana use will.

When it is all said and done, the final decider—willpower applied, expressed, meant, and followed as an absolute certainty: "I will beat this addiction and stop it now"—is the act that will make you free. If you are less than addicted, it will be easier, though still difficult. If you are addicted, you will have greatest success with the support of friends and family as well as a period of forced abstinence—not doing whatever you are addicted to—so your brain as well as your mind and desire will be clear and not under the influence.

We all know people who have stopped overeating, smoking, or doing drugs or alcohol with or without treatment. In the end they were all acts of the will. I am reminded of the story of a successful businessman, Rick, in his forties. He confided that from his mid-teens to his early thirties he was addicted to heroin. He went through treatment many times in facilities but confided that he had believed he could continue to use afterward and be able to control it. He couldn't. He finally hit rock bottom and believed, "I am nothing but a heroin addict." This of course wasn't the truth. He was a person with a heroin addiction—a critical difference. At that point he gained encouragement from others in his group therapy who had kicked their habits. He began to believe in himself, feeling he was more than a drug addict. He stopped his addiction, never to return, and he developed a healthier life with friends, family, and a career.

The case analysis of Rick's story is very instructive. First, Rick fought the truth, both psychological and experiential. If you are addicted you can never, never, never use regularly again without becoming re-addicted. There is no such thing as being able to use drugs or alcohol on a casual or "continuing but small amount each time" basis. Every follow-up study that ever tried to prove this showed absolute failure: within four years, if not sooner, re-addiction had occurred. Fight or violate a truth, and you create pain—in this instance re-addiction and relapse. Second, Rick called himself just a heroin addict, so he thought he was doomed. When he could realize the truth, that he was a person with a heroin addiction, he could move forward and give it up as he'd heard others in his group had done. When he latched onto this truth and made the full decision to never use again, Rick succeeded. He set himself free from the addiction and ended up creating a successful life.

Of course, if you are not and never have been addicted to any of these, you should be able to see why you should avoid them. If you are already addicted or close to it, seek professional help and become abstinent so that you can marshal the extraordinary willpower that lies within you to get free.

We all have within us dynamic and finely tuned, intricate, and vast natural brain systems. Nature has given these to us for being able to grow, develop, relate, handle challenges, and live well. Why hijack your natural reward system, why damage and change it, for the kind of short-term pleasures that lead to ruined lives? No, your systems are there for the high purposes of mastery and increase. The pleasure from drugs is false mastery. The pleasure from mastery and accomplishment is real, and you can build on it. That is a psychological truth.

Preference Problems

The primary preference problems are not knowing what our preferences are and being afraid to activate our preferences because we feel undeserving or unworthy. In the latter case, long-term guilt or conditioning created by a restrictive upbringing may prevent preferences from being expressed. Conversely, people who have many preferences can usually express and activate these in an orderly enough sequence to satisfy their desires.

Lacking Preference

Most problems with too little preference originate in childhood. The majority of children express preferences often and loudly, letting their feelings be known by crying out in frustration when they do not get their way. It is natural and the usual order of things in childhood to do so. More timid siblings can be afraid to try things out for themselves and instead follow a more assertive sibling's choice, never being original, always following and copying. During teens and young adulthood, this dependency manifests as they find more assertive or experienced people to identity with and to follow. If they do not eventually become their own person, developing their own individual preferences, they will in all likelihood need psychotherapy to break the pattern. Knowledgeable or intuitively good parents will spot this early and encourage the hesitating child to develop individual and unique preferences.

I performed this function during a patient's psychotherapy when the problem came to light. Bob, a young adult patient, recounted during therapy the numerous times that first his mother, and then his older brother, would invalidate his choices by saying, "No, you don't really want that; this [their choice] would be better." He became used to this preference-stifling process, and as a result early on in his life he quit choosing for himself and instead asked his mother or brother what he should choose, what would be best for him. It took many confrontations during therapy to get him to actually discover what his *own* preferences were, and more confrontations after that to get him to act on these newfound preferences. He initially struggled so much with self-preference and choice that I gave him several assignments to actually taste some new foods and select what he liked best and why. I asked him to do the same with clothing and types of music. By taking the risk and trying out many things—some he would keep as a preference, some he would discard—he became stronger at finding his own likes and dislikes.

My first awareness of how people can feel guilty and undeserving came during a noted lecturer's address in 1965 to the Department of Psychiatry, University of Utah's Grand Rounds, and afterward as he informally addressed my group of young psychiatric residents in training. The speaker was Robert Senescu, MD, Professor of Psychiatry and Chair of the Department of Psychiatry at the University of New Mexico School of Medicine. He described that people often become self-sacrificing and feel so undeserving that they do not do much of anything for themselves. He, too, had struggled with the problem for years and still felt "the torture of the damned" whenever he thought of buying a new car for himself. During the informal discussion session with us, I thanked him for calling my attention to the pattern, one I at times experienced. I told him I would now buy the sports car I had been eyeing. He chuckled and shook his head twice and said, "That's great, glad to have helped, but I'm still feeling guilty about the new Buick I just bought. I need to work on myself a little more."

Dangerous Preferences

Dangerous preferences seen in late childhood and adolescence need to be addressed to prevent serious problems later. Dangerous preferences include bullying or being afraid to stick up for oneself, stealing frequently or lying often, or the frequent telling of false, nonsensical stories to build oneself up. Bullying often develops in kids who have been physically abused in their families. If they are larger than the other kids their age, they may do to other smaller kids what was done to them and start bullying. Also, if they perceive themselves as larger or tougher than others, they attempt to gain power through fighting and, if successful, through bullying. They become mean, perhaps sadistic, enjoying the reputation of being tough.

Those who are afraid to stick up for themselves are usually smaller, are physically weaker, and fear being hurt. The other kids can see this in them and may taunt or even bully them if so inclined. The more afraid people feel, the more they are fearful of standing up and defending themselves.

Those who tell stories eventually are found out and are discounted or tolerated with a lesser view, an intuitive knowledge that they are trying to puff themselves up. If this pattern persists into later years, the storytelling may substitute for true accomplishment and impede success. Intuitively people realize that if some people tell stories about their accomplishments in a way that embellish them too much, they are not people of substance, and they tend to be dismissed as foolish.

Parents and schools can prohibit and then enforce compliance by punishments (always with explanations), restrictions, or carefully sequenced rewards. When teenagers start gravitating to groups involved in drugs and truancy, and they avoid more typical teen life, strong and lasting interventions must be put into action. These include constant supervision and engineering free-time activities. If necessary, professional help can be obtained that will assist the young person in removing the barriers and reconstructing more healthy preferences. Parents must be vigilant and decisive, or they can lose a naive, beloved child to the tragic outcome of drug addiction and life failure.

Conversely, overly restrictive and abusive parents—those who are too harsh or pleasure restricting (depriving)—can stifle the development of preferences. Their children may grow up to continue their own austerity program, now deeply inculcated through the earlier conditioning. They do not express preferences often, rarely thinking of them. If they think of an occasional preference or desire, they quickly shut it off, afraid to give it reign, inhibiting the urge through self-disapproval. For these individuals, it is important to encourage them to try out and develop tastes and preferences, and eventually develop their own likes and dislikes. They need to set aside their self-disapproval. In most cases, this is accomplished over time and with the assistance and help of an adolescent psychotherapist who is also a good behavioral coach.

Punishment in the form of self-denial, because of guilt feelings or the perception of unworthiness, can be hidden in people who display over-responsibility. These are usually diligent, accomplished people who have succeeded through being highly responsible and reliable. For example, Paula, an excellent nurse, told me she had discovered that her severe self-denial was a punishment for her many guilty feelings. Most of her guilt was irrational because she did not cause the problems she felt guilty for, but nonetheless she took responsibility for them. The guilt originated from her sense of over-responsibility. Because she was good at taking responsibility and had a history of successful outcomes, when something bad happened she would automatically look to herself as the negative causer; even if she did not cause the problem, by taking responsibility she just might prevent it in the future.

Since Paula saw herself as the responsible cause, and her logic required that she be punished for her guilt, she punished herself by self-denial. She told me that this pattern came to light during psychotherapy many years ago. The insight eventually allowed her to break the pattern and give reign to her preferences. Many overly responsible people self-punish to assuage the guilt from having taken responsibility, erroneously, as being the negative cause. Over-responsibility does not always require psychotherapy to discover and modify it. By just identifying the pattern and being conscious of its false logic, the pattern can be changed.

I would venture that many who are reading this now are having a self-discovery about their own cycle of over-responsibility, inappropriate guilt, and punishment. Two jokes succinctly describe the ludicrous nature of this pattern.

Did you hear about the overly-responsible and codependent person who fell out of an airplane at twenty thousand feet? On the way down someone else's life kept flashing in front of his eyes.

Did you hear about the overly-responsible person who bought "my fault" car insurance instead of no-fault insurance?

Other Problems with Preference

There are two other problems with preference: first, those who have only one strong preference, such as working too much and not budgeting time for a family, friends, or leisure activities; and second, those who are addicted, be it to alcohol, illicit drugs, or pornography. Both workaholics and addicts are consumed by their singular preference; it is almost the only thing they think about and the main thing they do. Almost without exception, addicts need professional help to change. Workaholics can develop new preferences if they deem it worth it at some point in their lives.

I've had several workaholics in my practice through the years. The largest number came from poor, austere circumstances. They developed a drive to overcome being poor and put most of their waking efforts into finding ways to produce money and gain power financially, so that they would never feel helpless and without means ever again. All of these people had families to whom they paid little attention, believing that providing money was what they should do to the exclusion of all else. Imagine the surprise of one such father, Delbert, who reacted with astonishment but a lack of understanding when his ten-year-old boy angrily cried one night and said, "Dad, you don't love me. You never do anything with me." Usually such a crying out will help a sensitive parent realize the need of his or her child, and the parent will make more time for him. Delbert was too aloof in his feelings to understand why his son wasn't satisfied with all the money he earned for the family. He had to be taught through psychotherapy to learn how to warm up to all the members of his family.

I have seen other instances of professional people, particularly doctors and lawyers, who have so much to do and who get such satisfaction from their work that they inadvertently and gradually slip into being workaholics. They will reorient their lives to include family, vacation, pleasurable pastimes, and so on, when something jolts their awareness—a comment from a friend, a confrontation from a spouse, or a request from one of the children for more time.

Finally, I see other people who slip into being workaholics because they are good at what they do, they are in demand, and they derive more satisfaction from this type of accomplishment than anything else. They derive too exclusively their sense of value from the work situation. As in the examples above, someone or a painful experience will start them readjusting their priorities.

Motivating Others

Over the years, I've had people ask me, "What motivates people?" Usually, these people are aware that I'm a psychiatrist who writes and occasionally conducts seminars. "If you could teach us how to really motivate people, that would be so great."

For years, I've pondered this question about what motivates people, and I've remained puzzled. After considerable time and contemplation, I concluded that people can only motivate themselves. Moreover, they can only do so if it is for a purpose that appeals to them, seems useful at the time, and is viewed as worth it. Otherwise, they will not do it. Instead, they will do something else that seems more worth it. What the people who wanted me to teach them were really saying was, "I want to motivate people to really succeed at what I am valuing and asking them to do."

One such person was a high school football coach who wanted his players to be fierce competitors. He wanted them to improve and work hard at acquiring skills. That makes sense if you are a coach. The other was a medical school professor who wanted to motivate medical students to become outstanding doctors. He also wanted to help motivate his own children to be as productive and accomplished as he. These were worthy goals, and he knew his own strong motivation had helped him become an outstanding professor and physician.

The coach and the professor were both inspirational and motivating. They accomplished this by conveying the values of a strong work ethic, teamwork for best results, lifelong productive patterns, and reliability. They were their own best life example, one with whom others could identify. As inspirational as this was, the students would still find their own dominant interests in life. Ultimately, their strongest motivations would be stimulated by the appeal of their own unique choices. What fits for one doesn't fit for another. The uniqueness of our talents, the extent of our skill development, our genetic predispositions, and our individual tastes and preferences will cause us to select our distinctive, purposeful passions. All of these variables motivate us to make our most important life decisions and to seek out our life goals.

Motivational Leaders

There are times when we come together for an agreed-upon purpose or goal. Any time an organization, business, or group exists for a purpose, it will have goals and leaders. Part of the leaders' challenges are to motivate. Some leaders are superb motivators, and others are less so. To be a time-tested leader and great motivator, certain conditions must pertain.

First, the leader must be able to command respect. The leader and motivator must have a reputation of accomplishment that precedes him or her, and a manner or style of successfully interacting both with groups and individuals. Respect is given to a leader who is admired for both past accomplishments and expressed future goals and intentions.

Second, the leader must be a good reality thinker who can help promote the qualities of realistic thought and truth, which is accomplished through an excellent communication style and exemplary behavior. This leader must be able to teach group members to think similarly, immediately correcting mistakes and illogic in a constructive and nonthreatening manner. John Wooden, the legendary UCLA basketball coach known as "The wizard of Westwood," compiled the best record of NCAA championships ever. Wooden used an instant teaching method as one of his tools. It was reported in an unusual publication, the *Journal of the American Medical Association* during the 1970s. Coach Wooden, upon seeing a faulty technique in a player, would stop practice, go out on the basketball floor, and physically demonstrate, "Do this, not this." The action was nonjudgmental and instantaneous (remember, "contrast springs an awareness"). His method was being suggested by the journal as a model for training medical students, interns, and residents.

Leaders and motivators communicate expectations clearly. They know where they are going, for what purpose, and how they are going to get there. This gives the road map, the purpose, and the image for the members to eventually accept, agree to, and actualize. The motivating leaders do this initially and frequently, reporting on progress realistically. The expectations have to be realizable. I like the expectation my older brother Jim placed on his high school football players. He successfully coached them to eight league championships in his ten years with them. He was an excellent teacher of both basic and advanced skills and a good tactician for developing successful plays to run. Beyond that he said his best psychological motivating tactic was to ask each player to play the very best he was capable of. This worked because it was realistically achievable and practical. He knew other coaches who unrealistically set the goal of winning as a must. At critical times their players would pressure themselves, creating mental pressure and stress, and they would usually make a mistake, such as creating a penalty, fumbling the ball, or overthrowing a pass receiver. The lesson here is that the leader's expectations must be within the participants' abilities and full control.

When people know they are creating something good and valuable through working together, they have an emotionally meaningful experience that both inspires them and solidifies the group's bonds of belongingness—a satisfying and profoundly touching experience, its own reward.

In a real way, each of us can utilize what good motivators and leaders do in order to help ourselves. The techniques are the same. By comparing and contrasting what we do—how we approach a subject, issue, or situation with what we believe a good motivator or leader might do—we can make better decisions and judgments while in essence being our own coach and even cheering section. For instance, when you want to motivate yourself to do a task or project, you can use a checklist of the following questions that a good motivator would ask.

1. Do I know what I want to accomplish and why?
2. Is it valuable or good to do this? Why?
3. Have I done something like this before?
4. If so, and it worked out well, how did it all happen?
5. What slowed the project?
6. What made it move forward well?
7. Do I really want to do it even though I agreed to? (Be truthful with yourself.)
8. Am I fully loyal to completing it?
9. Do I have a road map?
10. Do I know where to seek help or consultation if I need it?
11. Am I pressuring myself with unrealistic thinking? (chapter 1)
12. Am I doing my very best with this project?

Resistances to Motivation in Desired Endeavors

Knowing some of the causes and cures to the resistances against motivation that we experience can help us manage our motivations better. One cause of resistance is not knowing a subject matter clearly and fully enough to complete a task. When too uncertain about some aspect of a subject matter, research it more or rethink it in more detail, as accurately as possible.

For example, Jan thought fly fishing for trout would be fun and involving. She watched people fishing the river that ran next to her cabin and saw how engrossed they all were in their sport. She wondered how they knew what fly to use, what equipment, and what to do when a fish was hooked. It all seemed overwhelming, so she resisted starting. After a few years she mentioned this to a friend, Pat. Serendipitously, Pat had attended and completed a fly-fishing course in the area just a month prior. She encouraged Jan to take the course because it would answer most of her questions and teach her new skills. Jan did sign up, and over the years she became an able fly fisher who benefited significantly in her leisure time from the new pastime.

Bill bought a telescope to do some amateur astronomy. Halfway through the assembly, he hit a snag and was stopped. He couldn't figure out how to put several pieces of the telescope together. The instructions showed a part he couldn't find. He carefully went through the instructions several times. The part in question looked like it was already connected to another part in the instruction pictures, but when he compared that to the parts he had in front of him, he still couldn't find it. He put all of the rest of the parts together but could not get the telescope to work right; it wouldn't hold the position he put it in. He couldn't view his target and hold that view long enough to study it. He realized that most likely something was wrong, so he returned to the store's expert astronomy teacher, who had sold it to him. Indeed the part was missing. Finding the right part and adding it solved the problem.

A second resistance occurs when you don't take good enough care of yourself. You're out of balance, and your mind simply will not let you proceed until you treat yourself better. It could be that you are not getting enough sleep or playful recreation. Or, you are doing too much of the same thing, so a project becomes drudgery. You need to take some breaks. When you return to your task you'll be refreshed. "You can have too much of a good thing," is the adage. I would paraphrase it as, "Too much of one thing is too little contrast and too little novelty to stay fully interested."

Analyze the situations you resist and I'll wager you'll be able to see a pattern to them. The reason and the cure will be embedded in the pattern. The question to ask yourself is, "What are these resistances trying to tell me?" See what thoughts follow the question; give them credence and listen to them. Ask yourself the law of adaptive value to see how resisting is trying to help you at the moment. You will likely get your answer.

This happened recently to a medical colleague and friend. In what started as a casual conversation, he said he had an uneasy, flat feeling of late, and he felt a little purposeless. He was a successful internist who was busy and had more than enough work. He was doing well economically and personally. He had many purposes, but for a few months life had felt rather blah. It was hard for him to get going in the morning, to wake up and face the day with enthusiasm. He told me he had recently undergone a physical, including lab work and some other special tests, and all was normal. My friend suspected it was psychological in origin. He didn't have excess sadness and had plenty of energy once he got moving after awakening. He enjoyed his main hobbies and sports. He didn't have evidence of a depression that needed treatment. Still, he felt flat.

I suggested the law of adaptive value. "Why, in spite of your full and generally fulfilling life, are you now feeling flat, and to some extent purposeless? What is the flat, purposeless feeling trying to tell you? Your mind is your friend and is trying to help you. How is telling you that you are flat and purposeless a positive attempt to help?"

He thought for some moments and then realized he had felt similar many years before. As a young college student, he had felt flat and purposeless for a semester. These feelings left after he had made a decision to become a doctor. "That decision," he said, "contained so many immediate and long-term purposes and answers that I haven't felt that way again, until now. I know I need some big, new purposes in my life, certainly beyond those which I have done up to now. It may even be something beyond medicine. Or it could be a humanitarian use of my medical skills. I'm not sure yet, but I know it has to be something significant for my life yet fit with my family and medical practice as well. Thank you, friend, for pointing out a way to find a new direction and purpose."

Chapter Summary

1. Motivation is composed of an organizing purpose and an assessment of worth-it-ness, the value judgment about whether or not to attempt to fulfill the purpose.
2. Purpose is an organizing goal for obtaining something of benefit. This benefit can be for us, for a group or organization we are affiliated with, or for others who are the object of the benefit.
3. The law of adaptive value is a good tool for those trying to figure out a strange, seemingly illogical motivation or behavior in ourselves or in others. Ask how you can address these confusing or annoying patterns and find their underlying positive purpose and motivation. When you understand the underlying purpose for the annoying behavior, we can extract and use the purpose but drop the annoying behavior.

4. Motivation, with its purpose and worth-it-ness assessment, is a natural psychological truth. Humans can project into the future, consider consequences, and plan accordingly. These elements influence our choice of purposes and assessment of worth-it-ness.

5. Preference is an ever-present force and creates desire. Preference starts early in life and is about what our likes and dislikes are, about what our tastes and predilections are. We learn or discover our preferences in two ways: from our own experiences and from the experiences of others who are important to us. Through this process, we learn what works for us and what doesn't.

6. Volition is the power to choose and to direct ourselves in the ways we want. It is the force that organizes and focuses our self-powers, such as talents, abilities, energies, and responses to stimuli.

7. When our purposes tend to be short term, and we do not fully consider their long-term effect or consequences, we eventually create problems. Not curbing the desire for instant gratification has significant negative repercussions.

8. Too little desire happens in situations of depression, demoralization, health problems, or chronic and repeated defeats, especially when there seems to be no way to change outcomes. These situations can create a sense of hopelessness, of it not being worth trying again.

9. Unchecked or out-of-control desire is the opposite of low desire and can cause serious disastrous problems. Giving in to our desires satisfies short-term cravings but ultimately creates significant long-term issues.

10. The primary preference problems are not knowing what our preferences are and being afraid to activate our preferences because we feel undeserving or unworthy.

11. A leader must be able to command respect, be a good reality thinker, and communicate expectations clearly. Each of us can utilize what good motivators and leaders do in order to help ourselves.

12. One cause of resistance to motivation is not knowing a subject matter clearly and fully enough to complete a task. When you're uncertain about some aspect of a subject matter, research it more or rethink it in

more detail. A second resistance occurs when you're not taking good enough care of yourself. This throws you out of balance, and your mind will not let you proceed until you treat yourself better.

CHAPTER 10

———◆◆◆———

Search Out the New to Increase Your Understanding and Capability

Discovery gives us our greatest gains and a sense of exhilaration;
its truths evolve us, making us stronger and wiser. You can
learn methods that will increase your ability to discover.

Discovery is a basic process that gives exciting new information, knowledge, or wisdom. Evolution has paid off the sense of discovery with joyous, excited, pleasurable emotions, because discoveries seem to advance us—our knowledge and abilities, our progress—so much greater than other forms of learning. The learning and mental growth with discovery seems to be exponential. Without it, life would tend to be flat, menial, and lackluster.

Discovery is our great provider, satisfying our curiosity and offering answers. Without it, our lives would be dull and lackluster. We grow our minds with discovery, creating ever-increasing knowledge satisfying our desire to know and understand. Without discovery, we would still be afraid of the dark, and humanity would not have flourished.

The value and purpose of discovery is to increase knowledge, expand and improve our abilities, and provide new experiences or new ways to look at things. At the very moment of discovery, we experience an awe-inspiring "That's it!" The moment of discovery is a wonderful and enlivening experience. Discovery offers the new, the additional, the surprising; it feeds our mind with new tastes, delightful anticipation, and future dreams, and with new clarity and greater life-handling power.

Sometimes discovery unifies different ideas or provides the common thread that runs through seemingly unrelated experiences, allowing us to solve mysteries and create new concepts or theories. These new theories can change or correct existing science or even form a new branch of scientific pursuit. Take the Hubble Space Telescope, for example. Since its launch in 1990, the science of astronomy and astrophysics has seen tremendous discovery and change. The new data has revolutionized existing theories and ideas, forcing science to rethink the origin of the universe.

Methods of Discovery

Discovery is a powerful psychological truth and process, a fact of life. It happens to a greater or lesser extent in all of us. Like a vitamin, we need periodic doses of novelty, new experience, and mystery. We do best with an ample supply of curiosity and of seeking for new certainties and further new uncertainties to solve and make known. The need and process helps us grow.

Learning by Experience

By studying the process of discovery, at least studying our own personal process, we find important methods to assist us when we have questions whose answers are not evident. Perhaps the most widely known and universal method for discovery is learning by experience. As children we learned about little dangers the hard way: not to touch the hot stove, to use sharp knives carefully, to not go against our parents' wishes for fear of their disapproval. Our parents taught us to cross streets, to avoid fast-moving water, and to be aware of high places like ledges and cliffs.

Consequences always assist discovery. Our choices and behaviors teach us what works and what does not work. Sometimes we learned the hard way from our naive explorations into behaviors that are illegal but that we were not initially convinced should be. Hopefully these explorations or tests only happen once or twice. Getting a first speeding ticket may serve the useful purpose of slowing a teenage driver down, making him or her a safer driver. Trying alcohol when underage and then getting very sick from doing so is another example. Taking the illegal drug marijuana one time and thinking it isn't so bad, only to watch someone else progress to harder drugs and addictions—that can teach a painful lesson about the dangers of drugs. Unfortunately the one who got addicted didn't learn from a first experience. When a parent restricts the teenager's use of a car for a few weeks because of a traffic ticket, the teenager will likely learn a lesson not to repeat the traffic offense. Dare to ask a respected elder what he or she would do in a situation we weren't sure we handled well; then you can compare methods and learn from the elder's greater experience. Mainly we learn from doing, from our mistakes and successes. Feedback, approval, and disapproval from those important to us, particularly older and wiser mentors, is valuable for discovering what works.

For some, learning by observing others is as good as experiencing it themselves. The negative consequences or positive payoffs teach a great deal. It is not necessary to experience everything directly; fortunately, we can learn some things vicariously. However, learning by experience will always remain a trusted guide as we go about discovering the new and unknown.

Sampling and Trying Out

What do we do when we see an array of possibilities and do not know which we like, or which to choose because we have never tried any of them before? How do we decide which possibilities to pursue? How can we come to know? The answer is to try out as many as we need to before establishing a strong preference. For example, some arrive at college without a clue as to what major to pursue. By taking a number of courses, a natural preference will ultimately surface. Another way is to ask questions. Other people's opinions can give us a valuable starting point. This method is not the same as finding out for ourselves, but it may offer some needed perspective.

If a young person believes he or she would like to be an astronomer because of a love of telescopes and stargazing, it might be worthwhile to seek out an astronomer and discover what the professional life is like. The fact is, astronomy includes many tedious hours of directly looking at the new data coming in through a telescope, then further analysis and comparing the data with prior data, all requiring physics and math. For someone caught up in the romantic notion of being an astronomer, this could be a major turnoff. But to the person who loves analyzing data, it may be a perfect fit. Finding out the time and energy commitment of any profession may influence the choice by removing the romanticized notions. The same could hold true for someone looking at a law career. By actually speaking to an attorney and finding out what it's really like, a better and more informed decision can be made. Working as a law clerk for a summer could offer an experience close to what the actual profession is like.

Let us assume it's your first trip to a bakery. The smells are delicious, and you are faced with several displays filled with delicious-looking pastry options. You feel overwhelmed by the possibilities. How can you possibly know what each tastes like, and what you might like? You can't. So, what do you do? You start by choosing four or five and tasting them. Afterward, you might keep in mind those you liked best. If you do not like any of them, you discard those as choices. You continue to test, sampling and trying out each, and eventually you arrive at a few favorites.

For the sake of this discovery, you pick five, all with chocolate. These include chocolate brownies, German chocolate cake, chocolate chip cookies, Bavarian cream pie with chocolate sprinkles, and chocolate mousse pie. Over the next few weeks, you sample them again and again, but you still can't decide between the Bavarian cream pie and the chocolate chip cookies. One day you arrive at the bakery and spot a new pastry. It is a chocolate éclair, and you immediately love it. It clearly is your number-one choice and remains so for years. Going to the bakery happens a lot in life. We discover and then decide, sampling and trying out first.

The Information Sources

While talking to a successful book author, I asked from where his ideas came. Without hesitation he answered, "Newspapers, magazines, books, television." Though we do not usually associate these sources with discovery, the acts of watching television news, listening to the radio, and reading the newspaper or books offer material from which discovery originates. The author told me that his most successful book came about after he read an article in a small community daily newspaper. He said, "I take discoveries where I find them." By just keeping up with current events, we discover new facts, ideas, or subjects to explore further; these widen our interests and deepen our understanding of life and its possibilities.

It is important to stay engaged. When we attend movies, theatre, lectures, concerts, sporting events, and conferences, we are likely to come away with new information and perhaps a heightened interest or stimulation to discover more. Travel has long been a tremendous source of growth and new information, opening new vistas, experiences, and discoveries. We test ourselves with travel as well, seeking out new experiences and learning much about ourselves in the process. Everything we take from an outside source gives us discovery—if we take the time to consider and ponder it.

Analyze the Ingredients

Many times we have a sense of fulfillment or enjoyment after we do something, and yet we do not quite know what the reason is. The same can be true for negative feelings and assessments. "Why did the movie trouble me? What was missing in the billing from the wireless phone service? Why am I feeling so positive about my recent trip to Europe?"

In the last example about a group trip to Europe, analyzing the components or ingredients will offer the answer. If you want to know why a group experience was pleasurable, then ask those who participated about what they liked and disliked. Take that information and add it to a list you have compiled of every element that went into the experience. Include such things as accommodations, modes of travel with an assessment of ease versus difficulty, quality and type of food, mix of people, expertise of the guide, and so on. How did you like learning about the new culture? Compare the list with the other participants' preferences. When you put all that information together, you will have discovered what made the overall experience a good one. Next time, you will be able to plan new and better trips with the knowledge you've gained.

Years ago I ordered a Caesar salad in a Park City, Utah, restaurant. The waiter tossed the salad in front of us as was the custom of the restaurant. I didn't watch carefully as I was conversing with friends at the table, when I tasted the salad and noticed a marvelous flavor that seemed very fresh and enticing; it rose upward on my palate and left a wonderful aftertaste. I thanked the waiter for the best Caesar salad I had ever tasted and asked about the wonderful fresh aftertaste. He shared what he had done: "I added fresh European oregano." It changed forever my notion of a good Caesar. I began to make them with the fresh oregano, finely cut up. Soon my kids, grandkids, and friends would ask me to make my salads when there was a special occasion, such as a birthday or a stay at the family cabin. It all came from the waiter who had made such a great salad many years before, my noticing and asking about it, and his willingness to share his key ingredient.

Identifying the Multiple Causes: Has Anything Been Left Out?

Most of what happens to us or that we experience is caused by multiple influences. Here is an example. Three cars are involved in a fender bender, but no one is seriously hurt. It happened partly because Jim's car stalled as it headed south just after going through an intersection. Robyn, who was behind Jim, hit the brakes in time to avoid rear-ending him, but she swerved into the center lane before her car skidded to a stop. Bill, who was already in the center lane, briefly took his eyes off the road because his cell phone rang, and he looked to see who was calling. By the time he looked up, Robyn's car had changed lanes and was stopped in front of him. He hit the brakes, but unfortunately the pavement was wet and he slid into Robyn's car, then banked into Jim's. Bingo! A three-car collision.

If any of the various factors in this scenario had not happened, the accident probably would not have occurred. In this as in any case of multiple causation, all of the factors had to go together in the way they did to cause the accident.

Here is another example. Roger, feeling harried from work, arrives home to find Ginger, who is downstairs yelling something he cannot hear clearly. Ginger has just dropped and broken a bottle of weed killer in the garage. He yells out, "What?" from the top of the stairs. She calls back that she needs his help. Just then, the doorbell rings and she says, "Never mind, get the door! I'm expecting a delivery. I'll clean up the mess." After signing for the delivery, the phone rings, and Roger answers it. It's his boss, who needs to change a critical piece in one of Roger's projects; it means he will be working tonight. In the meantime, Ginger continues the clean up. Roger gets distracted thinking about the project and then goes down to the garage. A little chagrined with his delay, she asks sharply, "Where were you? It doesn't take ten minutes to sign for a delivery."

Already feeling imposed on by his boss's request, he feels a little defensive and put upon. Years before this comedy of circumstances would have evoked an argument with mutual accusations. Fortunately, Roger realizes the many simultaneous, time-competing events and rescues the moment. He accepts and acknowledges her being upset, and he explains his boss's new assignment and his innocent distraction. He empathizes with her frustration about the spill. She quickly understands, sees the humor in it, and laughs, saying "When it rains, it pours—both weed killer and projects." Together they chuckle, the moment rescued and further problems dissolved. They both understand the principle of multiple causation and trust that neither partner has any malicious intentions.

When we employ the concept of multiple causation in analyzing a situation, it is good to keep the question open for a while for factors that might have been left out. Sometimes we intuitively sense there is more but are not able to identify it. By keeping the question open, our awareness to additional insight is open as well. It is surprising how often an answer to the missing link will pop into our mind over the next few days. Outside of our conscious awareness, and because of the inherent certainty-seeking principle, our mind had been working on it.

Discovering Possibilities and Potentials

A useful exercise to train our mind to discover new possibilities and applications is to ask ourselves to think of five possible new applications of a new idea we have had. For instance, when I discovered that the violation of logical thought caused a pain, as in the instance of how the pain of mental pressure is created (chapter 1), I asked myself "How else might it apply? Could it apply to other types of psychological pain?" I found it did as I explored each of the pains of the mind.

Inventors think of new ways they can apply their inventions besides the original reason for those inventions. I learned a fishing technique in Alaska for large rainbow trout, which worked well when I applied it to my local rivers. Whenever you get a new idea or discover how something works, be willing to apply it to other things. If you cannot think of any, be creative, even coming up with slightly ludicrous situations. The important thing is to be open and not eliminate possible options. By doing this, we train our mind to think in an expanding and discovery-oriented way. Eventually this process becomes fun and easy.

When we plan a party or celebration or event that contains some uncertainty elements—such as weather, or a menu that depends on some hard-to-find products, or the uncertain number of accommodations for out-of-town guests—it is wise to think of multiple options. Explore different scenarios to handle the uncertainties in case they come to pass. By having multiple options available, by planning different contingencies ahead of time, we can be relatively certain to be prepared to handle all possibilities. If you have planned an outdoor event, and stormy weather comes, plan an indoor venue in case you need it. If your favorite seafood store has a run on smoked trout and is out, be prepared to use a different fish. Know of some additional sleeping quarters if extra guests come. Think ahead of what might occur and prepare for it. This process expands our mind and its capability to discover ways to solve problems; the more we discover, the more we are able to discover.

When teaching children to think of reasons why they caused a problem and to consider the consequences of their behaviors, we can ask them to give us five possible negative consequences. Often this is not easy, BECAUSE children tend to respond with, "I don't know." I teach parents to spread the five fingers of one hand, making each finger a possible consequence of the child's behavior. Help them get started. Tell them one or two consequences and then ask them to come up with the rest in half an hour. Generally, a child can do it, having identified with the examples. For instance, if a child repeatedly fails to do a chore, such as cleaning the garage, and others have to do it, ask the child why. The adult can supply the reasons, such as, "Maybe you forgot, or maybe you hoped someone else would do it," and then ask, "What could be some other reasons?" The child might say, "I wanted to play instead," or "I don't see why it has to be cleaned up." This last answer could lead to another teaching moment. If the child resists by being stubborn, let her know she has another hour to think about it, and she has to remain in the room while she does, with no distractions. Tell her if an hour will not do it, you will extend the time. Do not tell her for how long. This uncertainty dangle works because it is hard for children to tolerate. They will not resist for long. Do this, and you'll get some good answers and at least be assured they know how to think about consequences and aftereffects. They will also be better prepared to handle the complex situations of life, learning to think about possibilities and their consequences.

Scientific experiments employ the same basic elements as we do in discovery. These controlled experiments are used to validate hypotheses, prove or disprove theories, and discover facts and how things work. For life-handling situations, we can run experiments or do brief pilot projects to try out new ways of thinking or doing, then see what the results are. Try it. When finished, ask yourself whether things went better or worse the new way. Does the new way improve functioning, efficiency, and ease? In a word, does it work?

Cross-Fertilization and Syntheses

When two or more people get together and discuss a subject, they exchange information in the process. This information originates from each person's experiences and areas of expertise; as a result, each adds to the other. It often stimulates interest and rekindles new ideas to explore further or possibly find new solutions to problems encountered. Each participant adds something that was not there before. This process is known as cross-fertilization, and it happens all the time. It's is an important way to gain new knowledge, adding to what each of us already knows.

The synthesizing or cross-fertilization of different views and ideas usually happens after each participant has gone about his or her separate way. Each continues to think, review, and refine what the others added to the subject and then synthesize all of this at a deeper and more comprehensive level. Synthesis is the process of putting together the various aspects or bits of data into a new cohesive whole. It is a process of unification, at a new level, resulting in the formation of a new construct that can be applied in new, more powerful ways.

Questions for Discovering

Each of us makes personal discoveries almost daily. In fact, the process of making discoveries is worthy of a closer look. Ask yourself, "What made me desire to discover? How did I go about it? What was the value of the discovery? How did it change my awareness? What new capabilities did it promote me to develop? For what purpose? How did making the discovery feel?" When we ask questions about our discoveries, we quickly see how valuable discovery is and how good and exciting it feels. Many discoveries come from asking the question why, which sets our conscious attention and our motivation, our purpose, in the direction of inquiring and seeking information and knowledge. When we ask why, our minds consciously and subconsciously stay open and directed to the task of discovery.

The old saying "Curiosity killed the cat" does not apply to humans. It makes us stronger by leading us to discover. So does contrast, which gives us a new awareness when we compare the current situation with prior experiences. It all works together to give us the impetus and awareness to discover. Once we have the curiosity and have started wondering, the value of our questions comes into play. The five great questions—why, what, how, when, and where—focus the inquiry to the appropriate arena to find the answer.

Ask specific questions like, "Why is it happening so often?" or, "What is the nature of this feeling I'm having? Where is it coming from?" Further, "If I take this action, what will the consequences be?" When we want to know how something works, we ask, "How does this work?" Questions will yield answers, sometimes initially only partial answers, but eventually they will be full answers. As time passes and you gain experience, you will get better at asking questions, and your rate of discovery will increase.

Puzzling Behavior: Discover What Causes It

Early in my career, I puzzled over what appeared to be nonsensical behaviors that some patients kept repeating but that did not seem to get them anywhere. The patients were also puzzled by these unexplainable behaviors. There was Diane, who asked her physician husband to make doctor appointments for her with his colleagues, only to cancel them at the last minute; this caused frustration and strain in the marriage. Then, there was Bill, a geneticist who described frequent dreams of being back in graduate school and failing a math class; he awakened anxious but was then relieved it was only a dream.

I became convinced that we do things because they are worth it, and that pretty much everything we do is an attempt to master something in order to handle life. Our subconscious mind does not leave us defenseless or purposeless. It is our friend and is there for survival and handling life. It will even give us the most primitive of behaviors, fight or flee, when our repertoire is otherwise exhausted or deficient. It will not leave us with nothing.

How could I explain these seeming aberrant behaviors that did not seem effective and useful? Perhaps there was an element or remnant of a mastery attempt in them. Maybe they were useful at a former time in life, though not so much now, and were being used now automatically like a reflex, especially when a current situation or problem mimicked or had sufficient similarity to a prior one. In a previous situation it may have worked well. Now, it was aberrant and confusing.

I asked Diane, "How might this be trying to help you master or handle something in your life, even if your behavior does not seem to be for any good reason?" She too was very surprised and made a personal discovery:

during her depressions, she felt undeserving of receiving the benefit of the doctor visits. She had such a low self-esteem that she did not value herself even that much. Yet she could hold out hope that she might be worth it if her husband still valued her enough to make the appointments for her. We quickly went to work on her low sense of self-value.

As for Bill, while there was no history of prior failure in math, he did have some trouble with other grades and performance during a semester in graduate school. At the time, he was experiencing a relationship problem but soon solved it and went on to graduate with his PhD, quickly finding a good career in genetics. So why the dreams? When I asked how it could be a help, even though it seemed ridiculous, he quickly realized that whenever he was dealing with a new and frightening uncertainty, such as submitting a plan for more funds to complete a genetics project, he feared the funding committee would turn him down. The dreams occurred at times like this, showing him the future fears but symbolically portraying them in things he had succeeded at before—academics, math tests, and graduate school. The dreams' adaptive value were to displace the fear, the anxiety from his current situation, and place it onto an old success.

When he awoke after having another such dream, he could feel relief. He now realized he was reassuring himself. He had never failed at math, and he successfully graduated; his mind was supporting and encouraging him and trying to soothe him and reduce his fear about the future presentation.

When you find a confusing behavior in yourself, or if you are working on self-discovery, the inquiry can be a very useful tool for revealing the purpose of your behavior. Ask yourself, "How might this be trying to help me master or handle something in my life?" Then you can see if the answer is currently the best way to achieve your present purpose or if there is a new and better way. It's a favorite with me because it gets to the truth, fast.

Discovery of the More Obscure Within Ourselves

We have all had experiences of unpleasant and unwanted feelings invading our consciousness and being difficult to discard or clear away. These could be times when we felt irritated easily and did not want to be bothered. Or it would be a feeling of emptiness, sadness, or loneliness, perhaps even feeling rejected or angry, without knowing why. These feelings are most often triggered by recent experiences that parallel prior experiences that left unresolved feelings. The unresolved feelings surface during the new but similar experience and stay around because they are unresolved and have not been understood and processed consciously by our minds. To settle them, we have to discover their origins and why we felt the way we did; then we can move forward clear and resolved, ready to handle what comes next. When we do not know the origins, they linger, vexing us and contributing uncertainty and confusion to the original unpleasantness. To discover where these experiences originate and what causes them, try this.

The first step in identifying the source of the feeling is to place it in time exactly; for example, "It happened sometime this morning." To pin it more exactly, go back and recall all the events of that morning. What experiences happened, and what thoughts were you having? Do it as if you were a sports announcer broadcasting a play-by-play account. Go back in your mind and recall what you were thinking just prior to the onset of the unwanted and unpleasant feeling. Explore and describe the mental, emotional, and outside behavioral events, all the information about what was occurring until you pinpoint the moment when you got the feeling.

Typically it is something like, "I was watching television when I saw the main character's feelings get hurt, because the others went on without her, effectively leaving her out. That's when I felt down. If must have reminded me of my lonely, self-conscious feelings in seventh grade, how painful they were—one of the worst times of my life." Another scenario might be, "I was walking along a village road, looked up, and saw a town hall clock. It read 11:15 a.m. I got a chill and a wave of sadness just as I'm getting now. Eleven fifteen was the exact time we filed into the funeral parlor for a family service prior to my beloved grandmother's funeral when I was seventeen. She had emigrated from a little village like the one in which I was walking. Her life is now long gone, over. My life is going by so fast. Thinking about this has such a poignancy and sadness for me. I had not thought of her in a long time. I wish I could have told her more about what she meant to me, before she died. I'm feeling some pain about that, just now."

Pinpointing the exact time and then re-evoking the feelings by describing them moment-by-moment brings out the causative factors for the unpleasant feelings. It is usually an experience that contains people important to us and circumstances that we felt helpless to alter that caused us the hurt. When we experience events sometime later that have parallels to the initial experience, similar feelings are triggered and evoked.

Access Questions for Discovering

A very useful tool of discovery is the access question. It works well for organizing and recalling prior experiences of pleasures, such as joy, fulfillment, or delight. It can be put to good use for times of uncertainty when we lack confidence and can use support; it can give us courage too. It reminds us of when we handled painful situations and were able to resolve them.

Ask yourself the access question like this: "When, in memories of my experience, did I feel (for instance) joy?" Asking will bring up some experiences when you were joyful. Joan tried this and recalled that she felt joy when she put on a successful party for friends to celebrate their recent trip to Holland, where they witnessed the blooming of the tulips. They traveled by barge on that country's rivers and canals. Her clever decorations and thoughtful gifts delighted her guests. Later, they recalled the experiences of the trip with fun and laughter. Then she thought of when she gave an embroidered scene of a French countryside to a granddaughter. The granddaughter adored it and found it extra important because Joan had bought it in Paris years earlier. Her granddaughter's surprised delight evoked Joan's joy.

Like Joan, we can access many of the experiences of joy, satisfaction, accomplishment, and happiness we have accumulated in our lives by using the access question. We can do it for pleasurable reminiscing, whenever we want to. It's a great tool when we are feeling down or forlorn because it raises our spirits and reminds us how rewarding life can be.

If you can't recall many joyous moments, ask instead when you have felt satisfaction, or feelings of a job well done, or when you had done the very best you could in completing a project at school, in work, or while doing a hobby. It will remind you that you can accomplish things, giving you some supporting confidence.

Roger was feeling insecure and anxious about making a presentation to a hospital board for a proposed new short-stay surgery facility. To calm and encourage himself, he asked the following access question. "When in the past have I experienced fear and uncertainty before submitting my work or ideas to others for approval and had it work out?" Immediately he thought of his oral exams in medical school. He also remembered when he applied to the department of surgery at the medical school for his first job; he was understandably nervous but was accepted and had worked there successfully for a few years. More recently, he was nervous about becoming a department head of his hospital's surgical department, but he performed well and brought in several progressive surgeons and new techniques. He knew he was trusted and valued, so why not go ahead with a little more confidence? It worked. Of course his plan was accepted, and the hospital board gave him a vote of appreciation for his efforts.

Jane faced an uphill battle, holding on against creditors while trying to bring her new fashion line to the general marketplace. For a few years she had successfully shown her products in fashion magazines, attended trade shows, and even sold her designs at retail outlets in her home town. "Will I ever be firmly established and gain steady success?" she wondered. Is there something more I should be doing?" She thought back to a time when the going was even rougher. She was studying textiles and fashions at a specialized design school and had run out of money. Her mother was ill, and Jane was working overtime to pay rent and eat. She decided to focus only on her design goals and not let anything defeat her. She persisted and did not give up. Eventually, she made it through. With this memory to guide and support her, she decided the present difficulties would eventually pass; she needed to focus on her goal and persist, and she would get through somehow. Two years later, her product line was bought by a large fashion consortium, her new products were a success, and her financial problems were gone. She was glad she had not given up.

Discovery is an integral aspect to diagnosing and alleviating our psychological and emotional pains. It is important in making us stronger and getting us more breadth, depth, and understanding. Discovery assists in continuously increasing our life-handling capability. It is so important that nature pays us off with excitement and pleasure each time we learn something new, either about ourselves or something in which we are interested.

Chapter Summary

1. The whole chapter is about discovering and methods that work to bring about discoveries, and there are many. Learn to use them all, though you will probably have your personal favorites. The value and purpose of discovery is to increase knowledge, expand and improve our abilities, and provide new experiences or new ways to look at things.

2. Discovery comes in many ways, such as through experience, from the consequences of our actions, from sampling different options, and from sources of information, such as television and magazines.

3. Many times we have a sense of fulfillment or enjoyment after we do something, and yet we do not quite know what the reason is; the same can be true for negative feelings and assessments. To discover why, ask questions such as: Why did the movie trouble me? What was missing in the billing from the wireless phone service? Why am I feeling so positive about my recent trip to Europe?

4. Questions that focus your mind and your intention are the best and most powerful. The following questions will keep you on track to continuously discover.

    a) Why does this happen?

    b) How does this occur?

    c) What is the nature of this?

    d) What does this mean?

    e) What is this a signal about?

    f) How might this work?

5. When you find a confusing behavior in yourself or are working on self-discovery, ask yourself, "How might this be trying to help me master or handle something in my life?" See if your answer is currently the best way to achieve your present purpose, or if there is a new and better way.

6. We can access many of the experiences of joy, satisfaction, accomplishment, and happiness we have accumulated in our lives by using the access question. For example, "When, in memories of my experience, did I feel joy?"

CHAPTER 11

———◆◆◆———

Belonging and Your Basic Loyalties

Belongingness strengthens and supports our sense of self and gives us a sense of connection. Positive, basic loyalties strengthen us, while mixed and negative basic loyalties impair our success.

The sense of belonging—that very good feeling, like "home sweet home"—is a comfort to the soul. Each of us feels the value of being connected and supported, the warm and relaxed feeling of security when we know that we belong. Belongingness is a basic psychological truth, an element of our humanness, a product of our social nature and instincts. We innately belong to our family of origin; it is deeply felt and helps define us as we grow through childhood. "Hi, Mom, I'm home," says the first-grader returning after a day at school. We have to be with things (like home) or people (family, friends, or school class) long enough to have the sense of belonging. We internalize these belongings and carry them with us, yet we can quickly lose this sense of connection when conditions change significantly and rapidly.

When we perceive that we are disaffected, alienated, not belonging, too alone, and disconnected, we feel anxious (fear and uncertainty), perhaps disoriented, and sometimes even fragmented. In situations such as moving to a new city, or when severe illness, catastrophic accidents, and other disasters beyond our control strike, we become disoriented in our sense of continuity and belongingness. These are unpleasant states of mind and being, and we do not tolerate them easily for long. We work hard and fast to get the feeling of belonging back, to reconnect, reconstitute, or construct new conditions sufficient to restore the overall sense of belongingness.

The Sense of Self and Belongingness

Imagine you are the planet Saturn, and your rings and moons are your parents, children, family, and mate. You belong to this universe, and each element within it is part of who you are, yourself. Further out the rings represent your neighborhood, community, state, and nation. The furthest rings are your life views, philosophy, and spiritual beliefs. Together, you (the planet) and these rings are inseparable, each belonging to the other, a complete system interacting and contributing. It nurtures and comforts you.

Now imagine waking up one morning and finding some of the rings missing.

Our sense of self, who we are, is derived from and depends upon many components; not least of importance is our system of belonging. Carrie was in her late twenties when she came to me, and I had seen her periodically over the years. By the time she arrived at my office, Carrie knew herself quite well, and she wanted to talk to me about problems related to work issues. Shortly after sitting down, she blurted out, "I don't feel like I'm me anymore." I waited, a little concerned. She repeated the statement but hastily added to my relief, "I mean, I know I'm really me, but I do not feel like me, like my usual self. I feel a little lost."

"Tell me more about this," I said. "When did you notice it, and what was occurring?"

"I think I'm being fired from my job. I overheard my boss talking about cutbacks, and I'm worried that I'm not doing a good job." Before I could respond, she went on. "My dog Molly died Sunday, and I have had her since I was in high school. I'm sad and miss her. Then, of all things, the person I was going to share a new apartment with backed out." Until recently, Carrie had lived with her parents but needed to find an apartment when the family home was sold and they moved to a condominium. Carrie felt strange, different. "It's all too much, too fast!" she remarked. "Somewhere in the last day or two, I had this strange sensation that I do not feel like I am me anymore."

I was struck by the recent turn of important events. She indeed had sustained a highly unusual number of very important losses. We talked about what she might do, how she might think about this, and how she might deal with her work situation.

The next session she began with, "I feel a little more like myself this week." She explained that she misinterpreted what she'd heard at work and wrongly assumed she was being fired. After inquiring she discovered, to her relief and satisfaction, that they were quite pleased with her after all. With her work still in place, with one less major loss than she had believed the week before, she felt a little more like herself.

A week later, more had changed. She found a new roommate and was adjusting to living away from her parents. "I'm feeling more like my old self, but I'm still not quite there," she told me. As each element of loss was added back or replaced, I witnessed the return of her sense of self. By the next week, she was back to her full self. "I feel like me," she proudly announced, and then she told me about her new cute, little puppy and how lovable and adorable she was.

Carrie's experience is related to cultural shock, the confusing and sometimes frightening state we experience when we move to a new culture and have few attachments. Carrie experienced a "self-cultural shock," which is similar to what people feel who experience divorce. For a year or two, they feel disoriented, out of sorts, and set adrift. It is not until they create or recreate an adequate belongingness system—a new home, a new life, possibly a new mate—that they remove their displacement and replace it with the new attachments.

Years ago, while working in a child psychiatry clinic associated with the air force, I learned that families who were more adventuresome together, and who possessed a strong sense of family belonging, were better able to adjust to the relocation (its culture shock) required by the military. The secret was that they brought with them the valuable "portable" feeling of belongingness of their own families, and they enjoyed the adventure of new places and new experiences.

The term *belongingness* could be paraphrased as "being with long enough." It achieves a sense of comfort, certainty, security, and even home. Our attaching mechanism connects us to things we belong with. It has to attach to new and different elements when we go out on our own, to recreate the sense of connection and belonging. By doing this, we feel like we become ourselves again.

As we gain knowledge, capabilities, and developed skills and put them into practice, we can detach from old belongingness systems and reattach elsewhere to create a new sense of belonging. By nature, as we mature, our belonging elements grow and become more extensive. The broader and fuller our lives become, the greater the chance our belonging system will be strong and reliable.

Basic Loyalties

All creatures in the animal kingdom, including humans, are born with an innate relating instinct. Nurtured by parents, this relating instinct creates a deep belonging and bonding. Imprinting is even more primitive than bonding, as shown by the German ethologist Konrad Lorenz's[11] studies in 1935 showing that if introduced early enough, baby goslings would follow him around as if he were their mother. Because of the gosling relating instinct, they imprinted him.

Higher up the scale of socialization is basic trust. According to Erik Erikson, the famous psychoanalyst of the mid-twentieth century who wrote of the Eight Stages of Human Psychological Development,[12] basic trust is the first and perhaps the most important human developmental stage. It is an important achievement, necessary for solid development, later intimate relationships, certainly a smoothly functioning society. But even before basic trust comes what I have discovered to be basic loyalty, a more varietal and pervasive element in the bedrock of all our identities and personalities, whether or not we trust or can be trusted.

Because of our relatedness instinct, we essentially belong to and bond with elements of our early experiences. The combination of relatedness and early experience creates an automatic loyalty toward these early patterns; they become the basic bricks of loyalty that form part of the foundation of our identities. In many people, these basic loyalty patterns may even be called the cornerstones of their identity. They automatically give us much of the sense of who we are.

There are many variations of basic loyalties, but for our discussion we will look at three general types: positive, mixed, and negative. Simply put, positive loyalties make life go smoothly, mixed loyalties contain some energy-wasting and inefficient methods but still work to a degree, and negative loyalties create significant problems for those possessing them and those around them. Negative loyalties account for and explain stubborn refusals to change as well as many problem behaviors.

Negative Basic Loyalties

Billy was a charming, engaging, handsome eleven-year-old whose new adoptive parents brought him to me because of his disruptive and seemingly nonsensical behaviors. They'd adopted Billy a year earlier from the state's foster-home system and were struck by his enthusiasm and seeming appreciation. At the time, their youngest natural child was one year older than Billy, and they were excited to share their love and family life with him.

Billy's new mother was a physician, and his father was a respected university professor. They were highly organized and responsible and had already successfully trained their three children to be like them and to strive for early academic success. Before the use of cell phones, they employed a centrally placed chalkboard message system to indicate where each family member was and what he or she was doing.

Within two months of Billy's arrival, trouble started. Billy would not follow house rules and created troublesome episodes two or three times a week. He promised to clean up his room, but afterward it would be messier than before. He piled school books, paper, dirty dishes, and clothing in the center of the family room and refused to clean it up. Once, when they ordered him to clean up one of his family-room messes, he defiantly turned and walked away, ignoring the order.

The last straw came when he shoplifted a pair of sunglasses from the drug store. It was the very same pair of glasses his adoptive mother offered to buy for him after seeing his interest in them. He told her, "No thanks" and then stole them and got caught by the store's security team. He refused to offer any explanation as to why. Billy's behavior succeeded in disrupting this highly organized and well-functioning family with the willful obstructions he placed in the way. Why was he doing it? What was wrong?

On his first visit to me, after talking to his parents, I found out to my astonishment that he had been in at least fifty foster homes. After some research, I learned there were many reasons for his departure from each home, but only a few reported it was because of his behavior. I also learned that Billy had not seen his sister since he was six. They were taken out of an abusive, drug-addicted home and had not seen their parents since. The siblings went to the same foster homes through the first few placements and then were separated. Billy missed his sister greatly.

Even after a few sessions, I had little to go on, other than the obvious attachment issues and loss problems. The only data I had was his history and that he willfully created chaos in his new home. As time passed, two things were apparent: first, he trusted no one but himself, and second, he kept creating chaos. Perhaps Billy was patterned on these two things, and his early identity was organized around them. It made sense given his history. I suspected he had a "negative" basic loyalty to trusting no one except himself, and to living with chaos. This would explain his behavior.

When I gently explained this to him, he understood and actually agreed it was true. He felt like he did not belong anywhere and that he did not feel like himself unless he distrusted everyone, except himself. He admitted to creating chaos and that it was an ingredient of his early life. I explained how and why this negative basic loyalty could not work in his new family. I described what problems it created for them and what painful restrictions he was being subjected to for doing it. He could see it. I asked, "Would you be willing to work on changing it?"

He looked me in the eye and firmly said, "Absolutely not. I will not change it. It is me."

I asked, "But you could change it little by little. In truth, you will not lose who you are. You'll just add some abilities that will help your life." He continued his refusal, and I found out later that he continued his non-trusting and chaotic behavior. Billy perceived that he needed these negatives, to counter other people's demands and needs. It gave him the certainty of his identity—the only thing he had and the only thing that had always been with him.

The family called the next week and informed me with sadness, frustration, and a sense of defeat that they had sent him back to the adoption agency. His negative basic loyalty and the behavior it spawned was ultimately too difficult for them to deal with. I never did find out what happened to Billy, as he was moved to another state. I can only hope he eventually began to take to heart what I asked of him, or that therapists in the future could convince him he didn't need the negative behaviors to have an identity. He would at first likely be frightened to give up his negative behaviors, but with patience and encouragement he could gradually give them up. Like most things, it would take repetition and practice.

Another Example

Elaine convinced her boyfriend, George, to come to her therapy sessions. She had a successful career as a social worker, but tension between herself and George increased, and they were struggling to remain together. He was the father of her youngest child, and they had not married but planned to.

They came from different backgrounds. Though Elaine had been involved in the drug scene, and to an extent participated in some minor criminal activity with him a few years earlier, she extricated herself from this life and went on to graduate school. On the other hand, George had recently been released from prison after serving time for drug dealing, but he had not found a job and was not looking very hard for one. Frustrated about this, Elaine wanted him to come to therapy to work on his fear or reluctance or whatever it was that kept him back. In the three sessions, his dilemma became clear.

George was raised in a ghetto and knew the street life. Drugs, scams, making a quick buck—they were the things he knew. He had never been in the straight world and admitted he was terrified of it. He had no idea of how to proceed, and no amount of pleading from Elaine could convince him. "That's me, honey," he said. "I can't change. I've got to do the streets. That's all I know." Even at the risk of losing Elaine, he held to his position. He could not and would not change. George had a basic loyalty to his street-life identity, and he was terrified of giving it up and was convinced he would be a failure at anything else. Elaine and George did not last long and went their separate ways.

Is it possible to have loyalty to the street life? For George, it was a far more predictable life—even with its dangers, double-crosses, payback, and prison terms—than a life comprised of growth, mastery, and loyalty to the positive attributes of civilization. Is it possible to have a loyalty to not trusting? For eleven-year-old Billy, based on early life circumstances, it was a more predictable condition than trusting. Remember the movie *Straight Time* with Dustin Hoffman? The character he played had been in and out of prison for robbery most of his life. He was used to the "security" of inmate existence and panicked on the outside. The longer he was out the more anxious and nervous he became. Finally, Hoffman's character goes on a rampage and does a splashy robbery in a Hollywood jewelry store. As he escapes, with the police on his tail and sirens howling, he smiles and feels a sense of relief. He was going back to his prison world, his secure world; he was going back to the place of his basic loyalty.

Mixed Basic Loyalties

Mixed basic loyalties are far less pernicious than negative loyalties and have both positive and negative elements. Luckily, mixed basic loyalties can be modified, changed, and even eliminated. They usually reside in people who want to handle life well but who keep doing things that cause problems or hold them back from progress. Mixed loyalties are a product of early life conditions and worked well in those circumstances. But as we mature and enter a more complex and cosmopolitan world, these patterns get in the way and do not work well. They tend to be inefficient, waste energy, and require considerable compromise and adjustment.

As a child, Donald was very shy and easily embarrassed. He recalled being humiliated at school for his poor performance and described grade school as quite unpleasant. Donald doubted his ability and worried constantly about failing. At the same time, he was driven to succeed by both his own and his parents' high expectations. Even though he was painfully shy and embarrassed about his performance, and often teased because he was unsure of himself, Donald fought back mentally to succeed. The entire time he felt alone.

As an adult, Donald succeeded admirably in carrying on his parents' wholesale distributing business and making it very profitable. He developed good skills, yet he did so at a price: he still doubted himself constantly. When he drafted contracts for his established customers, he was self-conscious and embarrassed. He tried to hide these feelings, but inside he was unhappy and anxious. For Donald, his greater fear of failure pushed him to overcome the lesser fears of embarrassment and humiliation and resulted in his ability to generate good enough contracts to succeed. He characteristically would initially feel embarrassment, humiliation, and the fear of not succeeding as he worked up contracts, and then he would unmercifully pressure himself to perform well and succeed.

When Donald finally could see that it was his motivation and expertise that created his success in business. He no longer needed the embarrassment, humiliation, and fear to motivate and pressure himself to succeed. With this knowledge Donald gave up this mixed basic loyalty and relied on his good skills only. To this day, he only occasionally gets reminded, by re-experiencing briefly those old painful feelings, the remnants of an old loyalty.

Energy Drain with a Twist—A Pathological Blend of Basic Loyalties

Carolyn, a master at fixing problems and taking responsibility, came to me exhausted. She told me that after sixteen years of marriage she was frustrated and defeated, and she was considering divorce. She informed me that her husband, Irv, kept giving her problems to solve and dilemmas to fix. It was only after years of fixing one thing after another that Carolyn finally realized that Irv had been directing her activity much of the time. It went like this: Irv would mention a household problem, a difficulty with one of the children, or his wish for her to prepare a favorite meal. Carolyn would comply and solve the problem, and after thanking her, Irv would tell her he was concerned about something else—for example, the dog shedding hair in the living room. Carolyn would take the cue and brush the dog or take measures to keep it out of the living room. When she finished, he would tell her she had done a good job, but then he'd mention some other chore or problem that needed her attention. One thing led to another in a never-ending sequence.

Carolyn and Irv had developed a pattern. Irv would make a request or point out a problem, and Carolyn would take care of it. As soon as she finished, he quickly mentioned another one. This pattern went on endlessly, until her anger and frustration broke loose and she threatened divorce. He was incredulous and could not understand why she felt that way.

As I sat listening to Carolyn describe this situation, I had a mental image. I saw Irv sitting in an easy chair at the center of a merry-go-round as it turned round and round. He would throw a problem off the spinning platform like a little rubber ball, and it would bounce away. Carolyn chased after it, trailing it across the pavement until she could grab it and then return it to him. He would look at it, thank her, and then throw a different ball, and off she went chasing it and returning it. Round and round they went for years. No wonder she was exhausted!

When I presented the idea of this mental picture to Carolyn, she could see her folly of always trying to solve the problem and giving Irv the certainty of the solution. Irv was always uncertain and, because of it, kept presenting new problems and concerns. Irv could not become assured, and Carolyn, for her part, could never help him be assured and certain. He had a loyalty to uncertainty, and she to certainty and fixing things. Carolyn tried to have Irv become certain with the problem solved. (By certain, I mean definite, holding the answer, complete; by uncertain,

I mean the solution or answer to the problem remained doubtful.) Their patterns combined to form this painful existence. Both were angry at each other, she because he would never get certain, he because she did not see all the uncertainty he did.

This special pattern, an energy drain with a twist, is quite common with couples and in parent-child relationships. It always results in shared consternation and confusion, which both parties create. The pattern initially defies logic and never changes, unless a deeper look reveals its nature. It can be changed, and actually eliminated, when one knows the hidden key to this vicious pattern.

How could Carolyn get Irv to stop? What was wrong? I got a clue to solving this perplexing problem when I worked with a physician and his wife, Diane, discussed before, who were having problems. In this instance, a particular vexing series of difficulties arose when the wife constantly complained of a variety of health problems with physical symptoms. Being a doctor, the husband made many attempts to help, assisting her with medical referrals. The husband made the appointments for her because he knew the physicians and she had requested him to do so. With every appointment he made, she canceled at the last minute. This cycle continued for a long time until he became angry and demanded to know what was going on. "I will not let this matter rest," he told her, "until I know why." He was firm and determined, and she knew it. An hour or so later, she finally admitted, "Basically, I do not feel deserving of the benefit of the care you have set up for me. I do not feel worth it." It should be noted that the wife suffered from chronic low self-esteem. "But when you keep making the effort, I think maybe you think I'm worth it, and I cling to that hope." I could now see why she kept recreating the situation. By his caring actions, she could at least have some reassurance that she might be worth it. She was borrowing from his concern for her. It was fragile, but it was her only hold on having some hope of self-esteem, of possibly being worth it. Diane was depending upon his continued willingness to make the efforts in her behalf. This important discovery has been discussed before; it is repeated to show how this insight helped Carolyn and Irv.

For Carolyn and many others, this discovery offered a solution. Hard as it was, Carolyn needed to stop the pattern of reassuring Irv, the perpetually uncertain one. She needed to quit fixing and leave it to Irv to "sink or swim." She informed him, "It is up to you, I'm not doing the solving anymore," and remarkably the vicious cycle ended. The energy drain with a twist was defeated. The fix-it person could let go of always fixing. The uncertain person had to "sink or swim," do it for him or herself, earn the value of being capable, or not.

Positive Basic Loyalties

Positive basic loyalties are easy to identify and understand. We all have many of them and become automatic at using them. If we have been at least moderately successful so far in our life, we are using them well. To discover your positive loyalties, ask yourself, "What is it I can always rely on in myself to pull me through, especially at a difficult time? What attitude serves me best?" Recall how others see you; what have they told you about the kind of a person you are, or what do others identify as your most valuable attributes? Many times, others see us more clearly than we do.

New positive basic loyalties can develop when you become particularly good at something over time. I have developed new loyalties in dealing with certifying agencies and state entities in my medical directorship positions. I didn't know how to do it in the beginning; experience was the teacher. I am now sought for this ability—a new basic loyalty I can rely on. Any skill you develop and can rely on becomes a positive basic loyalty.

Whenever you fall prey to self-doubt or become nervous or uncertain at the start of a campaign or project, ask yourself what has worked for you in the past. What strengths have you relied on to help you succeed? By recalling the past, you identify positive basic loyalties that you have employed successfully, and the result will calm doubt and uncertainty. Positive basic loyalties are really quite pleasant to realize. They include loyalty to mastery, an increase in knowledge, and a drive to discover. Others include love and care and empathy and being a good friend, assuming responsibility, and being productive and generative.

Positive basic loyalties can include our habits and our style as we approach tasks. Some study closely, paying attention to detail before they act. Others look at situations from a large overview, make decisions on where or what to start taking action, and then proceed. Still others dive in enthusiastically and somewhat impulsively and ride the power of their strong, energetic drive. Just about anything that works for you, particularly over time, is a positive basic loyalty. They tend to be non-conflicted and efficient, unlike the mixed basic loyalties that require compromise and extra energy to make them be successful.

Geographical Belongingness

Places and geographical areas evoke and solidify our sense of belonging just as people or important behavioral traits or styles do. For instance, if you were raised in the mountainous country of the intermountain west, you probably long for the sight of the familiar mountains when you have been away for a long time. You feel comforted and then comfortable when you are back in them. The same holds true for the Midwesterner with his or her attachment to the prairie and big sky. Anybody I have ever met who was raised near the ocean feels the same way about the beaches and ocean vistas of their childhood.

Belongingness with Familiar Things

Things as everyday as one's own comfortable bed or well-worn desk are things that give us a belonging. Anytime we are near to or involved with something for a long enough time, we will obtain a measure of belonging with it. Simply said, we get attached to things.

Belongingness Disrupted by a Move

What happens to us when we move to a distant place and relocate to a foreign culture for a while? We are often stimulated with the new adventure, but at the same time a part of us feels disoriented with our familiar attachments gone; we experience cultural shock. It takes an average of three months to attach to enough new situations to make them familiar. Although they will never replace the old belongings kept alive in our memories and our longings, they give us enough so that we become comfortable and familiar with people, places, and things. The more hesitant one is, the longer it takes to develop the new attachments and belonging. The great adaptors, on the other hand, have developed their methods and abilities so that they get comfortable and attached more quickly and fully than most.

Example of a Master at Creating Belongingness in New Locales

Sandra had often moved to head up new hospitals in their development phase. Her company valued her start-up skills as a hospital administrator and moved her every two to three years. She was a master at establishing herself in new circumstances, and she purposefully set out to meet members of the local city government, from the mayor to police and fire chiefs. She would meet the local school principals and counselors and invite them all out for a tour of her hospital. Then she would set out to develop referral sources and hold marketing seminars at rooms she rented in city government buildings, so she and the hospital were visible to city magistrates and thus integrated into the community. Much of this was done for launching the business aspect of her hospital, but it was for her personal life as well. Her ability to integrate shortened the time of her not belonging and uncertainty. We can all take a leaf from her style. Become assertive and purposefully focused to connect with the many important elements of our new community; join clubs or organizations, seek introductions, and get involved. In that way we connect faster and more fully.

Loss of Belongingness and Anxiety

Interestingly, being out of belongingness can create anxiety within us, giving us some frightening uncertainty and risking to our quality of life. There is a direct relationship between lack of belonging and anxiety. In a sense, anything we are anxious about suggests an element of future risk that our desired result may not occur. When we are used to being married, a divorce creates much anxiety and disorientation. Many of our automatic reliances are torn away, including the belief of growing old together. These painful disorientation feelings often last for a year or more. The support of friends and psychotherapy can certainly help during this trying period. Eventually the trauma subsides, the new life becomes routine, and new relationships develop.

Loss of Belonging through Death

Death of close loved ones can put us into a dizzying spin of grief and lost belongingness that takes much energy and pain resolution to eventually overcome. The massive loss of belongingness includes the daily contact, activities and conversation, emotional and physical intimacy, and the future together with its dreams and plans. We are inherently social beings, so we rely on our loved ones a great deal for our sense of belonging, connection, our security, and even our identity to an extent. The loss causes us to initially disbelieve the truth of the loss. We will experience the raw wound, the ripping away from our attachment, and it will hurt. The pain of the lost attachment causes us anguish, terrific sadness, uncertainty, and confusion. Some of us deny the reality of our loss or try to bring the lost loved one back, but of course we cannot. We strain to reach and hold that which has just gone. We at times feel empty. Over the next weeks and months, the loss sinks in more. We realize we can and will go on. We remember the good times and the bad times; often the memories bring tears, mostly of sadness but some of gratefulness, for what we had that is no longer. We have moments in our quiet thoughts and dreams that the person is still there, in the present remembered activity. Gradually, over months, and not smoothly but with punctuations of pain and sadness, the level of the grief and the duration of painful episodes diminishes. After a year or two, our own living takes up much more of our time, involvement, and energy. Even so, some nostalgia and intermittent brief sadness will probably remain for a lifetime.

The Value of a Good Social Support System

The best natural antidepressant, well-known to mental-health professionals, is a good social support system. We are social beings as a species, though there is variation in what each individual's requirement for social contact is. A good social support system of family, friends, and acquaintances buoys us up and gives us the opportunity for responsible and considerate involvement with others. The broader, deeper, and more emotionally intimate the elements of our system are, the better it is for us. We are graced, comforted, and valued, even loved, by and through our relationships, which give opportunity for us to be givers as well as receivers of personal acceptance, caring, and service.

Increased Options and Access

Belonging gives us all a certain type of valuable power and ease of access. The broader our system of belonging, the greater the number of options available to us. The familiarity and ease available from belonging gives us greater numbers of sources, people with varieties of expertise, to assist us by our merely asking. As members of the belonging, we are given automatic acceptance and access to all; the same is expected of us if others ask our advice. It is both an efficient and effective way for humans to get along. In former times extended families, kin, tribes, or clans provided these valuable things. Modern-day life and job mobility required by corporations, or special schooling out of one's geographic area, have eliminated much of the old, automatic belongingness system. The only viable answer and strategy to this is to develop the ability (which you carry with you) to create new and suitable belongings wherever you go.

The Value of Groups and Clans

Probably the most lacking element of belonging in modern life is the loss of the moderate-sized group or clan—fifty to five hundred closely associated people. Because tribes, clans, and geographically close extended families are a rarity now, other organizations can be substituted: neighborhoods with organized get-togethers, leisure time clubs (golf, tennis, hiking, etc.), churches, service organizations, alumni organizations, symphony guilds, and professional organizations. If you are missing this important element, it should be worth the effort to find it because of what it can uniquely give you—a rich source of exchange, involvement, opportunity, and access, thereby increasing your liaisons, which add to your adaptability and thus your strength. Belongingness increases psychological strength by providing more connections, more learning, and more partnerships. Broad and deep belongingness has the potential to increase our strength much more extensively.

Close-knit groups of this size also provide good matches for the young members to identify with and have their skills nurtured. There is a greater chance that children's innate talents and skills will find a welcoming reception through similarity when there is a greater number of role models from whom to choose a figure to idealize and identify with. Matching skills and talents of the young with willing elders of similar talent and skill provides teaching, mentoring, and good role models, as well as mutual understanding and support to the young where parents alone may not suffice. For instance, if a child is musically inclined but the parents are not, a musically talented aunt, neighbor, or congregation member could be an encouraging or teaching source. A relative or club member with superb athletic skills would recognize and be able to facilitate good emerging skills in well-coordinated youths of his or her acquaintance. This automatically happened in tribes or clans of yesteryear. It can still happen through belonging to a similar-sized group in the modern era and engineering the connections.

Belonging with Your Own Self-Processes

Eventually as we come to know ourselves through how we characteristically function, and consciously know many of our positive basic loyalties, we gain a greater sense of belongingness and awareness with our own self. We then develop increasing trust in ourselves and realize we can rely on ourselves to often produce what we are aiming for, to fulfill our intended goals. This generates confidence, a self-belief of likely success that we can take with us wherever we go. This enhanced sense of belonging, *belonging with our processes*, helps support and insulate us as we go through the many changes and losses which life brings. It is a great strength to have. It helps neutralize or minimize the disorientation and loss of sense of self that we would otherwise experience from big changes and losses in our lives. Belongingness is one of the inherent, basic psychological truths.

Chapter Summary

1. Each of us feels the value of being connected and supported, the warm and relaxed feeling of security when we know that we belong.

2. As we gain knowledge, capabilities, and developed skills and put them into practice, we can detach from old belongingness systems and reattach elsewhere to create a new sense of belonging. By nature, as we mature, our belonging elements grow and become more extensive. The broader and fuller our lives become, the greater the chance our belonging system will be strong and reliable. It is worth reviewing from time to time to see if we are missing any important elements.

3. The valuable feeling of belongingness strengthens us. When we lack this valuable feeling, we have painful uncertainty, even anxiety. These feelings can be used to point to the areas of belongingness we do not have but would be wise to develop.

4. We belong to and bond with elements of our early experiences, which creates an automatic loyalty toward these early patterns. They become the basic loyalties that form part of the foundation of our identities, automatically giving us much of the sense of who we are.

5. There are three general types of basic loyalties: positive, mixed, and negative. Simply put, positive loyalties make life go smoothly, mixed loyalties contain some energy-wasting and inefficient methods but still work to a degree, and negative loyalties create significant problems for those possessing them and those around them. Negative loyalties account for and explain stubborn refusals to change as well as many problem behaviors.

6. Belongingness can be disrupted by a geographical move. It takes an average of three months to attach to enough places, situations, and experiences to make them familiar.

7. Close-knit groups, such as churches, service organizations, alumni organizations, symphony guilds, and professional organizations, provide good matches for members to identify with and to have their skills nurtured.

SECTION 3

Enhance Your Relationships and
Communicate in the Best Possible Ways

CHAPTER 12

———◆◆◆◆———

How to Grace and Honor Your Relationships

Love and positive valuing can mean different things to people from different family backgrounds. These differences can influence your relationships.

In our most important relationships, we sometimes have to experiment to see what works well and what doesn't, in terms of communicating love. This chapter will help you discover the hidden pitfalls that can hurt your valued relationships; it will also show you how to remove those pitfalls. Sometimes it's simply a matter of discovering the differences and similarities in the love patterns you learned from your family during childhood. To begin, let me show you what can happen in the early years of marriage.

A Problem That May Arise Early in Marriage

Ron and Maxine were well suited for each other, and their patterns coordinated smoothly during the first years of marriage. They had chosen each other because they liked and admired the other person and for what they each had already become in life. From the outset, they liked the full photograph of the other person, so to speak. In the fifth year, they began to fight and ended up in my office explaining their problems. I was surprised to receive the call because I had seen each individually a few times during the previous two years, for individual matters, and neither mentioned any difficulty or conflict between them.

To my surprise, each described the other's shortcomings and told me how the other person did not serve their needs well. Each accused the other of "not loving me as much anymore." Since I knew both patients, I was fascinated by these assessments. What was wrong?

I learned that the shift in the relationship began when Ron started criticizing Maxine. Ron wanted more praise than Maxine gave him for completing a successful real-estate development. Inwardly, Ron began feeling that Maxine took him for granted and was not interested in him enough. He felt a little cheated and started finding fault, showing less patience and exhibiting more anger. As his irritability increased, he demanded to know, "Why don't you love me more? Why don't you cook my favorite meals anymore? Why is the house always a mess?" Ron said further, "Why don't you take a class and better yourself? I'm progressing and you're not."

Maxine reacted with hurt and surprise. She wondered, "What is wrong? Why is Ron being this way?" At first, she listened to the criticism and tried to understand what was happening. Finally tired of being berated and filled with consternation, she retaliated, "You're not the man I married! All you do is criticize me and moan! You don't support or help me with the kids. I never get a break. Once you were considerate to me, but those days are long gone! You love your work more than me!" She stomped out but not before telling him, "To hell with you!"

What happened? For sure, each was dealing with more in life than they did earlier in the marriage. Ron's business was growing and demanding increased time and focus. They now had two children, and the responsibilities of parenting consumed them, more so for Maxine because she was the primary caregiver. Consequently, there was not as much time together and the expressions of love, desire, and devotion were fewer and less often. Not incidentally, each had an aging parent who suffered from illness and needed help and support.

The Hidden Cause

But the most important cause (and cure, when they saw it) was something else. They had unconsciously changed the pattern of how they viewed each other and then began to expect something different from the partner. It started with Ron, but Maxine soon joined in. Each wanted the other to be a function of his or her own *inner wish* of how they wanted to be related to. When the partner did not fit this changed expectation, bad feelings erupted, followed by accusations and criticisms. What had been mutual appreciation and admiration had changed, without agreement, into expectations and demands. Why? Ron wanted Maxine to praise him more on his success in real estate, which provided the family funds. Maxine wanted to be told and shown directly that she was valued by Ron, more than he valued his work.

Strange as it may sound, previous childhood powerlessness and disappointment provides an answer. When, as four- or five-year-olds, we could not have our way with a parent, we vowed to ourselves, "One day, when I grow up, I will have it be my way. I'll get what I want!" Long buried in the unconscious mind, that old wish and promise to the self can become activated in adult intimate relationships, particularly mating relationships. This old self-promise surfaces when some prior balance gets upset and then the rules change, from appreciation to demand and then criticism. By its nature, this infantile and unrealistic change cannot work; it causes pain and disruption and must be exposed and released for normalcy to return. These unrealistic, infantile, omnipotent expectations lay dormant for years before surfacing, but for success they must be seen, released, and given up.

When Ron and Maxine became aware of this, they saw it in themselves and realized what had occurred. By seeing and understanding how they shifted into a childhood expectation, they were able to get back to the positive feeling they possessed before. They reaffirmed their "old photographs," their successful relationship view of admiration, appreciation, and value for each other.

This situation is not unique to Ron and Maxine; it could be one of the most widely experienced problems that otherwise healthy couples face. For Ron and Maxine, it took three psychotherapy sessions to understand and solve. In the twenty years since, they slipped into the unworkable pattern two more times and came to see me. Each time they were surprised they were doing it and were easily able to stop.

The Solution

If you find you are having more criticism of your spouse and feeling less loved, you could have unwittingly slipped into these infantile expectations and power vows. Likewise, if your spouse surprisingly and wrongly accuses you of not loving him or her anymore, the same reason could be causing it. Short of going for therapy, one of you could bring up the possibility that either or both of you may have inadvertently changed from appreciating, admiring, and loving each other for being what you originally saw and loved into instead a pattern of wanting, even demanding, that the loved partner *change* to fulfill your own selfish expectations. Admitting this possibility openly, honestly, and earnestly could go a long way to producing a cooperative search and a solution.

The Way Love Was Expressed in the Families of Origin

A frequent complaint I get from one spouse is that, "He doesn't show me that he loves me." After inquiry, I find out from this spouse that receiving gifts and tokens of endearment means, "I'm loved." Usually, the other spouse says, "She's always giving me gifts. That's fine, but she doesn't tell me she loves me. She doesn't talk to me about our love. She complains that I don't show my love, even though I tell her all the time."

Some families of origin show love by giving gifts or by doing acts of helping to demonstrate it. They usually do not express love verbally. In contrast, other families share and tell; they express love verbally and usually do not give so many gifts. It is important to learn your partner's pattern of love expressing—that is, what constitutes or defines love and consideration in his or her family of origin. Once you have learned this, you can fit that pattern if you choose. If you feel your partner's pattern of love expression is "just not you," explain your own family's pattern to your partner and come to a mutual understanding. It seems a little thing, but it has big consequences. Keeping aware of some simple but powerful truths about intimate relationships goes a long way in producing harmony, reducing conflict, and engendering mutual positive regard. Gary Chapman[13] has written on this subject; see his book for more explanation.

The Pattern Clash

Just like the patterns of love expression, people are a composition of many patterns and styles. Each of us has our own identity, our own bouquet of patterns. No two people are exactly alike, but the patterns of mates and good friends generally sequence well, which is one reason we choose each other.

Unfortunately, even well-selected mates do not always sequence well. We clash, have misunderstandings, and argue. In most instances, no one is intentionally trying to be a bad or negative influence; it is just an inadvertent pattern clash. It is really too bad that when these patterns and styles clash, we cannot see them for what they are, instead taking them personally and responding in kind.

I often define an argument as two people trying to stab each other from their own point of view. I have observed that people are highly motivated by their own point of view, which if held too tightly causes some self-defeat or even ostracism by others. People are both *impelled* and *impaled* by their own point of view. The question is, how can we identify clashes in styles and patterns and disarm them from becoming arguments that harm our relationships?

An Example

Patti and Jim were both capable of being opinionated. When their opinions on a subject clashed, each held tightly to his or her respective views, and arguments sometimes resulted. For many situations this was healthy; they simply agreed to disagree because they respected each other. However, when they encountered situations where much was at stake, it sometimes got ugly. For example, they periodically discussed making changes to their investment portfolio. This important subject required problem solving and decision making, and invariably they hit a snag because they held very different opinions. Each held tightly to his or her position and would not budge: Jim's more risky, fast turnover investment strategy versus Patti's more conservative, slow growth-stock approach. They claimed it had to be their own way and viewed their beginning position as the final position.

Jim had been successful through taking risks. He did not like the more conservative approach his parents used in their financial life, so he reacted negatively to Patti's view. Patti's parents suffered a financial disaster while she was still a teenager, and she was concerned this might happen to herself and Jim. Patti viewed the conservative approach as the safest and therefore the best. It was not until they had many intense and painful arguments that they concluded they were at a hopeless impasse and sought a third party to facilitate solving the problem. Afterward, with work and patience, they developed problem-solving techniques that served to neutralize inflammatory situations and find satisfactory solutions.

What techniques or ground rules did they learn? First, they agreed to be conscious and considerate of the other person's opinion. They learned to acknowledge that the other person's opinions were important and came through experience and good decision making. Second, they learned to take their partner's opinions seriously. Third—and this was very important—they learned to allow their partner an opportunity to fully present his or her thinking, experience, and emotional investment without interruption. Fourth, each became committed to listening to the other with an open mind, stressing empathy and respect. Fifth, they gave each other the opportunity to ask questions, which engendered greater understanding and clarification.

Not surprisingly, after learning more information the other possessed about investments that they never alone could have considered, they could reach compromises and solutions. They agreed to develop a plan including both investment strategies. 30 percent risky and 70 percent conservative. The big bonus was how much more they understood each other and why the other had developed such strongly held beginning positions. They also learned that by changing their beginning positions and realizing that new data was important and valid, they could be better informed and situated. Neither Patti nor Jim alone knew all of the financial aspects of investing; only by combining their considerable knowledge could they make better and more informed decisions. Perhaps the greatest benefit was the cessation of the arguments and hostility. From then on they could laughingly say, "We were just having a pattern clash."

The Techniques of Resolution

There are six techniques and attitudes to apply if you are to resolve a pattern clash successfully. First, listen to each other's understanding of the situation. Second, show respect for each other's position. Third, avoid dogmatism or tyranny and be willing to depart from the beginning position you held when new data coming from the discussion seems plausible and useful. Fourth, begin to synthesize a new, more informed position or viewpoint that is acceptable to both. Fifth, recheck to see if you both agree to the new solution. Sixth, check to see that both of your feelings are settled. If settled, you are done; if not, you have more to discuss. These techniques can be used for any emotionally charged situation, helping us to keep an open mind and develop better understanding.

A Second Example

Renee and Richard were both divorcees with children from former marriages. Each had different notions about child rearing, and each was somewhat vulnerable to the demands and manipulations of their own natural children, something the other could see. At the same time, each had a history of special and meaningful ways of relating to their own children that was not fully appreciated by the other. These situations cause some of the common dilemmas of blended families.

When Richard's children visited from out of state (Renee's children lived with the couple most of the time), the differences in parenting styles created minor but sensitively felt conflicts. Wisely, Renee and Richard developed a method to arrive at a synthesis of agreement that allowed differences in the uniqueness of parenting styles, while downplaying favoritism and always leaving the door open for discussion. Each agreed to hear and accept critiquing, even constructive criticism, about vulnerable issues such as favoritism or guilt manipulations used by the kids that the other was blind to or handled poorly. Renee and Richard's goal was to create an ongoing system to serve their blended family. This goal kept them rational, and they were able to function effectively in their blended family life.

Truly and Fully Understanding Each Other—Clearing the Misunderstandings

People who have chosen each other as mates for a long-term relationship usually have similar goals and similar care and concern for each other. When they have a big misunderstanding or other barrier to smooth functioning, it is because they have inadvertently been unable to make something clear to the other person. Usually the cause is a misinterpretation on the part of one, followed by a defensive or accusative retort back from the other. Sometimes one or both is already upset by a recent experience that is not even connected to the partner. The upset person's tenseness and irritation come across by mistake, and the other is taken by surprise and naturally reacts negatively; then hurt, reaction, defend, accuse, and further hurt follow. It is an argument, a big one.

The Corrective Technique: Someone Takes Responsibility to Start

The best way to clear things up is that one person has to be willing to take responsibility to start the process. This is best done by a statement of how that person views the relationship, what he or she wants to be happening, how he or she values and desires the best for each other and the relationship, and how there is sorrow for something obviously unintended getting in the way. The initiator also needs to state the valued presumption that the partner appears generally to feel and desire this same way. After setting this tone, the initiator reveals his or her intention in the situation that became a problem, the purpose involved in why he or she said what was said, and an apology for clumsiness or unwanted attitudes, tones, or irritations that contaminated the desired communication. At this point, a physical hug helps to underscore the basic love and affection.

For instance, let us see how Renee and Richard have learned to do this. Renee feels upset about her belief that Richard criticized her for what he thought she had said to a friend, so she says, "Stop telling me how I'm wrong!"

He reacts by getting defensive and telling her, "Quit telling me how to act. You don't even know what I meant!"

At that point Renee wisely realized they've gone from misunderstanding to mutual irritation and some anger. Wanting to clear the problem up, Renee says, "You know I love you, and we know we love each other. We're probably having a misunderstanding. It isn't worth it to argue. We want the best for our relationship. I'm sorry for my retort. and I know you probably are too. I meant that Sally had a lot to deal with, was probably stressed. and so should be careful how she proceeded. I didn't mean it that she had better watch out or else. I'm sorry I was a little clumsy in how I said it. I'm Sorry I attacked you when I said, 'Quit telling me how I'm wrong.'"

Then the Other Partner Reveals

The other partner, in turn, reveals and acknowledges his or her intention, purpose, and preferences for the relationship's best functioning. Both parties then have agreed, in a larger sense, that they share the same value and best desires for the relationship.

Ron smiles and hugs Renee, saying, "I love you, I'm sorry too. I felt hurt, so I attacked, which only made it worse. I could have stopped and asked what you meant before reacting. Next time I hope I will. You know that I love you." At this point, the couple can discuss what had created the problem in the first place, and what measures they can take to reduce or eliminate the creation of similar difficulties in the future. Doing this brings to light all of the causative factors that derailed the clear communication and quality relating.

By creating this cameo of reality in exact detail, you can analyze it fully and understand it, and then the relationship can get back on track. Renee and Ron both realized that at times they don't hear correctly or misinterpret from the tone, presuming an intense tone means anger or attack when it could really be worry or concern. They realize they have to be very careful to make sure they try to understand not misunderstand, to reduce or eliminate conflict.

Sometimes one or the other who are in an interaction will remain angry and possibly defensive, apparently unable to let the feelings go and attempt to be together. At that point, it would be wise for either person or both to say, "I now can see that this is still upsetting, so let's move beyond it to other things until we feel able to solve it."

Chapter Summary

1. Discover and learn what love and positive valuing mean to each of you, from your origins. Often these will be different for each of you. Think back and describe experiences and examples from your pasts so you can both understand where each of you is coming from. Then, dare to try each other's ways. Your partner will appreciate the attempt and you will be encouraged to use it more often.

2. Arguments about how things should be, or heated discussions about differences of opinion, are often just pattern clashes. Do not let these situations have enduring, negative, painful power with you.

3. Remember that misunderstandings are truly lacks of mutual understanding. To remove them, considerately create understanding by using different words and explanations until you are each clear.

4. Be willing to leave your starting positions and viewpoints, and hear each other out in order to move toward a synthesis of new agreement and a course of action that you both endorse.

CHAPTER 13

———◆·◆··◆·◆———

Clear Communication

Two people cannot have the same mind. Further, no two people have exactly the same perception. Our inner images are our own, slightly different from others, even on the same subject.

Clear communication is important. Unfortunately, sometimes we do not realize our requests are unclear, and then we become irritated at having to repeat them. Other times, we fight the truth; we realize there is a misunderstanding, but we ignore it because of the additional effort required to clear it up. At its best, communicating articulately, succinctly, and concisely conveys an exact idea, concept, or request. The more exact the similarity, the greater the clarity of understanding. However, it is hard to communicate exactly considering human complexity, which is why so many misunderstandings occur.

Misunderstandings: Recognizing and Fixing Them
Misunderstandings arise often during everyday conversation. While looking at the TV room's disarranged furniture, Julie says to Bob, who

is down the hall around the corner, "I need some help; could you please rearrange the furniture in that room?"

Uncertain which of three rooms she's referring to and exactly what pieces of furniture, Bob asks back, "What furniture? What do you mean?"

Julie is quickly frustrated at having to repeat herself, and she says sharply, "Just what I said! The furniture in the room needs rearranging."

Reacting to the sharpness and irritation in Julie's comment and still unclear on what she wants, Bob yells back, "Damn it, what room? Which furniture?"

"Over there," Julie shouts, and she points to the TV room as Bob comes around the corner and down the hall.

"Well, why didn't you say so?" he retorts.

"That's exactly what I told you," Julie reiterates, feeling angry and frustrated.

"Well, make it clear next time," Bob chides.

Julie and Bob have just created and experienced a classical misunderstanding. Bob did not know which room or furniture Julie meant. Looking into the room, Julie was clear in her own mind; she did not consider that there were other rooms nearby that Bob was also considering, so she was frustrated at having to repeat herself. He was frustrated because she, in frustration, repeated the same message without clarification.

The Fix

Misunderstanding is just what it says, not an understanding. Obviously, the way to correct it is to realize a misunderstanding exists and then take measures to clear it up. Bob could have asked, "Which room, what furniture?" because he was thinking of three different possibilities. Julie could have realized he truly did not understand and then changed her message to, "I'm looking at the TV room. The furniture is out of place from the group watching the game last night. Could you put it back in place?" Either option could have solved the problem. By stating more clearly, giving more information, or asking clarifying questions, such situations can be avoided. If Julie had asked, "What else are you thinking about? I'm talking about the TV room and the party last night," then the situation would not have developed.

The sooner we realize a misunderstanding has occurred, the sooner we can take steps to clear it up and to prevent the further inefficiency and compounding frustration. What happens so often is that we make a request when busy, with many other things on our mind, and it lacks clarity. When the message is not received accurately, we get irritated and frustrated at having to repeat it again. *At the earliest point of misunderstanding, the best resolving technique is to restate the request in a different way, attempting to make it more easily understood.* Unfortunately, sometimes we do not realize our request is unclear, and then get bothered at having to say it again. Other times, though, we fight the truth. We realize there is a misunderstanding but ignore it because of the additional energy and effort it will require to clear it up.

Clear Communication

Whether at home or work, clear communication that is understood is important in interactions, particularly when giving directions or assigning tasks. After the warehouse manager, Gerald, requested Will, the stocker in section H, to get five of the red-labeled supply boxes of electrical outlets ready for a delivery, he continued by asking if Will was clear about the order. Will started to say he understood, but then he realized there were two different types of "red labeled" electrical outlet boxes, one for home use and one for industrial use. He asked Gerald, "The home-use size or the industrial size?"

"Gosh, I did not realize both had red labels," Gerald remarked, surprised. "Let me quickly check … Uh, the industrial. I think they are labeled with the abbreviation 'Ind.' The home use is labeled with an H. Both are numbered 265, so get the Ind. 265, not the H. 265."

"Right. The Ind. 265, five boxes, coming up. That's what you need?" Will both asked and informed, restating the order for both correctness and redundancy.

"That's it, five boxes industrial, Ind. 265," Gerald confirmed. There would not be a mistake. Gerard and Will used the techniques of cross-checking and restating, letting the other clearly know what was in each other's mind. That way, they eliminated misunderstandings and could most clearly approximate being of one mind.

Communication Enhancers

Cross-checking with clarifying techniques—and a method called self-referring communication, which will be shown shortly—enhance clarity dramatically and help eliminate misunderstandings that can frequently occur. As you will see, the further value of self-referring communication is that it acts respectfully toward others, bypassing potential defensiveness or shifts in responsibility that can stimulate wariness and uncertainty. It creates an environment where communication is clear and rewarding.

No matter how carefully we try to communicate clearly, communication will not occur all of the time; there is no foolproof method. Good intention and technique go a long way, but if misunderstanding occurs, it will generally be taken more lightly.

The Click of Certainty?

Many times we believe we are truly communicating when we are not. Consider the case of the "click of certainty." It is the feeling or sense of certainty and clarity at the end of communication, when you are truly on the same page with someone else and in full agreement on both an external and internal level. You and another person have clicked, and you both know for "certain" that you have really communicated.

This topic came up in a therapy session with couple Betsy and Tom. They talked about a recent conversation in which they had achieved the click of certainty; each fully understood what the other meant. The click came when they were describing how exhilarating a day of powder skiing had been a year earlier at Jupiter Bowl in Park City; it was a fun and fulfilling day, ending with a good dinner. Both experienced very similar feelings, their mutual discovery felt quite good, and they enjoyed the shared memory of it. But when I asked a few questions—"Which part of Jupiter Bowl did you ski? What was the weather like? Where did you eat?"—each described a different part of Jupiter Bowl, different weather conditions, a different restaurant, and even a different month of the year! Neither realized they were talking about two different though similar experiences, until I asked for more detail. I had inadvertently exposed the lack of full exact communication.

The above experience and many others have prompted me to often say, "Communication isn't." So what are we to do? The best we can. Though we can get quite good at communication, we unfortunately can only approach total exactness of clarity.

How You Say Things Counts

Mr. Chapin, the manager, said loudly and firmly, "Get the data sets, all of you, as fast as you can. We need to go over everything one last time before we file our final bid." People scrambled to obey the order, all feeling some fear and pressuring themselves to do as told. It was a tense time for all, but they got it done.

A rival firm's bid manager, Mr. Jamison, requested its data sets a little differently. "Folks, I know we have a very important opportunity coming up to win this job. It means a lot to this company's future and our own futures. Please bring your data sets and your best ideas to our final meeting so we can prepare the best bid possible. Are you with me?" Enthusiastic affirmatives were followed by hard work from everybody on the team.

These two similar tasks, but very different experiences, were created by how the instructions and communication were handled, from what attitude was conveyed by management and what the bid team members felt hearing the message. How you say things counts.

When Jill told her six-year-old boy to do a task, he balked, and she had to threaten punishment before he complied. The exchange was unpleasant for both. Andrea, on the other hand, explained to her six-year-old her desire that he could help her and the family by doing the task. It would be much appreciated. Was he willing? After a brief hesitation, he cheerfully answered, "Sure, Mom."

The principles of good verbal communication start by stating the truth of your awareness—that is, verbalizing what is it you are thinking. It can be difficult, but you must take the responsibility to do it. Then, state the request or desired action you would like. Be invitational: "I would like to have you with me on this," or "I would like you to come with me; are you willing?"

Analyzing the Impact of Statements

Once, in teaching a continuing education class, I conducted an exercise in communication. I had the adult members of the class ask each other out to a movie. The subtle and not so subtle awareness of feelings the askers evoked were revealing. Take this example: "How would you like to go to a movie?" At first glance it looks simple and straightforward. However, the responses told a different story. One student said, "I feel like the asker is putting the responsibility on me. I don't know if he really wants to go to a movie. It seems he wants me to decide." Another student added, "It makes me feel like the asker doesn't know whether or not he even wants to go, he's uncertain." Both agreed that the asker was shifting responsibility to the person asked. Everyone in the class felt slightly uncomfortable, a little wary, and uncertain.

In contrast, here is another approach. "I'd like to go to a movie tomorrow night. Would you like to come with me?" Most agreed that they felt comfortable with this, but some commented, "I still feel like the asker is shifting some responsibility to me—that he maybe would not go unless I went with him." This was a response to a subtle shift of responsibility that many in the class had missed but could now see. When another asker tried, "I'm going to a movie tomorrow night. I'd love for you to come with me, if you'd like," everyone liked this approach best and felt comfortable with it.

Difficult situations that may create conflict can be brought up in a similar manner. For example, "It seems to me that we are having some difficulty agreeing to the same course of action dealing with our teenager.

Can we talk about it, first to see if we are having difficulty, then to discuss ways we each think we might solve it, and then to see if we can solve it? How about it? Are you willing?"

Summarizing

The principles of good communication come through again. Take responsibility to state the truth of your awareness, to state your perception, and to suggest and invite participation in a course of action. Next, ask if there is agreement or willingness. This is so much better than, "You need to change your way of dealing with our teenager," which accuses and engenders defensiveness. Or, "It's your fault the way our kids are acting," which blames and engenders both defensiveness and retaliation. Remember, angrily accusing or blaming usually receives a like or similar response. Nothing useful will have been accomplished.

On Being Invitational Rather Than Accusative

If you are angry, you can say, "I have some upset (or angry or troubled) feelings about this situation. I don't know if I'm seeing it accurately or not. Are you willing to discuss it with me and help solve this problem?" It's hard for someone to turn down an invitation to help on a situation that is emotionally affecting you both. If the inviter prefaces his or her emotional concern with self-responsibility ("I have these feelings") and does not blame ("I do not know whether I'm seeing this accurately or not"), but rather invites the other's assistance in solving the problem, the chance of coming to an agreement and full communication is greatly enhanced. For example, Sue has invited Dick to discuss with her a situation she sees as a problem. She presents it in a nonthreatening manner, owning her own feelings. "I have some troubled feelings about you and Johnnie (their ten-year-old son) going off and leaving Katie (their nine-year-old daughter). It appeared to me, from my way of looking, that she was left and was hurt by it. Can you give me a reason why you didn't take her? I think she needs to hear that from you."

"Hmm," Dick said." I thought she was happily involved in what she was doing. I shouldn't have assumed. I should have asked her. I'll talk with her." A few minutes later Dick approached Katie and carefully wrapped up his conversation with a caring expression. "I'm sorry I didn't ask my daughter to go with us this morning. I thought you were busy. I should have asked you and not assumed. How about you and I have a special father-daughter activity? You get to choose."

There is another useful technique, called care package communication, that helps establish connection in delicate, potentially explosive situations. In this, the initiator realizes ahead of time the receiver might easily get defensive or take offense at the subject matter; the initiator knows this from prior experience. The initiator, Dick, states thusly, "Sue, I have it. Can I mention it to you, knowing I am being careful and considerate of your possible feelings, ahead of time?" With a communication so carefully wrapped in a container of consideration, the receiver, Sue, can feel safe to agree to hear and prepare not to be greatly hurt by what will be said.

All of these techniques are parts of a method I call self-referring communication, which emphasizes the self-responsibility to speak up, to initiate, and to reveal one's own awareness about the subject and the purpose for bringing it up. This technique then becomes invitational, by asking, "Will you join me?" While no method or technique for communication works all of the time, self-referring communication works better than anything else I have tried.

Chapter Summary

1. For best communication, it is very important that you take self-responsibility to say your desire, your wish, or your awareness with no strings attached.

2. At the earliest point of misunderstanding, the best resolving technique is to restate the request in a different way, attempting to make it more easily understood.

3. The principles of good verbal communication start by stating the truth of your awareness—that is, verbalizing what is it you are thinking. It can be difficult, but you must take the responsibility to do it. Then, state the request or desired action you would like. Be invitational rather than accusative: "I would like to have you with me on this," or "I would like you to come with me; are you willing?"

4. Take responsibility for cross-checking to make communication more likely successful and certain.

5. Use care package communication. In this, the initiator realizes ahead of time the receiver might get defensive or take offense at the subject matter and wraps a container of consideration around his or her communication, inviting another to listen to what must be said.

6. How you say things really does count.

SECTION 4

The Stances and Attitudes That Produce Success

CHAPTER 14

———◆◆◆◆———

Psychological Stances and Monitoring Positions

Your attitude and intention influence your outcomes, your personal well-being, and your social pleasantness. You can learn to replace restricting, and often unsuccessful, negative stances with successful, life-handling, positive stances. You can select what always works best.

Readiness and monitoring stances—attitudes, if you like—are self-fulfilling prophesies; they create the way we hold and carry ourselves. We lead with our attitudes, and as a result we stimulate certain responses in others. For example, if we are peevish, irritable, angry, or accusative, we evoke defensiveness, retaliation, or resentment in return. But if we are accepting and interested, we stimulate giving, cooperation, and acceptance as a response. It is like the old adage, "If you want a friend, be friendly." If you want good results, offer good attitudes and feelings. Consider the examples below.

Similarities of Physical Skills and Psychological Skills

At the conference championship basketball game, one-half second remains on the shot clock, and your team is one point behind. Jim, your best player and a 90 percent foul shooter, is at the line with the chance to tie or win. In the midst of the fans going wild, Jim steps up to the line, places his hands carefully on the basketball just where he wants them, sets his body, breathes deeply three times, gazes intently at the basket's rim, crouches, then pushes off his lead leg and releases the shot with a flick of his wrists. Basket! The fans are jubilant as pandemonium breaks out. He shoots again, making the second free throw. Victory! Jim and his teammates, the conference champions, are mobbed by supporters.

Psychological Readiness Positions

Jim's aim, body alignment, and release were right, his technique practiced and perfected, and it paid off. His readiness position and his monitoring of the motion of his free throws were excellent, and he succeeded at a very important time. So it is with psychological readiness positions, the conscious intentions of holding ourselves as we live our lives—planning, encountering, overcoming problems, and facing new unknowns. When we do not consciously set a good stance or pattern and agree with ourselves to use it, such as, "I will be ready for anything, open to suggestions, and accept interruptions rather than fighting them," we instead may use a poor one and become easily overwhelmed or too strongly influenced by what we encounter. Many situations in life can throw us off course or upend us. These situations make us more prone to error, less efficient, sometimes disoriented, grouchy with others, and generally less successful.

In golf, when a player's alignment and stance are wrong before hitting a shot, the ball's direction will be off-line. In life, if we employ a poor or unsatisfactory readiness and monitoring stance, such as, "I hate this! I do not want it! I will fight it!" we create chaos, misunderstanding, and conflict. For example, the economy has been through tough and volatile times with the stock market during 2008–2011. Many investors, particularly the less experienced, say, "Oh my gosh, what if my stocks lose a lot of value? What will I do?" The answer of course is to stop being paralyzed with fear and get the best professional advice you can—which could be to get out, to buy more bonds, or to change over to gold. Calm down and take your advisor's advice. Ultimately, make your decision, be vigilant, and continue to reevaluate your decisions in a calculating manner.

Another example could be fear of losing your job. Instead of worrying, figure out a strategy to prevent job loss the best you can, and figure out possible safety nets. The best strategies include always doing the best you can, being on time or arriving early, staying a little late to complete important items, and letting your boss know how much you like the job, how devoted you are, and how you would like a future with the company. Ask if your boss has any suggestions for new things you could learn. Be open, willing, a good worker, committed, and eager. Most of all, be pleasant to work with. Then, if you still lose your job because of job cuts, money problems in the company, and the like, realize there is unemployment money, friends or family, temporary job agencies, and employment agencies to lean on during those times of unemployment. Answer fear with best-possible solutions.

A nine-year-old who fears he will mess up his piano recital might think, "Oh my gosh, what if I mess up? What will I do?" He might take this stance: "If I do, I do. I will still get through it. I'll live, no matter what. I'll still have friends. My parents will still love me. I'll do the best I can do for right now." These stances work.

However, for those interested in a good, satisfying production, these stances do not work. It is essential to set our readiness and monitoring stances with something more like this: "I will agree with myself to be open and accepting initially. I will consider and reserve judgment on issues and opportunities before I decide." Or, "I will look at life as an opportunity for new experiences: to learn from, to help me increase, and to enhance my existence." These conscious readiness and monitoring stances result in greater quality of life and optimism. Without them or similar patterns, we tend to have greater disappointment, pain, and pessimism.

Have you ever heard people around you, perhaps even yourself, grumble about a new requirement at work? How often are said statements such as, "Why is management requiring that? Don't they get enough out of us?" or, "It'll never work. We won't be able to do it." Or even something like "They just keep demanding more and more. I guess I can do it, but it might burn me out." Contrast those with more useful and successful stance. "Well, I guess management has their reasons. They believe in our abilities; lets' give it our best and see what happens." This latter stance is more likely to result in group cohesion and positive motivation, with much less resistance.

Consider the following story: After a Naples, Florida, Chamber of Commerce spokesperson finished talking to a group of businessmen from the North about opportunities in Florida, two men approached with questions and comments. The first, a man from Ohio, asked, "I'm thinking of coming down and setting up a branch of my business here. How friendly and receptive would I find the people?"

The spokesperson asked, "How have you found people when you have opened other branches? How have you found the people to be in Ohio toward your business?"

The man responded, "Generally receptive and positive."

The spokesperson told him, "I think you will find that here in Florida too."

The next man, from Minnesota, asked about opportunities but expressed concern that his stores were not doing well and customer satisfaction was down. He believed the stubborn Swedes in Minnesota were to blame; they had a negative attitude toward his store. The spokesperson paused briefly and replied, "You know, I'm afraid you will find some of that same attitude in Florida. I would think twice if I were you, before committing to come here."

Negative versus Positive Self-Fulfilling Prophesies

Saying, "Oh my gosh, what if …?" results in a state of fear and a sense of being overwhelmed by uncertainty. It gives power to what might happen, not to how you will deal with the situation. The solution is to deal with this fearful, open-ended question matter-of-factly, completing it with "then it will," which takes the momentary power out of it. Follow with, "Let's see the best way to handle it." Then proceed to thinking of ways to solve the situation.

"All is lost, oh no …" This bad position predicts dire results, leading to moaning and groaning, blaming, denying, and excessive emotion. Instead, how about, "Hmm, I'd better assess the damage, contain it, and then chart the best course." The point is, do not give a result or a feared result overwhelming, disastrous power over you. Continue to look for best ways to proceed; keep moving in a useful way.

I am reminded of a sensitive, easily embarrassed boy who missed a layup in a junior high school basketball game. He felt embarrassed, and at the timeout he sulked on the bench, teared up, took a position of a humiliated person, and said, "I can't play anymore, I'm no good." The coach put his hand on the lad's shoulder, then put his arm around him, and told him how valuable he was, that everyone misses layups, and even Michael Jordan, arguably the best basketball player of all time, said he had missed more last-second game winning shots than he had made in his career. Further, the coach said as he patted him on the back, "Get out there! The team and I need you no matter how many layups you make or miss!" It worked.

You can provide yourself with comments similar to what the coach told the boy if you find yourself over-reacting to a situation with embarrassment, humiliation, and a feeling that all is lost. When that initial reaction gives way to the observing, wise part of yourself, and you assess your situation more objectively, you can calm down and come up with better solutions in the short and long term. ("How can I prevent these situations in the future?")

"This is terrible; it always happens to me." This victim stance tends to lock a person into a defeatist position of being powerless and having things *done to* them. People who use this stance predict poor outcomes. After making this prediction, they give up easily and hope others will see their plight and step in to help. This stance fosters dependency and manipulations. How much easier is it to say, "Life is opportunity. What's the best way?" or, "I will handle this in the best way possible."

Successfully Achieving Goals Without Having the Pleasure of Accomplishment

"First I will do this, then this, then this, and then everything will be fine." This stance helps us reach many goals, but we can easily get caught up in it. By setting one goal after another, we forget to take time for other rewarding experiences and opportunities. There *is* such a thing as delaying gratification too long. This stance takes our life out of a good balance, one where achievement, leisure, relationships, and rewards work in concert, and replaces it with an incessant striving for accomplishment. Why not set your stance with something like, "First I will do this, then that, but I will make sure to take breaks, keep my life in balance, and often smell the roses."

If you tend to have the pattern of incessant striving, here is a way your conversation might go before you learn how to do differently and smell the roses. When one of your young children or your spouse comes up to you and asks you to play or go to a movie, the reflex is to say, "I have to do the dishes, then vacuum, then run to the bank, then return the phone calls that have piled up, then meet with the neighbors about the noise problem, and then maybe I can have fun, because everything will be taken care of." Of course other things tend to come up, further absorbing time. The family and you lose out to the monster of continuous accomplishment and delaying for too long the fun elements of life. This stance can be used so continuously that it becomes the only thing someone does, being busy accomplishing, squeezing out personal relationships, not having leisure time, and becoming a workaholic only.

When we become frustrated or feel defeated, we often assume a stance such as, "I cannot handle it anymore. This is too much." With this stance, we draw a limit around ourselves and refuse to budge. We deny the adaptive side of our nature. Try saying, "I'm having trouble handling this. I probably need a break. I will consider whether or not to get additional help."

When we get tired, angry, and irritable about tasks piling up, we tend to say, "Nothing else had better happen, or ..." The trouble is, something else usually does happen, and because of our limiting stance, we blow up in a fit of anger, maybe even rage. Avoid this situation by saying, "Wow, what a pile-up. It'll end eventually. I don't have to get it all done now; I'll switch gears and simply deal with each thing that comes up. If something needs my immediate attention, I'll change my plans enough to accommodate it by resetting my priorities and putting less important things on the schedule for later." This stance puts you back into the feeling of self-control and allows frustration to dissipate.

In chapter 1 we learned how we create mental pressure by using crucial and absolute thought stances, the "I must do this" or "I have to prevent that" imperative. When we change that stance back to one that is based on truth and reality—"I will do it to the extent I am able"—the mental pressure goes away.

Use the Principles of Psychological Truth

Bad or nonproductive readiness and monitoring stances eventually limit us and cause psychological pain. Good or positive stances follow the flow of reality, the truth of the thing, of how things really happen. They also include our choice and our application of self-power techniques to create good living. Reality and truth are the strongest forces we have. Develop stances accommodating reality and truth that are the most productive and feel good, rather than resisting or denying reality and truth, which causes pain and is inefficient and ineffective. Then you use psychological truth, which will always give you the best results.

Here are examples of such stances. Say to yourself (or if you are a leader, to others), "I have this job to do. It is important, and now is probably the best time to do it, so I will do it to the extent I am able, the best I can." This way is far better than irrational ways such as, "I have to do this, I have to get it done. I can't stand for any more to pile-up, so it has to be now." The first statements fit reality and the truth about anything future and was positive. The second statement was absolute and crucial, fought logical truth, and was complaining.

A Workplace Example

I showed a draft of this chapter to a banquet manager at a five-star hotel in our community. He read and acquainted himself with the contents, and he could see the various negative readiness positions and monitoring stances his employees were using, particularly when they felt time was running out to prepare for a banquet. They usually succeeded but felt stressed and pressured while working. They said, "What a lot to do. How will we ever do it?" or "Oh no! Not all of this. There's too much," and even "I guess we'll be working overtime tonight doing another big project."

The banquet manager met with them and explained some of the realistic and positive ways to look at their work: they should mentally hold their tasks and the times for completion in a more positive way, greeting whatever came as an opportunity to learn and handle, and to do this as well as they were able. Immediately they all felt more upbeat, able, and unpressured. They felt light rather than heavy, no longer fearful and worried as they carried out their tasks. He later heard them talking positively instead of negatively about the jobs ahead. They said things such as, "We'll do what we can. What we can get done will be good enough. Let's do it! I believe we can. Let's help each other whenever we need to. Let's pitch in. A little more effort and it will be done." He also heard, "We can't do any more than we can do, so don't sweat it and just keep going. We'll be okay. We have a good team. You all are part of our success, through your skills and efforts. I appreciate that and am proud of you. We can get this done. I'm with you all of the way. So let's pitch in and do something good for the community."

Over time, his department moved from its former average performance to being the top performer in the hotel. He gave much of the credit to what he had learned from this chapter and passed on to his employees.

People are willing to listen to people they admire and respect; they will follow an admirable leader. At times I have asked people the characteristics of admired persons. Most people answer that they look up to leaders, sometimes a family member, friend, or a neighbor, who typically seems certain of him or herself. This person is confident and seems to have an understanding of how things work. The person appears to genuinely care and show concern for others, and makes them feel important and capable of contributing something of value. They feel good in this person's presence. This individual was respected and returned respect. The respected person carries him or herself in stances of sincerity and willingness, without significant limiting attitudes. He or she values others and is careful to communicate clearly. This person always gives his or her best at what he or she does and has developed good abilities in areas of expertise. In short, this individual uses good readiness and self-monitoring stances.

Getting out of the Hot and Heavy Zone

When you find you are in the hot, embroiled zone—the "Oh no, all is lost" or the "We'll never get it done, there is too much to do" situations—here is how to get your mind and yourself cleared and out of it, to set a new stance.

1. Stop, then stand back (pull back and observe).
2. Evaluate: What's going on? Why are you this way?
3. Reassess: How else can I handle this?
4. Strategize new possibilities, new ways to set your stance. For instance, change from "Oh my gosh, all is lost," to "Hmm, hold on here, what is the best thing to do next?"
5. Reset your stance, such as:
   a. "I'll get some help and develop a better way."
   b. "It isn't so overwhelming. I can slow down for a moment. There is always tomorrow. It will look better after a good night's sleep and a fresh perspective."
   c. "I see a way. I'll do what I am able."
6. Proceed.

Like our star basketball player Jim, whose free throws won the game, if you want to perform at your highest level, use good readiness and monitoring stances. Once will be enough to prove the point. Polish your skills and be able to perform the best you are able to do. Whether at basketball or in living your life, the principles of wise self-stances and self-monitoring work the best.

Chapter Summary

1. Notice what you think or say to yourself as you face a task or start a project; this is your starting stance. Note the self-monitoring statements you make to yourself as you are doing the task or project.
2. When we do not consciously set a stance or pattern and agree with ourselves to use it, we instead may use a poor one and become easily overwhelmed or too strongly influenced by what we encounter.

3. In life, if we employ a poor or unsatisfactory readiness and monitoring stance, such as, "I hate this! I do not want it!" we create chaos, misunderstanding, and conflict.

4. Saying, "Oh my gosh, what if ...?" results in a state of fear and a sense of being overwhelmed by uncertainty; it gives power to what might happen, not to how you will deal with the situation. Deal with this fearful, open-ended question matter-of-factly, completing it with "then it will." Then follow it with, "Let's see the best way to handle it."

5. By setting one goal after another, we often forget to take time for other rewarding experiences and opportunities. This takes our life out of a good balance and replaces it with an incessant striving for accomplishment.

6. When you find yourself embroiled in a negative stance, follow these steps: 1) stop, then stand back, 2) evaluate what's going on, 3) reassess how to handle the situation, 4) strategize new possibilities, 5) reset your stance, and 6) proceed.

CHAPTER 15

---◆·▶◀·◆---

Mattering, Influence, and Self-Esteem

All of us matter, having influence and impact, merely by being visible and taking up space. It is, however, when we do something, attempt to convince, or cause something that we become a bigger influence.

We all want to matter. We want to feel that we have importance and know we are special, at least some of the time. We especially want to matter to those close to us, our family, friends, and associates. Most important, we want and need to matter to ourselves. Mattering positively gives a sense of value and delightful recognition. It tells us we mean something unique and defines us in an affirming and accepting way.

Positive mattering is both being a beneficial influence and the self-realization that we are of value to others. We can also receive this sense of positive mattering when others recognize and tell us that we are a valuable and contributing, positive influence. The verbal expressions others give us, such as "You really matter to me" or "You are so valuable to us. Thank you," are pleasant and rewarding acknowledgements. These expressions make us all feel momentarily valued and feel good. They tell us we positively matter. They become reinforcing, stimulating us to do more.

For positive mattering to truly work, it requires some form of expression or communication. A wonderful example of positive mattering that goes both ways is the warm and even joyous greeting between children and their grandparents. Byron fondly recalls how at the age of eight his grandfather proudly set him on the local tavern's bar and introduced him to his friends as "my grandson." Although it happened decades earlier, Byron recalls it as if it were yesterday, still filled with warmth and love. Dolores blushes with delight when she explains how her young grandchildren excitedly squeal, "Grandma!" and run to give and get a big hug from her every time they visit. "It really makes my day," she exclaims, her eyes twinkling and filling with tears. We can all share in her delight as our own fond memories are kindled.

How Positive Mattering Happens

All positive mattering is built on a foundation of involvement, care, genuine concern, and contribution. At times we may not even be aware that we are currently positively mattering to others, because we are simply doing things the way we know how, almost automatically. Others may silently admire our functioning and the attributes we show that we ourselves are used to doing. More often, though, our mattering positively will be when we put our best foot forward, show care and concern and respect to people, and genuinely attempt to like and appreciate them. They will respond to our warmth as well as the various elements of value we offer—more experience, answers to problems, encouragement and emotional support, positive regard, and concern for their welfare or rooting for their success. We give them the positive expression that they matter. In turn they appreciate and value us, showing in various ways that we positively matter. That is the reinforcer.

Sometimes positive mattering is a state of awareness and realization. When we realize how delightful and valuable it feels to positively matter (as with the joyous greeting of grandchildren or our own young children), we will want to pass such delightful and joyous experiences around more often. These experiences punctuate our days with momentary high pleasure and make our world a better place, or at least make for "a great day." How nice it is to point out true and valuable things others do and give them a positive lift. It is important to not sugarcoat less meaningful things or give phony praise; it needs to be truthful and meaningful to count, to be valuable.

The best advice for implementing expressions and actions of positive mattering is to act when you become aware that something from someone matters to you. Tell your children the joy they so often bring you, and in what way. It is more than saying, "I love you." It is saying, "I really value you because of what you do and how it influences me (or others)." We miss opportunities to express positive mattering every day. How many times do we wish we had told others who have moved away from us to other jobs or locales, or died, how important they were to us, but we cannot now because they are gone? Learn from that and be quicker and more willing to offer those valuable expressions to friends, teachers, or mentors.

Negative Mattering

Unfortunately, some of us have had little to convince us that we matter in a positive way. When we are served a regular diet of negative mattering through the expressions of anger, spite, scorn, criticism, contempt, or frequent blame, we hurt inside. Can you recall times you have witnessed an authority figure shaming someone in front of others? This is an experience of negative mattering. How different this is from the way John Wooden, the great UCLA basketball coach, changed behavior. He would say, "Do this, not this" and demonstrate. This simple and straightforward method gave his players good instruction, and they did not feel shamed. They felt privileged to learn more from a great coach; it worked well, and they improved their skills.

Consequences of Negative Mattering

I have often worked with teenagers who perceived one or both of their parents as "always angry" or "always disapproving" of them. They felt they only negatively mattered to the parent. The parents would be dumfounded when I informed them and would blurt out, "But I really love my son (or daughter). I just want the best for them." That was my signal to immediately have a family session, clear up the misconceptions, help them improve communication within the family, and promote more realistic and useful expressions of mattering. When we experience negative mattering, our first response is usually to become defensive. We may withdraw, feeling dejected and even depressed. The aftermath of these negative expressions has long-lasting repercussions: they erode self-esteem and create barriers in relationships. It can be overcome in an immediate situation if someone is wise enough to see it, stop the process, and explain that this wrongful approach was used but really wasn't meant fully and that the child truly matters positively. However if it happens a lot and over a long period of time, it will require both psychotherapy and actual different positive valuing by caretakers, who will now treat the child better and help him or her to stop reacting automatically as if he or she only matters negatively. This pattern becomes such a habit that children will tend to almost always perceive themselves that way, even in new and positive circumstances. They have to be taught to not see themselves negatively.

Children who are frequently treated with negative mattering not only develop a negative self-image, but they learn to deal with the world-at-large from that position. They are angry and resentful, and have a difficult time fitting in. They begin to intentionally do bad things and even delight in them. They are empowered by being a "bad kid." They act out, reaping negative payback on society, all from a self-view of, "I'm bad, so it is justifiable to hurt others." They develop a convoluted loyalty to this process and continue to self-define and reinforce themselves in this negative way. Individuals who believe they negatively matter need psychotherapy to help view themselves and the world differently. The problem is, they will not or cannot seek help on their own; it takes school authorities, law enforcement, or juvenile courts to intercede and send them for treatment, because they do not realize they have a problem.

Indifferent Mattering
What may even be worse than negative mattering are the long-term effects of indifferent mattering. Low-impact environments where there is a lack

of love and expressions of caring, where a child's emotional needs are poorly met, can create low-grade depression and a state of emotional monotone, where life is experienced only as a drab existence. The lack of love, of positive regard, of felt care and concern can result in long-term, negative consequences. We will see in the case that follows how this can be overcome, but it will require work and changed circumstances.

Ronnie's Case

Ronnie, an eleven-year-old, was sent by a school social worker to our mental-health center. He came to his fifth-grade teacher's attention when, during an art assignment, he drew a picture containing a house and trees with a solitary boy figure standing outside. Unlike his classmates who reveled in bright colors, Ronnie's drawing used blacks and browns to create a drab and lifeless scene. Alarmed, his teacher called in the social worker to evaluate him and his home situation.

Ronnie's father had been hospitalized for the past two years at a veteran's hospital with a serious neurological illness. Depressed from his illness and robbed of his ability to speak adequately, the father withdrew and did not want visits from his wife or son. To make ends meet, Ronnie's mother was forced to work two jobs, leaving him alone for long periods, and then she was tired when at home. To complicate matters, the mother was not an emotionally demonstrative person; she lost her mother at age three and was placed in an orphanage by her father, who was a truck driver and did not want to be, or could not be, involved in her upbringing. He visited only occasionally and died when she was twelve. She left the orphanage after high school, met her husband, married, and gave birth to Ronnie when she was twenty. He too was an only child. This emotionally impoverished mother had not been very involved with Ronnie and left him home alone with only a set of daily instructions.

Early in therapy it became obvious Ronnie believed he really did not matter. He was lonely, had few friends, and blamed himself for his situation. When he made mistakes at school, he expressed a deep self-anger and even spoke of hating himself. Ronnie did show a spark of life and relatedness when he talked about a school friend who'd moved away when he was in third grade. He also could recall some good times wrestling on the living room floor with his father and going fishing occasionally, but that was long ago.

Much like his mother, Ronnie really did not think he counted for much. He was emotionally withdrawn and often indifferent to people and situations. He rarely got excited or found interest in things that other children normally enjoyed. He possessed a large degree of self-hate and blamed himself inappropriately and illogically for his misfortunes. Inadvertently, Ronnie had been treated with indifferent mattering. In Ronnie's case, it took a long time and a lot of interest and effort from therapists at the mental-health center to improve Ronnie's self-view, his family situation, and his socialization. Fortunately, as a result of care and involvement, he grew into adulthood much improved and ready to face life's other challenges.

The message is clear. When we are not exposed to a sufficient amount of positive mattering, we have a much weaker and more pessimistic view of ourselves and general outlook. However, when we positively matter, we are more resilient, handling disappointment and misfortune with greater staying power. When we have the conviction that we positively matter, we have an added element of psychological strength. The result is we treat others in a more caring fashion, looking for their good points and holding them in positive regard. When we express our positive mattering, other people feel it and respond in kind. It does matter.

Discouragements, Depression, and Perceptions of Mattering

We all get discouraged from attempts that do not work out. Life is replete with disappointment, and we are saddened by the loss of people we know or love. When in the brief throes of these hurts, we sometimes feel we do not matter much, probably because we feel lost and down, and we recognize we lack the power to prevent the unwanted happening. Usually the feeling that we do not matter passes as we realistically assess what happened. We recognize the truth of our helplessness, begin to adjust to it, and get on with life. We may blurt out, "I do not matter!" in a momentary regressive protest, hoping, like a small child calling attention to his or her dilemma, that a parent or loved one will attempt to soothe us. We quickly get over that, too, and move on. It can be more of a problem when people are depressed and more seriously dejected for a longer period of time.

I have encountered people so devastated by depression that they begin to really believe they do not matter enough to go on. They believe they are valueless, worthless, and even bad. They become convinced they are unlovable. As their depression deepens into despair, they conclude they do not matter enough to friends, family, or that special someone to go on living. This perception is so painful and anguishing that life does not seem attractive enough to continue. The case of Milt, a sixteen-year-old high school junior, illustrates this.

Milt's Example

Milt was a big, friendly, athletic kid who had many friends. Though inwardly shy and self-critical, he came across as confident, humorous, and energetic. He was an excellent skier and had won a place on the school ski team.

Milt was referred by his mother, a professional, divorced woman I'd successfully treated for anxiety and depression earlier. She had become concerned about Milt's recent change in behavior. He was withdrawing into his room at night, spoke less frequently, and did not seem to talk on the phone to his friends as often. The day before his mother called me, he skipped a day of skiing, telling her, "I don't feel like going." I scheduled an appointment for the next day. Unfortunately it was a little late, but luckily not *too late*. The night before the appointment, he overdosed on aspirin in a suicide attempt. I saw him after he was medically safe. He told me the following details as I probed in the first interview.

It seems Milt's depression began and gradually worsened after returning home from Christmas vacation at his father's house in a distant state. His father ran a ski resort and had been busier than usual because of mechanical problems with a ski lift. They had not skied together as much as planned, and

Milt felt a strong disappointment, though he did not mention it to his father. Back home at school, he developed a new interest in a girl in his class. They talked often, went on an enjoyable movie date, and both felt an attraction.

Next, Milt told me some of his friends were planning a poker game for Friday night, and he had not been invited. He told them earlier in the week that he planned to take his new girlfriend to a church dance that night, so they assumed he was not available and had not asked him to join them. As it turned out, his new girlfriend was unable go to the dance because her family decided to leave town for a brief winter vacation. These two disappointments and Milt's distorted misinterpretations combined to create a deep and immediate crisis.

He brooded all week, feeling crushed and rejected because his friends had not even asked him to play poker. Crestfallen, he stayed home from school and did not even get out of bed after saying good-bye to his mother, who left early for work. He felt no good and worthless, like he did not really matter. Dejected, he reached out to pet his loyal dog, lying on the bed at his feet, but for some reason the dog got up, stretched, and jumped off the bed instead. That was the final straw! "Even my dog doesn't care about me," he concluded, and then took the aspirins.

Milt's distorted thinking that he did not matter is common in people who are depressed. They feel so bad inside, so worthless, so full of pain, and such a burden that they feel everyone would be better off without them. They are so terribly burdened by the experience of depression that they unwittingly project this feeling onto their loved ones, assuming everyone considers them a worthless burden. Actually, the burden they project onto others is really the burden their depression places on them.

During his treatment we found that Milt was particularly vulnerable to loss and disappointment. Three factors set him up for depression: the impact of his parent's divorce, a family predisposition to depression, and a long-held tendency to excessively blame himself and feel overly guilty for mistakes or circumstances that did not work out as he wanted them to.

Milt's slightly illogical thinking patterns became distorted with the recent disappointments of not enough time with his father, the invitation that never came for the poker game, his girlfriend leaving, and finally his loyal dog turning away. He saw himself as the great negative cause for bad things happening and concluded that he did not matter to anyone. When I laid out a more realistic view of the events leading up to his depression, Milt quickly saw how ridiculous his thinking was. His treatment progressed well, and he did not require medications (his was a psychological depression). Though not trouble-free, Milt went on to have a successful life.

A few years ago, he referred his adolescent daughter to me for some self-esteem and minor depression problems. It was a testament to the successful treatment he received. "You helped me; do you remember?" he asked.

"Of course I do," I responded. We visited for a few minutes, and then he said "You helped me back then, and I thought you could help my fifteen-year-old daughter now."

Helpful Techniques

Frequently during psychotherapy, patients experience a self-loathing phase or express very negative feelings about themselves. They apologize for their existence and for being such terrible company. I listen very carefully, and together we analyze the root of these feelings and recent causes of these negative self-viewpoints. At a timely point, I deliver a resounding challenge to their distortions. This challenge clears the illogic very decisively from their thinking. I say, "How I view you is up to me, not you. I have my own view, and it is not negative. You cannot change my view. You are helpless to do so. Like it or not, you are not powerful enough to be the cause of so many negative things." By slaying their omnipotent negative thinking, an avenue for positive possibilities opens up. Further, when they talk about how they do not matter, I confront that too, at a timely point. "You matter, whether you like it or not. You take up space. You eat food. You are visible. You have impact and effect, merely by existing. You are an influence, to an extent, to anyone who comes in contact with you. That is a psychological truth. Let others decide in what way you matter to them. You and I will figure out how *you* think about the way you matter. We will look at what is logical and what is not and what that does to you." This kind of confrontation shifts the focus to a more fruitful and productive path.

Would frequent expressions of positive mattering have helped prevent Milt's depression? Maybe, maybe not. Illogical thinking patterns can be tough adversaries. If they had been corrected in childhood, they would have had a more preventive effect. Nonetheless, if we treat each other with recognizable and direct positive mattering, it will produce an awareness of being of value and serve as a positive motivating element.

Influence

Ask yourself this question: "What kind of an influence do I want to be?" By its nature, this question requires us to take a deep look at our values, motives, goals, and most important the influence other people have had on us. In a way, the answer revolves around the influences that have shaped and motivated us. Influence plays an important role in who and what we are, yet many of us are unaware of its true significance.

Influence occurs in many ways, but its best vehicles are example and teaching. The example of other people offers us a new way or new option we might identify with and then try out for ourselves. When we read about someone who has overcome tremendous hardship or difficulty to reach great heights, we think, "Hey, if they can do it, so can I!" Teaching transmits ideas, concepts, and knowledge that can give us the capability to make things happen. When we are not being influenced by examples or teaching, we learn from our own experiences and from seeking answers through introspection or other explorations. This process of influence is how we grow from the inexperience of childhood to the functioning of adulthood; we go from pupil to professor, from neophyte to expert, from insufficiency to sufficiency. At every crossroad along the way, influence plays a very important role.

Examples

My most influential teachers in school were those who required and even demanded excellence. To get the reward of their respect and a good grade, students had to perform at a high level. At the same time, the teachers did not expect more than one could realistically give; neither did they expect more of less capable students than they could give. These teachers were interested in the best each student could give. Looking back, I now see they were all realists whose classes were always under good control. They possessed a sense of humor and employed it at appropriate times, never to shame anyone. They were always fair and listened if you asked a question respectfully and maintained decorum. We feared some and respected them always, wanting to do our best. They expected us to do so and were able to influence us. We knew they cared because periodically they told inspirational stories of former students who went on to do great things. They admired and respected those former students, and we could see they held them in high esteem. We knew there was a possibility they would view us that way too, someday.

In college, the instructors who stand out most wanted both excellent performance and a no-nonsense approach, but they also allowed us to enter a realm of respectful mutual admiration. Because we were closer now to intellectual equality and adulthood, we were viewed with peer respect and were expected to produce with less direction and to assume more responsibility.

The Influence of a Particular Professor

In medical school the professors that stood out had achieved international fame. They were tough, requiring high responsibility and completeness in our patient assessments. They placed a premium on truth and accuracy.

My favorite professor was the toughest of all. Because of his formidable reputation, the anxiety generated in us was probably not helpful, but I soon found he was approachable and a man true to his word. When we started our rotation on his service, Dr. Maxwell Wintrobe warned us he would be tough, just like we expected a football coach to be who believed we could win a championship. He proved true to his warning, but he was fair. He did not suffer fools or foolishness easily, yet I flourished in his class—partly from fear but mostly from respect for his expertise and his scientific and clinical value to the medical world. At the time, he was the author of a textbook that was considered the bible of hematology, a worldwide standard in the field. Because of his influence, I almost became a hematologist.

During my internship I recall saying to myself, "I will not stop short of pursuing a diagnosis as accurately as possible. I will not give up too soon." Dr. Wintrobe's words still echoed in my mind. Once when discussing a person who was bleeding from the bowel, I told myself, "You must continue until you find the bleeding source." It was Dr. Wintrobe again whose influence drove me to find answers. He had a similar rule for iron deficiency anemia, often caused by subtle bleeding somewhere in the body. "You must find the source and treat it," he taught. "Do not just give iron pills." The bleeding was usually in the small or large intestines or the stomach. In women, it could also be excessive uterine building.

Bleeding sources are discovered by a test for blood in the stool, direct examination rectally, by pelvic exam in women, and by a sigmoidoscopy, colonoscopy, or gastroscopy (tube into the esophagus, stomach, and upper small bowel). In the days Dr. Wintrobe was teaching, we would send a string on a weight down the throat into the stomach and small intestine to see at what point, measuring the length of the string after pulling it out, that a stain of blood might be, thus locating the bleeding point and helping develop a strategy (often surgery) to fix it. I incorporated his rules in my psychiatric practice. To this day, I continue to seek and sift through the uncertainty until I find the answer, until I discover the new certainty.

Influential Leaders' Characteristics

These characteristics have been mentioned before but bear repeating. When I am teaching patients a point, I have often asked, "What kind of person do you really look up to as a leader?" In almost all cases I get a similar response.

A leader is seen as competent, knowledgeable, and confident. A leader seems wise but even so always asks others for opinions. A leader accords respect and gives attention and time to the questions or observations of others, from the least qualified to those with the greatest capability. Each person feels understood and listened to without interruption. A leader has integrity and truly cares. A leader is a problem solver who campaigns for what he or she values and believes is the right thing to do. Finally, a leader believes in possibilities; no obstacle is too great to overcome.

After the profile of a leader is fleshed out, I ask my patients whether these characteristics should be ideals to try to reach, characteristics to emulate. I then tenderly draw comparisons to circumstances or situations where they might be giving up too easily, giving in to uncertainty, and shying away from taking a stand because of the fear of being disliked or displeasing others. I advise them in the future to make comparisons with the profile of an admired leader when considering how to proceed, what to portray, and what to dare.

Parental Influencing

When people wonder what kind of a parent to be, I first suggest let nature take its course and let their instincts unfold naturally. After all, how they have been parented will automatically come out. The things they did not like, they will try to avoid, though they may do them occasionally to their chagrin and horror—such things as raging as their father did or inducing guilt like their mother did. Conversely, what they did like, they will consciously try to do. I inquire about their idea of the characteristics of an ideal mother or father. For an ideal mother, they invariably say unconditional love, support, and caring, yet a mother who will be tough when needed. The ideal mother teaches values and rewards her children. In some important areas, she emphasizes accomplishment. She uses discipline to thwart negative behaviors and to teach a better value. Almost every one of us sees the ideal mother as being understanding, having integrity, and being wise. We also see her as having a life beyond her children.

When describing the ideal father, many see good fathers as kind, approachable, encouraging, loving, and supportive. They want someone to be proud of and to be respected by others. The ideal father should possess integrity, being strong and decisive and tough when needed. Studies have shown that adult children value and respect parents for having and adhering to parental rules. Parents were admired for being strong and not giving in when their teenagers tried to get their way. In the long run, kids want to feel safe with the strength of parents' love, support, encouragement, structure, and rules.

Two Special Hospital Administrators

As a medical director in several psychiatric hospitals, I have significant contact with hospital administrators. Recently I had a delightful and inspiring experience with two very special administrators in finding a creative and thoughtful solution for a difficult and rapidly deteriorating situation with a patient.

Our staff was caring for an older depressed patient who was grieving the death of his daughter. Not only was he devastated by the death, but he'd just had major surgery that left him weak, partially disabled, and requiring physical therapy. At the same time, his insurance was running out, and he clearly needed further care. The man was divorced and had no other children, and his best friend had stopped by to say that his own cancer had returned and was terminal. Our patient was alone. What was he to do?

We had an emergency meeting of the staff and the assistant administrator, who had supervisory oversight of the combined hospital and skilled nursing facility complex. The psychiatric staff hoped the nursing and physical rehabilitation facility could provide a bed for another three weeks or more of treatment. It was doubtful the patient's insurance would cover the cost, and he had no other resources. Both the nursing facility and the rehabilitation facility's management resisted the idea. Among other cost-related concerns, they did not believe they could provide ongoing psychiatric care.

The assistant administrator, a dignified, clear-thinking, and caring person who is also the hospital's ethicist, brought up questions about the opportunity to take responsibility for continuing care, even if it meant charity care. She asked everyone to consider this option. Some agreement was reached, but the final decision fell to the head administrator. He was called and joined the meeting, listening to all the facts and concerns. He agreed to provide charitable care as was needed until the patient could safely be released to home. There would also be attempts to qualify the patient with insurance for his physical care needs. If unsuccessful, charitable care would be provided. During that same period, the psychiatric staff would continue providing and directing care after his transfer to the long-term nursing facility. Both administrators brought about a cooperative decision that would adequately handle the problem. They obtained agreements from the staff, and we all left the meeting feeling we were doing the right thing.

I was touched by this display of unruffled, competent administrative problem solving. I realized how much I respected both the assistant and the head administrator. Over many years I had always seen them function with good self-control and caring. During discussions they offered time for all opinions to be expressed and considered while possessing a sense of equanimity and calmness. Clearly both had integrity that engendered confidence and resulted in significant respect from those who worked for them. Both had the ability to provide the influences that made each member of the staff feel special and valuable. The result was that all of the staff members experienced positive mattering. These two administers are the best I have ever experienced. They are good leaders and inspiring influences. Their efforts and decisions, and the staff's interventions, were successful for my patient. He got stronger, went home in a month, and got adequate and continuing relationship support through attending our structured outpatient psychiatric group therapy several days a week with others who had suffered losses and dealt with grief and depression.

Impact-Effect-Response Cycles

There is a basic cycle to all human interactions that is a psychological truth. It goes like this: The one who starts an interaction, the initiator, provides an impact. This can be a behavior, an emotional reaction, a request, an idea, or a teaching experience. The impact is sent and causes an initial effect in the receiver. When it causes a surprise, the receiver is startled at first and then scared or delighted; that is the effect. It is mostly involuntary, a reaction on the part of the receiver. A speaker speaks (the impact), and the listener hears it (the effect) and then thinks about it and later asks a question (both thinking and asking are responses).

After the impact and the momentary effect occurs, there is a consciously given response on the part of the receiver, such as, "What are you doing?" or "I like it," or "Quit scaring me." Of course there are many possible responses, plus the continuing responses over time. The person sending the initial impact sees the immediate effect and the given response, all of which affects the sender. This cycle is repeated, going over and over again, from one person to the other and back. Why is this important to know?

This cycle also happens in physical situations. If some unruly person hits you (the impact), you are knocked backward (the initial effect), and then perhaps you yell at the hitter, strike back, remove yourself from the scene, or perhaps call for police (all responses).

First, influence is a description of the change caused by both the impact sender and the receiver who responds in turn. Influence is a bridge, one side built by the impact person, the other by the receiving and responding person. For example, a revered hockey coach and retired hall-of-fame player teaches his star forward the secret of doing his patented scoring move, showing how to best start it and then deliver it, a secret he had not revealed before. His star forward is grateful to receive the special technique and decides to perfect his own version of it to become an even better player. Together they form a bridge of influence. The amount and type of influence will depend on what is sent and how the receiver perceives it. Therefore the influence we create will be contingent on the value, the power, and the presentation of what we send. If the receiver perceives value and is positively stimulated or gains something useful or important, he or she will have received a positive influence. As in the example, the sender can now be seen as having had a positive influence by giving a successful technique. The receiver gains new know-how and puts in the effort to perfect this new technique for himself.

Impact Downs

A typical example of an "impact down" is taking a job, assignment, or activity that does not fit our style, talents, or interests. This type of activity does not let us see the results or positive conclusions of our efforts. Impact downs are de-energizing, causing a sense of flatness and leaving us empty. They require some kind of change to remove them. A good example is Jan, who had just such an experience with her first job out of college.

Jan graduated in commercial art and was excited to tell me about the job she'd just accepted: she would produce artistic posters for commercial purposes. It was exactly what she wanted, and she could not wait to start. A month later, Jan was feeling down and flat. She described her job as unfulfilling. She produced posters by computer and was not doing the hands-on creative work she desired. The act of creativity fed her: producing a quality, creative piece of art gave her zest, pride, and a real sense of accomplishment. Unfortunately she discovered this was not possible from her new job. At the same time, she could not read the effect of her efforts. It seemed she could not positively matter or have any unique influence or impact. The result was that her morale and mood suffered.

Jan was suffering an impact down. Her job did not suit her individual artistic expressive temperament. Her efforts left her unfulfilled and meant little to her; she was not getting the effect and response that truly meant something to her. I suggested a change, and she agreed, starting a job search immediately. A few weeks later, she bubbled with excitement as she told me about her new job. Even though it paid less, she was able to use her creative and artistic talents directly. What *she* created would be reproduced and distributed widely. Her new position was hands-on and fit her perfectly, making an enormous positive change in how she felt.

Needless to say, we are all different. The value of the type of effects and responses we receive depends upon our unique characteristics. What fits your style? If you are in an impact down, it is time for a change of some kind.

Self-Esteem Cycles

When we are able to produce the effects and influence responses similar to what we intend, we are pleased and experience a moment of good self-esteem. Being able to predict and then obtain desired results builds self-esteem. But alas, self-esteem is fleeting and requires replenishment. We replenish by producing new cycles of success and then seeing the desired effect of our efforts.

Some people are revered and sought out because of what they do or have done. A friend of mine once told me as he was completing an important five-year church assignment, which endeared him to many people. "I'm going to miss being revered, having the close contact with people over their intimate, concerning issues."

In the 1970s, I consulted for a time with a group of creative photographers and then taught with them in continuing education college courses. I had the honor of teaching alongside Ruth Bernhard, a revered "grand dame" of West Coast photography. Students flocked to Bernhard and gave rapt attention as she walked around an area and pointed out how light influenced various objects. She taught her pupils how she saw and increased their sensitivity to the world around them. Afterward, she critiqued their photographs, pointing out things they did not see, suggesting how they might amplify the effect they were trying to produce, and complimenting them when she saw excellence.

How did she achieve such a revered status? By being an excellent and available teacher and a superlative creative photographer. Of course, her great artistic photographs stood the test of time. Like all great artists, Bernhard's photographs ultimately stood apart from her, possessing their own identity and value in the world. Undoubtedly her art contributed to her status, but it was the influence of her teaching and her ability to convey personal and direct value to students and upcoming photographers that solidified her place of reverence. She gave frequent audience to her students and mentored them with both technical precision and nurturing care. She continued to teach into her eighties.

To find lasting influence, stay involved. Keep on producing and sending impacts, and you will continue to feel the esteem, the value, and if you have earned it, the revering.

Chapter Summary

1. All positive mattering is built on a foundation of involvement, care, genuine concern, and contribution. Mattering positively gives a sense of value and delightful recognition; it tells us we mean something unique and defines us in an affirming and accepting way.

2. Children who are frequently treated with negative mattering not only develop a negative self-image, but they learn to deal with the world at large from that position. They are angry, resentful, and have a difficult time fitting in. They begin to intentionally do bad things and even delight in them. They act out and have a self-view of, "I'm bad, so it is justifiable to hurt others."

3. Indifferent mattering may exist in low-impact environments where there is a lack of love and expressions of caring, and where emotional needs are poorly met. Indifferent mattering creates low-grade depression and a state of emotional monotony, where life is a drab existence.

4. A feeling of not mattering is common in people who are depressed. They feel so bad inside, so worthless, so full of pain, and such a burden that they feel everyone would be better off without them. They are so terribly affected by the experience of depression that they unwittingly project this feeling onto their loved ones, assuming everyone considers them a worthless burden.

5. Influence occurs in many ways, but its best vehicles are example and teaching. The examples of other people offers us a new way or new option we might identify with and then try out for ourselves.

6. The one who starts an interaction, the initiator, provides an impact; this can be a behavior, an emotional reaction, a request, an idea, or a teaching experience. The impact causes an initial effect in the receiver, which brings a reaction on the part of the receiver.

7. Influence is a bridge, one side built by the impact person and the other by the receiving and responding person.

8. A typical example of an impact down is taking a job, assignment, or activity that does not fit your style, talents, or interests. This type of activity does not let you see the results or positive conclusions of your efforts. Impact downs are de-energizing and cause a sense of flatness, leaving you empty.

SECTION 5

Handling the Situational Anxieties
and Understanding Their Value

CHAPTER 16

———◆·❋·◆———

Methods of Handling Situational Anxieties

You can handle the varieties of situational anxiety that can occur in life in the best ways possible. You just need to know and apply valuable truths about the signals, messages, and meanings that come with situational anxieties. This chapter will equip you to face circumstances that threaten your quality of life.

Some have termed the last half of the twentieth and beginning of the twenty-first century as the age of anxiety; others call it the age of uncertainty. The truth is, both terms are related and describe our cultural and societal condition. Never before in recorded history have we had so much stimulating us. Increased oversight and regulations from federal and state sources place more demands upon us at work. We deal with vastly increased amounts of information from the contributions of science and the proliferation of media methods. Advertisements are everywhere, in all types and forms, competing for our attention. Computer and duplication technology, aimed to help efficiency and powerfully increase information access at the same time, make it easier to quickly bombard us with more requirements. The constant news about national and international crises, terrorism, environmental problems, and psychological traumas also contribute to this hyper-stimulation.

From the time we get out of bed until we retire many hours later, we are bombarded by a seemingly never-ending barrage of modern trials and tribulations. We have so many new opportunities and choices that no previous generation has had to endure—but endure and thrive we must, if we are to live well. It all calls resoundingly for an increase in self-capability that recovers and retains clarity, that manages wisely, and that develops new knowledge to handle the perpetual increase of outer stimulation and inner awareness and growth.

No matter who we are or where we go, and no matter how we try to avoid it, anxiety and uncertainty happen to all of us. The issue is what can we do to eliminate or minimize the ill effects of anxiety and uncertainty, use their value well, and increase our capability.

Change and Anxiety

First, know that both anxiety and uncertainty are positive early warning signals designed to alert us to important situations, issues, or lessons we will encounter soon. Good examples of these are the times we get anxious before starting new jobs or moving to new places, relocating our families. We can reduce the turmoil by preparing ahead of time. When starting a new job, we can ask those already working there what we need to pay particular attention to so that the first days go as smoothly as possible. When moving to a new neighborhood with a family of children, it helps to contact new schools and neighbors to reduce the uncertainty and the anxiety from leaving the familiar and starting into the unfamiliar situation.

Threats to Our Current Quality of Life

Anxiety also comes when we perceive either consciously or subconsciously that there is a threat to our preference of what we believe constitutes an important element of our quality of life. It is a warning signal that something in the near future could have negative consequences or turn out differently than what we want. Our current and preferred quality is at risk. This happened to Bill and Madge when they found out that the state-planning commission decided that a new freeway would be placed in their neighborhood. It would not only be a threat to peace and quiet, but also some property would be condemned—maybe theirs— and property values would probably drop. They had fear and uncertainty about a future event over which they had little control, an event that could affect their quality of life. The status quo was at risk. They took the warning signal (anxiety and concern) seriously and met with neighbors to find out just how certain the plans were. If built, where exactly would the freeway go? What were their rights, and what were the possible legal actions they could take? Later they attended public hearings and voiced their concerns. Eventually the freeway was built, but much further out, in a nonresidential area. Their anxiety lessened when they started taking action, and it disappeared when the threat evaporated.

Anxiety is both a warning and a reminder that there are no guarantees. Unpleasant though it is, anxiety occurs for our benefit. After we are warned, we can take the necessary steps to attempt to obtain or keep our quality of life preferences, or if unable, to accept reality and adjust to what comes.

A Comparison of Frightening Uncertainty and True Physical Danger

Specifically, frightening uncertainty is a component of anxiety; it gets our attention and tells us there is a danger to our quality of life. This same frightening uncertainty is related to the danger signal we experience when we fear physical harm or even the possibility of death, such as coming upon a rattlesnake, a bear, or a cougar while on a hike, or catching a life-threatening infection that requires immediate medical help. The purpose of the fear and uncertainty (to the outcome) in the physical danger signal is to warn and prepare us to ultimately become safe. In anxiety the purpose is to warn of the threat to quality of life so we can take steps to preserve it. When it comes to physical danger, there are ways to improve our safety, such as preparing for an attack by increasing our defenses or avoiding the circumstance by removing ourselves from the scene; in some situations we can attempt to negotiate a resolution. Another approach is to take the offensive and attack, removing or annihilating the threat. The point is, physical danger causes us to take action in the best way we can. And so it is, too, with anxiety if we are to handle it best, though the situations and consequences are different than those of physical danger.

The Signal and Message of Anxiety

The job of our anxiety signal is to immediately get our attention. It not only alerts us to a problem and tells us to find a solution or resolution, but it refuses to leave until we do. If we attempt to ignore or otherwise refuse to deal with it, we impair our quality of life by feeling constant anxiety. By causing us to face and deal with circumstances, our anxiety signal alerts us to learn new lessons and gain valuable capability in order to retain quality. If you do not learn this lesson, you will always have to comply grudgingly with the new circumstances rather than develop skills and insight to both retain and evolve your quality of life by mastering each anxiety. "Master you will, master you must, or live a life of increasingly severe limitation."

What Anxiety Feels Like

Because anxiety surprises us and gives us the unpleasant feeling of frightening uncertainty, many miss or do not understand its real message. We conclude something is desperately wrong and seek medical attention for our symptoms: sweating palms, shaking, racing heart, difficulty breathing, and a deep visceral gnawing in the chest. Some believe they are having a heart attack. Sometimes the anxiety signal creates pressure in our head and brain, making us fearful that we are going crazy or having a stroke. Milder anxiety can diminish our ability to concentrate; we read a page or two and are unable to recall what we have just read. We start over again, but the same thing happens. I tell people, "Words or thoughts will not stick on the blackboard of our mind when we are having anxiety." Anxiety can also affect our memory briefly, probably for the same reason that words or thoughts will not stick.

In spite of how unpleasant the anxiety experience can be and how understandable it is that you would like relief from it, do not run the risk of not using it well. If you fail to extract its message and learn from it, you face a bitter, open-ended time of anxiety, filled with repeating the same problems and making the same mistakes again and again.

Anxiety has great importance in the behavioral sciences (psychiatry, psychology, sociology) because of its prevalence. It exists as a primary problem itself. Anxiety can also be found alongside a variety of other psychiatric illnesses (co-morbid), or it can be actually stimulated by other psychiatric or physical illnesses that are a threat to your quality of life.

In its mildest forms of apprehension and nervousness, anxiety affects everyone occasionally. It occurs with upcoming significant events such as school tests, important contests, inquiries from the IRS, planned surgeries, and economic risks. In its more severe forms it comprises the clinical syndromes classified as anxiety disorders, such as generalized anxiety disorder, panic disorder, and often post-traumatic stress disorder. In these clinical syndromes, the anxiety continues unabated and often won't shut off with insight alone. Although these clinical syndromes are generally beyond the scope of this work, they possess many of the components of everyday anxieties we will deal with in this chapter. Remarkably, the more serious anxiety disorders resemble the more common types in definitions and meaning, especially in situations that evoke them, in methods for handling them, and in finding solutions to alleviate them. At the same time, like so many of the psychological and emotional pains of the mind, anxiety points the way to truth discovery and good thinking.

Medications are frequently given in clinical disorders but are not always required. If an individual is experiencing very painful episodes of anxiety or panic but still has the ability to think clearly enough to function and find some relief by applying accurate and potent thinking strategies, he or she generally does not need medication. If the anxiety is so great that the patient cannot think clearly or sleep adequately, or even becomes depressed and perhaps suicidal, then medications are useful and often required.

When people go through large, life-changing events, such as divorce, they feel anxiety, have much uncertainty, and often feel great self-doubt. They are lonely, feel disoriented about their life, and lack their usual sense of belonging. In divorce they experience a host of losses—the former good times, the planned future, the dreams developed together, and the once-loved spouse. New hardships are created, including the need to reorganize financial responsibilities for children who exist and a move for one of the spouses. Property settlement may be difficult and conflicted. Family and friends divide their loyalties, causing further disruption to the former continuity. There is uncertainty at every level and the pain of grief. Solving these issues with useful advice and counseling from trusted sources can help. Ultimately, solving the problems through effective thought and action brings the resolution. Like so many things of the mind, mastery is the answer. The bonus of mastery is the gain in capability and confidence we experience, and the building of new circuits of accomplishment in the brain and mind. We increase. Even if medications are required to quiet our brain, we can still create new circuitry after the calming effect of the medications takes place.

The Types of Commonplace Anxieties

Once we have discussed the types, sources, and solutions for many of the more commonplace anxieties, we will examine growth anxieties. These anxieties are brought about by our commitment to a conscious and continuous exploration of discovery and increase. By knowing of them in advance and by being prepared to deal with them, we are able to grow and function with a high degree of efficiency and success. These include fear of the unknown, a wish or tendency to avoid the new, clinging too strongly to the old (psychological security threats), fear and uncertainty about whether or not the new growth task being ventured can be handled or mastered ("Am I up to it? Is it worth it? What if I don't succeed?"), and the fear of irrevocability ("Can I get back to where I was?"). When these growth anxieties emerge and we handle them, we develop new comprehension, concepts, and understandings that result in an increase of our psychological strength and capability.

Nervousness or apprehension occurs when there is an upcoming event that concerns us. These are forms of anticipatory anxiety; we experience them when we focus ahead and anticipate the significance of various outcome scenarios. How we rank the importance of the future happening determines the level of anxiety we experience, from simple nervousness ("I want to get it over") to more apprehension when consequences could be more serious ("I hope the IRS doesn't find something wrong, then fine us as a result of the audit").

With a particularly concerning threat, we might experience our muscles tensing up, have butterflies in the pit of our stomach, and feel a pressure sensation in our mind. We become fearful and uncertain about what will happen next, hoping things will turn out okay. The question is, why does our mind signal us with such unpleasant sensations? The clear answer is so we will not ignore the situation, and so we can prepare as best we can to increase our odds of a good outcome.

Most of us know these uncomfortable feelings and have learned to take apprehension for granted, as a part of daily life. Still, some of us attempt to avoid or deny situations and, in doing so, complicate matters and make them worse. The worst thing we can do is avoid a situation or flee from it like from an enemy. When we avoid and deny, we are like the ostrich that puts its head in the sand. I tell patients, "An ostrich that puts its head in the sand may get bitten in the fanny by a lion."

Avoid Avoiding

By avoiding our mind's warning signals, we increase the likelihood of creating an even worse situation. With the IRS, for example, if something is found and we owe more, we must deal with the problem immediately or get stiffer fines and penalties later. Also prior to the audit, we can reduce the uncertainty and fear by consulting a good accountant. When we flee from situations, fear and uncertainty escalate, and we are swamped in the negative effects, ultimately making us feel worse. As hard as it may seem, it is far better to face the truth, acknowledge the anxiety, and understand its signals; only then we can prepare and aggressively tackle the problem.

When we do this, the anxiety soon dissipates and leaves entirely by the time the situation has been completed.

The Panic Attack

The panic attack is the most alarming and unpleasant of the anxieties. It is also called an acute anxiety attack. Not everyone experiences panic attacks, but a large percentage of us will have one or two in our lifetime. Unfortunately, some people are plagued by frequently having them. We know there are both psychological and biological causes for panic attacks; the latter runs in families and often requires medication to manage or eliminate. In both causes, there is a sudden outpouring of adrenaline into the system. This release of adrenaline is in response to a perceived threat to one's identity or one's sense of self. The mind fears being overwhelmed or overcome by some frightening circumstance or situation. This could be the fear of being left all alone, or the fear of being too controlled by others with little or no choice to act for oneself. Panic can also arrive when we fear being hurt physically, similar to how we have been hurt before.

We experience a panic attack both in our bodies and our minds. In the response to the flood of adrenaline, our hearts race and pound loudly, the pupils of our eyes dilate, and our gaze widens. We may tremble and shake. Our chest may hurt, causing us even greater fear because we think we are having a heart attack. We may feel pressure in our temples or head, as if it might explode. We fear we are having a stroke or that we might be going crazy. It is no wonder people end up in emergency rooms with their first panic attack. When we experience a panic attack, we may actually realize what is causing it, or we may be completely at a loss and without a clue.

It is important to learn or decipher the meaning of the panic attack and how our mind is trying to help us. When we correctly analyze the psychologically caused panic attack and then master the situation that brought it about, our mind will stop giving us these troubling warnings because we simply do not need them anymore. The initial primitive reflex meaning of the panic warning is, "Get out of there, you are in danger!" Or it can be, "Don't go there!" or, "Don't let it happen again!" The mind reads (interprets) our situation in a stereotyped way and then reflexively warns us. When we analyze and understand the situation, we can correctly conclude it is not truly dangerous or will not take our identity away. We can then consciously take control and tell our mind, "Thanks for signaling me, but now take a rest." At this point, our conscious self, the part that is in control, decides how to handle it. It is important to reassert our self-control when a panic attack occurs. We are able to accomplish this only when we know the specific meaning of each particular panic signal.

An Example

Doug, a thirty-six-year-old divorced physician and patient in psychotherapy, described a panic attack he experienced two days before. He was alone on his day off at his new condominium. His fiancé, who was out of town with girlfriends, was due home the next day. He had been missing her but was a little disgusted with himself for being jealous that she and her friends were together while he was alone at home. He was wishing he was stronger and more mature, and hadn't experienced this jealousy. Suddenly he felt panic. His heart began pounding wildly, and he feared he was dying. He checked his pulse and found it fast but not dangerously fast. He was not in pain, nor did he feel faint. He accurately diagnosed that he was having a panic attack and assumed it was from the fear of being alone. He decided his mind was warning him that he could die if alone. Calmly and coolly, he told himself, "You won't die. It's just a panic attack. You're making too much of being alone." He talked to himself like this several times over the next hour, and the panic subsided. He confided to me that if it would have lasted much longer, he was ready to take medication to calm himself. Luckily it was not necessary.

In part, Doug correctly analyzed himself. I added that it was interesting that his panic occurred just before his fiancé was to return. "What might that mean?" I asked. A moment of silence followed, and then he noticed a slight feeling of fear and a brief sense of panic. There was something more to this situation. He then realized that his strong dependency on his fiancé, and other females in the past, was a threat to his identity. His panic was warning him of his fear of being all alone and his fear of being too dependent on a woman, both of which were threats to his personal identity. The panic display warned him about giving away too much self-power to this dependency. It could cause him to give his fiancé too much control over his life, and he knew that would be unhealthy for both of them. From that time forward, in therapy and in his personal life, he made great strides toward a more balanced, developed, and autonomous self. In this instance, the panic signal was like a friend who helped him modify his behavior and develop himself more fully, while at the same time he shed a weakness. The combination of Doug's initial interpretation of the panic and my contribution made the general message of the panic understandable and specific enough for him to evaluate what the threats actually were.

General Anxiety

Generalized anxiety, also known as generalized anxiety disorder, usually occurs when major changes in life happen that we are unprepared to handle. In later life, these changes are usually large things like the death of a spouse, loss of financial security, or loss of an important physical capacity. These losses require significant life adjustments before we can regain or insure future quality of life. Generalized anxiety may make us tremble, as if we are having an earthquake inside. The foundation of the security we have depended on is missing or has undergone a major rearrangement or remodeling. Generalized anxiety may come when we anticipate and then actually leave home for the first time as a teenager or young adult. College freshmen experience high rates of anxiety because they experience so many changes, new expectations, and new uncertainties. I call this period from eighteen years old to mature adult responsibility the age of uncertainty.

Before an anticipated marriage, some of us experience general anxiety. The new life requirements of marriage seem to bring this up in susceptible individuals. Art, a young friend, was anxious for three weeks prior to his marriage. When I saw him a month later, he told me, "Things are great."

When we are laid-off at work, anxiety often erupts for a period and then subsides. Middle-aged people who undergo major job changes are particularly vulnerable to generalized anxiety. This happened with Wally at age fifty-two. After the company he had worked in for twenty years merged with another, his job description changed. He had trouble handling the changes and became very anxious; it took him five months and another job reassignment before he could settle down his anxiety. In our current economic reality of mergers, downsizing, and corporate failure, each of us is likely to experience anxiety because of the associated job uncertainty. As with all forms of anxiety, general anxiety is a signal telling us that an important aspect of our quality of life is threatened or has changed; we can no longer fully rely on our former situation. All major life changes may cause generalized anxiety. The anxiety will subside and go away after we have sufficiently changed or rearranged our life—that is, adjusted to meet the situation. The college freshman gets used to the change and starts to enjoy new freedoms and increases in individual responsibility, getting better at handling them as the months go on. Those who lose jobs find new ones and adjust their life accordingly; they soon get used to the changes in some of their patterns that the job change forces. Shortly after newlyweds are married and they get into routines, adjust to each other, and start making their way as a new couple on their own, they start enjoying the adventure of making life decisions together, and soon the anxiety disappears. The most important aspect for eliminating anxiety is to strengthen our abilities to master and handle the new life requirements. If instead we avoid directly handling the situation, the anxiety may last many months, becoming ever more unpleasant. If that happens we find ourselves retreating from life, hiding from responsibility and becoming fearful and avoidant. It is far better to master these things instead.

The symptoms of general anxiety occur at any time day or night and may last for weeks or even months. The symptoms include ongoing apprehension, difficulty concentrating, tremors, perspiring palms, and excessive underarm perspiration. Heart rate often increases and stays at mildly elevated levels (90 to 110). There can be mental pressure. Acute panic attacks can overlay or superimpose general anxiety when self-doubt, a threat to identity, or a loss of self-confidence reaches high levels. Not surprising, individuals with general anxiety seek medical and psychological help.

When viewed objectively, general anxiety is a call to mastery, alerting us to handle life in new and better ways. It is a reliable guide that disappears after we achieve a good enough quality of life in our new circumstances. At the same time, some people experience such a severe form of general anxiety that they are unable to function effectively. The thinking process becomes foggy, and they have great difficulty concentrating. They may have trouble sleeping and eat poorly. When general anxiety rises to this level, medications often make a significant difference. In the majority of cases, medications help calm the anxiety quickly and reliably. Once a person suffering from this severe form of anxiety becomes calm again, he or she can take the necessary steps to fix his or her life and come to terms with new circumstances. In the end, mastery comes about psychologically; the result of developing sufficient ability to handle the changes encountered in our lives.

One Formula, Many Different Causes

Anxiety has a number of causes, some more obvious than others, and it often accompanies depression. Because depression negatively and profoundly affects quality of life, anxiety can be viewed as a signal that quality of life is at serious risk. It is worth noting that various physical illnesses stimulate anxiety because of their effect on quality of life. These include life issues after a heart attack—what to do differently or the same. Heart rhythm problems can cause anxiety. Inner ear problems that affect balance often have an anxiety component. The physical limits imposed by multiple sclerosis can bring many anxieties. Whatever its cause, anxiety is a reliable communicator telling us that something is wrong.

The last anxiety I want to discuss is post-traumatic stress disorder, which also carries a meaning with its signal. In post-traumatic stress disorder, one has what appears to be an overactive protective response, based on an overwhelming frightening or catastrophic experience. With this disorder, the frequency and severity of the signal actually become disabling. It is a warning signal that will not shut off and causes many panic attacks that act just like the panic attacks previously described, but all are related to a particular trauma experience.

Typically, the person with post-traumatic stress disorder has a one-time experience that is dangerous or life-threatening, or severely identity-threatening psychologically. The afflicted person has panic episodes but also is easily startled, for instance, by seeing movement out of the corner of the eye. The act of being startled has a protective function, warning the person to watch out for quickly moving objects that might hurt him or her. Dreams and nightmares occur often and are usually about frightening or dangerous people or situations, quite similar to the content of a recent prior trauma or dangerous incident. If an individual has been injured in a crowd, he or she will avoid crowds. Visual reminders of the trauma—for example, seeing a company car with the company logo on the side, reminding the person of the place or location where the trauma occurred—may trigger a panic episode. This happened to Fred, who had been seriously hurt by an attacker while working for his former company. He had developed post-traumatic stress disorder and suffered panic attacks when he would see that company's trucks when driving around. The sight of the company's name would set off a cascade of fear and panic in him, until he was cured two years later. He required counseling and medications and job training for a new profession, but he developed confidence that he could control his panic, even severe episodes while driving. He would pull over to the side of the road, take his medication, wait twenty minutes while the panic subsided, and then drive on. Over time, these episodes happened less frequently until they stopped.

Both the brain and mind have developed exaggerated fear responses to warn of imminent danger long after the causative dangers are gone in people with post-traumatic stress disorder. These fear responses work overtime to protect the individual when this is not necessary in actual reality. They keep firing, become self-perpetuating and strongly overreact to any new perceived danger or and old remembered danger. They do not shut off. They become an illness; post-traumatic stress disorder. Psychotherapy, desensitization techniques, and medications are often required to quiet these abnormal reflexes.

Abundant brain imaging studies (PET scans, MRI scans, and fMRI scans) during the past two decades show altered brain structures and abnormal brain pathways in people with post-traumatic stress disorder. These studies show reduced size of the hippocampus, the anterior cingulate cortex, the amygdala, and perhaps the insula. Additionally, these structures and the medial prefrontal cortex show altered reactivity, generally less activation than the same structures show in normal people's brains when provoked with fear-inducing stimuli. The altered brain structures of those with post-traumatic stress disorder compose the neurobiology of post-traumatic stress disorder. An excellent review article by Sarah N. Garfinkel, PhD and Israel Liberzon, MD summarizes the many brain imaging studies of the past two decades in the article "Neurobiology of PTSD: a Review of Neuroimaging Findings".[14] It provides the reader a detailed summary and excellent biography of individual studies.

These reflexive and protective pathways give the sufferer of panic attacks from post-traumatic stress disorder certain false beliefs that they must master and release before they become better. A type of false belief might be stated this way: "You've been injured before, in this type of circumstance (such as being in a crowd), and you will be injured again. I'm warning you, get away from this place." Another false belief might say, "The world is not a safe place. You've been injured before and can't count on being safe. You cannot trust; you must remain on alert at all times in order to be safe." In other words, the sufferer is being told by his or her brain and mind that he or she must protect him or herself at all times. The result is a loss of trust in safety and well-being.

For those who suffer from post-traumatic stress disorder, the most important adaptive and useful truth to regain is that we will probably be okay most of the time, and we can go about our business without worrying too much about safety. Generally, we can trust we will be safe. There are exceptions; the case of war is one. But if we get into uncomfortable circumstances or situations with known security risks, we will be careful. We all know there are uncertainties in life—accidents and crime *can* happen, but they probably will not. We can take preventive steps and handle difficulties when they arise. It is not worth it to be on hyper-alert all the time, because it gets in the way, detracting from quality of life and from the ease of living. There is a point when we have prepared well enough; we do not have to be perfect at always protecting. This more relaxed way or approach is good enough. This kind of healthy viewpoint about life, lost to the anxiety sufferer, allows us to go about life normally. The person with post-traumatic stress must get back to this viewpoint and utilize it in daily living, before he or she is well.

In cases of post-traumatic stress disorder resulting from ongoing physical or sexual abuse during childhood, the memories and associated emotions need to be recovered and re-experienced by the patient, then reassessed as to their appropriateness. These victims often have inappropriate shame and guilt, as did Jane, a patient who had been sexually abused by an older brother when she was ages eight through ten. It is as if they had been willing participants capable of making adult decisions to agree to the forbidden activity—at least, that was how Jane saw it when she first discussed it in therapy. Jane, as with other victims of sexual abuse, had to realize that at the time her mind was that of a child, not of an adult, before she could understand and sort out her emotions, finally getting in touch with her childhood situation of being innocent, vulnerable, easily led, afraid, and helpless. Then she could respond with appropriate emotions, including anger and chagrin at being violated. Now she could take action, seeing to it that justice and retribution occurred when possible. People so abused will keep having nightmares and remembrances known as flashbacks until they settle these issues with themselves and their perpetrators. These individuals will have to relearn to trust in intimate relationships, or learn it for the first time. When they finally accomplish this, their symptoms go away. This happened with Jane, and she was able to eventually resolve these issues and report on her brother.

In our state there is a mandatory reporting law. We encourage our patients to take the responsibility and report it to police authority. If a patient victim will not, we as health-care providers must do so. In this instance, the brother was sixteen and so was court ordered for treatment. When adults go to court, they are often given prison sentences and obtain treatment during their prison stay. Jane's brother had to be removed from the home and placed in a foster home without younger children during his treatment in order to safeguard Jane.

In some cases, a remnant of the reflexive warning signals will not shut off. These individuals must ultimately assert self-control over their mind and brain pathways that are giving them the false warnings. They do this through realizing the truth and empowering it, asserting that they are no longer in the original circumstances and are safe.

Once more we see that psychological pain comes from being off-line with the truth of actual current reality. We know the actual current reality, but when illogical, overprotective beliefs are generated, the pain continues. When the post-traumatic stress sufferers are able to fully realign their minds and beliefs about trust and safety to the psychological truths of normal existence and the general truth about how things really are, the symptoms go away.

Growth Anxieties

Remember the definition of anxiety earlier in this chapter? Anxiety is a state of frightening uncertainty concerning a quality of life issue; it is a signal that our preference is at risk. We may or may not be able to obtain our preference; anxiety merely alerts us to the risk. In accord with this definition, there are specific growth anxieties that we may encounter when facing new life challenges or when we consciously choose to evolve ourselves. These include separation anxiety, initiation anxiety, and merger anxiety. When we are able to identify growth anxieties—knowing what they are, what they do, and what hidden (unconscious) fears they contain—we are able to handle each with greater understanding and ease.

Forms of Separation Anxiety

We learned in the mastery mechanism that as we depart from what we know and our collection of certainties, we venture into the unknown and into uncertainty. It is from there that we make new discoveries and new learning. At first, our mind may perceive this new unknown as a threat or a danger to our security. After all, we do not know what it is, and we have never been there before, so we may initially conclude it could be harmful to us. Our mind may interpret this new venture as leaving what we already know, totally separating from it. For some, this evokes abandonment and separation fears, stepping out too far from one's base camp of certainty. This type of frightening uncertainty and anxiety can be paralyzing, or at least very unpleasant. It is as if the unconscious mind takes all our certainties, all of the known elements of our self, and gives it a symbolic power as if it were our mother whom we have never left, never separated from. We rely so much on our certainties, just like helpless infants afraid to separate from their mothers, that we are afraid to leave them and try new unknowns. Of course, we do not really leave our old certainties; they are part of us, go with us, and can be used as reference sources or confidence givers from their prior accomplishment. We tend to forget this when we become so fearful of a new unknown.

In child and adolescent development, the theme of separation anxiety plays out over and over again. In fact, the concept of separation and individuation, well-known in the science of child development, says we must separate to become an individual. Even though the scientific concept is not as simple as I'm making it, it is still true that we cannot remain dependently connected to our mothers forever. We cannot realistically depend or rely on our parents indefinitely if we are to mature. We must separate off into our own life, make our own choices, stand on our own two feet, and take the risks of living if we are to become autonomous. After all, it takes eighteen to twenty years for a human to accomplish this task. Perhaps the complexity of the process, the slow maturation in humans, and the prolonged dependency all contribute to why we have separation anxieties. Early on in life they protect us and are normal. If too frequent or too long-lasting as we get older, they become clinical problems. However, we can experience them briefly when leaving known and secure circumstances. It could be a problem our evolving brain has not fully comprehended and solved yet, or it could be that we are venturing (aided by information technology) further and faster into our future than in any time in history. As a species, we may not have developed sufficiently enough yet to successfully do this without some separation anxiety. Whatever the reason, these growth anxieties occur in most of us.

An Illustrative Analogy

As stated above, growth anxieties include separation anxiety, initiation anxiety, and merger anxiety. They are most easily described and understood through the analogy of an apple and tree. Consider you are an apple still attached to the tree. The apple represents the part of yourself that will soon venture out to discover and learn. The tree represents your origins, your parents if you are a child, or your old and current self until now. The fear involved in separation anxiety, known to us from depth psychology, is that separation means death in the unconscious—both death to the life-giving mother and death to the unprotected and helpless infant. It is a state of psychological symbiosis, each needing the other to exist, each unable to survive without the other. If you are to break from your tree, the unrealistic but powerful unconscious fear is you will fall to the ground and die, and the tree will bleed out its sap at the wound where you were attached. Consequently, if you separate, you kill yourself and your mother, or you kill your old and new self and cease to exist. This unconscious belief is at the root of separation anxiety.

Initiation Anxiety

Initiation anxiety and fear occurring beyond the separation anxiety is the idea you will not be able to handle the new environment, away from the security and nurturing of the tree. There are too many unseen dangers, too many overwhelming tasks. What will you do? How will you know what to do? The reassurance I offer people is that the apple carries capabilities with it. Its seeds can germinate, take hold in the soil, and sprout a new tree. We all carry inherent ability to master; we have knowledge and various skills useful for successful living. Unlike the apple, we carry our old self, our acquired certainties with us, for use at any time.

Merger Anxiety

The last anxiety in this triad is merger or engulfment anxiety. Many people have unconscious or sometimes conscious fears they will lose their sense of self or individuality if they form new close relationships with other people or organizations. They resist and avoid rather than utilizing the value the new alliances offer in helping reach a goal or advancing themselves. Let us go back to the apple for a cute part of the analogy. The lone apple on the ground sees a horse grazing on the grass and coming closer. The apple fears the horse will eat it, and then it will cease to exist. The horse does eat it, but never worry, never fear, because of course the apple seeds have a protective coating and pass through the horse's intestines only to be deposited in a nice pile of fertilizer, which helps the seeds to germinate and grow a new tree. We have more ability and internal protections than we give ourselves credit for. We all pass through self-growth cycles, many deliberately chosen by us, before we gain a measure of confidence and trust in our own inherent and developed life-handling abilities.

Chapter Summary

1. In today's world, we deal with a seemingly never-ending barrage of modern trials and tribulations.

2. Anxiety and uncertainty are positive early warning signals designed to alert us to important situations, issues, or lessons we will encounter soon. We can reduce the turmoil by preparing ahead of time.

3. Anxiety also comes when we perceive either consciously or subconsciously that there is a threat to our preference of what we believe constitutes an important element of our quality of life.

4. The purpose of the fear and uncertainty in the physical danger signal is to warn and prepare us to ultimately become safe. In anxiety the purpose is to warn of the threat to quality of life so we can take steps to preserve it.

5. The job of our anxiety signal is to immediately get our attention. It not only alerts us to a problem and tells us to find a solution or resolution, but it refuses to leave until we do. If we attempt to ignore or otherwise refuse to deal with it, we impair our quality of life by feeling constant anxiety.

6. There are many forms of anxiety. Because anxiety surprises us and gives us the unpleasant feeling of frightening uncertainty, many miss or do not understand its real message.

7. Like so many things of the mind, mastery is the answer to anxiety. The bonus of mastery is the gain in capability and confidence we experience, and the building of new circuits of accomplishment in the brain and mind.

8. By avoiding our mind's warning signals, we increase the likelihood of creating an even worse situation.

SECTION 6

Solve and Remove the More Severe Psychological Pains and Complexes

CHAPTER 17

————◆◈◆————

Guilt, Remorse, and Psychological Depression

You can rid yourself of the long-term pain of remorse, persistent guilt, or anguishing psychological depression. Once you understand the illogical beliefs that create and maintain these pains, you can release them by using the pertinent psychological truths.

Many of us suffer hurtful feelings because of our past actions. However, we need to understand that we now have the benefit of hindsight. When we realize we would do things differently if we could go back, we have learned something valuable and can use that insight to guide us in the future. Harnessing truths for future benefit is the wisest use of the past. When we engage in this type of analysis, we are able to release the regret, guilt, or shame we have carried and forgive ourselves. Let me show you how some of my patients have been able to do this.

A Sad Case and a Difficult Dilemma: Guilt, Shame, and Remorse

Many years ago, Mabel came to see me; she was seventy-eight years old at the time. Mabel was obviously uncomfortable and opened the session with hesitations that punctuated the story she wanted to impart. Through tears running down her cheeks, she told me she had undergone an illegal abortion when she was only seventeen years old. She had never shared this information with anyone, she told me. "You are the first person to hear it." Mabel was still very ashamed of this chapter in her life and still experienced the burden of extreme guilt and remorse. She had secretly hidden this scarlet letter and its anguishing pain for sixty-one years. To this day, she continued to suffer deep guilt and shame, and it robbed her of any chance for prolonged peace of mind or well-being.

When Mabel was seventeen, abortions were illegal. Few doctors performed them, and those who did risked losing their medical license and being sent to jail if found out. At that time, abortions were not accepted by society or the courts—and sadly, neither was the option of an unwed mother keeping her baby. Typically, unmarried pregnant teenagers were sent to homes for unwed mothers, and after their child was born it was placed for adoption. Because Mabel's family was poor, this option was not open to her, so she secretly had the abortion.

Not only had Mabel never forgiven herself, but she had never really explored her feelings about this event. Although she decided to have an abortion for reasons that seemed important enough at the time, she now had totally forgotten or discounted them. The real reasons, the truth of why she chose as she did, were strangely lost to her; instead she focused on the guilt and shame she felt. She was consumed by the fear of discovery and the yoke of shame she believed she would have to suffer if others knew what she had done. She gave the possibility that others would condemn her so much power that she bowed her head in shame and guilt, as if everyone was aware of what happened and had already ostracized and condemned her. Mabel did a far more thorough job of condemning herself than others could have ever done. In the process, to a degree she robbed herself of all her life could have been.

Later, I marveled at how long we can carry a pain—for a lifetime—unless we master its cause. Pain will stay with us until we master it. The truth Mabel had conveniently forgotten, or had not allowed herself to fully understand and accept, was that she had chosen, for some purposes, to have the abortion, even risking her health and breaking the law to do it. It was that important to her to not have the baby. The truth was, she believed her whole life would be ruined if she carried the baby. The boy she got pregnant with no longer loved her. Her parents and friends were excessively proper, and she believed they would severely condemn her. She was ready to graduate from high school and had a good job opportunity waiting. Finally, she did not feel psychologically prepared for motherhood.

Based on these reasons, Mabel did not carry the pregnancy to term and could never give the baby up for adoption. She made her decision. Of course, she felt guilt and shame for stopping the baby's opportunity for life; she had chosen her own self-reasons over the baby's life. Surely the burden of this choice would be hard to resolve, perhaps never fully resolved, but she did not even give herself the chance. From the time of the abortion forward, she empowered a cycle of self-condemnation, guilt, and shame. She discounted the conflicted reasons that motivated her in the first place and gave them no further power. Instead, the continuous cycle of guilt, regret, and shame consumed her, and for sixty-one years she suffered without much relent.

When we suffer from feelings of regret or guilt over our past actions, we can master and release these feelings if we recall the original reasons we chose our course of action. We need to offer ourselves the latitude to acknowledge that it was our best effort at the time, given our analysis of the circumstances. In addition, we need to understand that today we have the benefit of more experience and can see the consequences of our past actions more clearly. If we conclude, after reviewing the past and knowing why we chose as we chose, that now we would have done things differently because of greater understanding, we have learned something valuable for our future use. This is the wise use of the past, the ability to harness its truths for future benefit. We then are able to release the regret, guilt, or shame and forgive ourselves. When we review and fully comprehend our original reasons for doing something, then view them with the clarity and truth of our gained experience, a powerful tool is created for releasing pain.

Mabel had not done this yet. We had only one psychotherapeutic session. She felt relief getting it off her chest, and to a small extent, off her conscience. After hearing my comments (see below), she felt some self-acceptance. From her current adult perspective, she could more clearly see the dilemma she faced as a frightened, ashamed, and condemned teenager. She better understood her plight as a pregnant teenager adrift in a non-understanding and unaccepting world. "Could not you understand," I asked, "some other girl in similar circumstance—a friend at the time, a granddaughter now, someone else?" She pondered this awhile, sighed, and seemed to agree a little more.

I will never know how completely she faced her dilemma or if she came to terms with it, because she never came back. She wanted to clear her conscience and confess before she died. Shortly before meeting with me, Mabel had an operation for uterine cancer, which she probably saw as punishment for her sin, although we never got that far in exploring why she came to me at exactly that time in her life. When she left, she told me she'd accomplished what she'd come for. I will never forget Mabel. While considerable time has passed, and I'm sure she has long since departed this life, I hope her last days were free of this long-term burden.

Long-Term Guilt and Remorse in the Overly Responsible

Long-term guilt and long-held remorse account for major pains that plague many people, particularly individuals who possess a high sense of responsibility. People who are at times overly responsible are always willing to go the extra mile to take care of others and things. In some strange combination of responsibility and caring, the overly responsible individual sometimes goes too far, taking blame and guilt for another person's actions.

We all know that drug addiction and alcohol abuse waste lives and are tragedies to the addicted persons and to those who love them. It gives us great pain when a loved one succumbs to this; we feel angrier toward a parent or spouse with a similar problem, because we know for sure that we are not the cause of their addiction. They are their own cause, but their actions can greatly affect us painfully and negatively. Their obstructive effect on our life evokes our anger. But a sibling—or even more tragically, a son or daughter—who is addicted hurts and pains us deeply. This pain is understandable, but we still desire the best for those who are suffering. We have an idea of what terrible things they have experienced and know what horrible things the future has in store for them. We do not want that for them or for ourselves.

Instead of leaving it there, many overly responsible individuals feel guilty about the other's failure. They assess themselves with blame and take responsibility. I have heard parents lament, "I feel so guilty; I must have done something wrong. I certainly did not act perfect when I was raising my child, but …" The statements of self-blame, responsibility, and guilt start like this and then are repeated year after year until they have a life of their own.

Over the years, I have treated many drug and alcohol addicts. I have developed and implemented hospital chemical-dependency programs and listened long and well to the addicted. Almost universally, they rarely blame a parent or anyone else; the overriding cause for their addiction is their personal choice for the drug. Obtaining and using the substance is their sole purpose—they believe it is worth it, and that they can get away with using it and still live life. The point is, each person who uses these drugs chooses to. As faulty as their motivation and logic are, they have a purpose, and to them it is worth it.

Eventually these individuals believe they have no other identity than to be drug addicted, and they give up on themselves. Of course, the idea of having no other identity possibility is untrue; it is more a function of their discouragement combined with the love of the drug. Once again, they fight the truth of reality and create a pain, a downcast self-wanting to give up. It is only when they begin to realize and then believe they could give up the drug that they have a chance. Sometimes this comes through examples from others, and other times it is because they find or discover a new life goal that is more appealing or more important. These new goals are such things as a satisfying relationship, a new child, a career opportunity, or even an exciting and intoxicating new hobby or avocation. This truth, that they could give up the drug for a better purpose, becomes a powerful motivating force. When they understand they could be free rather than enslaved, they realize the promise of other opportunities.

For the parent, seeing this real truth about addiction and dispelling the false beliefs and misplaced responsibility can clear the guilt. The sad truth is, the heartache that your loved one will not fulfill the desirable dream you may have for him or her—not at this time, at least—will probably resurface occasionally. It is a hard truth to accept, but it needs to be acknowledged if you are going to become free of the guilt and anguish.

The Mechanism of the Irrational Guilt

The guilt felt by the parent is an attempt to explain this horrible, unwanted, helplessness-inducing situation. Much like one of the initial unrealities we think about in an early grief reaction, the lament. "If only I had been there visiting, she would not have driven to the store and been killed in the accident," is analogous to this guilt statement, "I must have done something wrong. I failed my addicted son and feel so guilty." In both cases, the individual is taking the position of being an omnipotent negative cause, the responsibility causer for the problem. The logic of the omnipotent negative cause is as follows: when you assess yourself as the negative cause, you believe you had done something wrong that led to your offspring's drug addiction. This allows you to believe that with another chance, you could offer your son or daughter something better so that his or her addiction would disappear. This logic obscures the following omnipotent belief: you could be the positive cause of your offspring not ever becoming a drug addict, and that if he or she did, you could cure the addiction and make his or her life work well. The omnipotent negative cause belief (fantasy) keeps alive the underlying omnipotent positive cause belief that you can create only good for your offspring.

The Ridiculous Nature of This Belief

In the final analysis of this belief, because you are the cause for bad, then you could be the cause for good. After all, you are omnipotent, are you not? The answer, obviously, is of course not. The omnipotent cause belief is formed deep within the mind as a near-delusional defense, against true but almost intolerable helplessness.

No one can overcome another individual's free will. What sometimes looks like overcoming someone's free will is simply the other person agreeing with your wishes and obeying you. They do this because they perceive it is worth it. Just as *our* free will must select its own purposes, so must our children's. The guilt-ridden parent must see this truth if he or she wants to release its pain. He or she cannot be a negative cause, and he or she cannot be a positive cause. Even in the extreme case where a drug-addicted parent introduced his or her child to the drug, it is still ultimately up to the child to choose whether to continue. The parent in these rare and extreme instances is a partly contributive influence, but it is still up to the individual to choose for him or herself.

Best Use of Remorse and Guilt

Guilt and remorse can rob quality of life. No matter how many mistakes we have made, the best way to proceed is to learn not to create similar problems in the present and future. The best use of remorse and guilt is to view them as attention-getting signals. Each signal carries this message: Learn from the past and do the very best you can now for the present and future. Let guilt and remorse be signals of experience rather than creating the punishment of painful suffering.

Bonds That Bind, Created by Guilt, Can Be Cut

Guilt can also create what I call long-term bonds that bind. This situation develops in relationships and is formed by a guilt-based agreement between two people. For instance, it may develop between a mother and her adult daughter. The mother, anxiously over-dependent on her daughter, panics at the prospect that her daughter may move away to a distant city, where her husband is seeking better employment. The mother believes, "I will die if my daughter moves away." It is even worse if the mother has a cardiac disease. The daughter who contemplates moving feels guilty, sharing the irrational belief: "It will kill my mother if I move." The result is that the daughter is kept hostage through guilt, and the mother believes she needs her daughter around.

In order to break the bondage of this unreal guilt, the truth must be viewed with an unwavering eye. The mother will not die because the daughter leaves; the mother will only die if her cardiac disease worsens, or if some other cause of death occurs. The irrational nature of this bond between mother and daughter must be exposed. The elements of this confusion about caretaking must be unraveled by the psychological truth of actual cause and effect. Before the daughter can become free of the guilt-binding factors with her mother, she must view the true reasons, if her mother died from the disease, not the false reason, the daughter's leaving. Then she can release herself, and the guilt will disappear. Remember, violate a psychological truth, and you create a pain.

Believing Something Is Necessary: Prescription for Depression

Two patients had strikingly similar episodes of early teenage depression. Bob and Sue each recalled having a moment of great personal discovery, the kind of discovery associated with independent thinking and coming of age. However, when each shared this newfound discovery with their mothers, each was crestfallen when the parent failed to affirm the merit of their idea. Bob had discovered that he had to decide why to take an elective class, and not simply follow his older brother's footsteps and take the same elective. He had discovered the importance of making his own personal choices and how strong it made him feel to do so. Sue had discovered that she didn't have to wear the same type of clothes as her peers at school. Formerly she felt compelled to dress exactly like her friends and would be frantic if she didn't know what they were wearing. Now, as she made her own choices, she felt a fresh sense of originality; some of her friends now began to view her as a trendsetter. How deflating it was that her mother didn't get excited for her. In essence, Bob and Sue were met with indifference. Wanting maternal support and believing they needed it plus an approving acknowledgment for their new ideas, they each fell into a depression when none was forthcoming.

Like all young people, they were hungry for a vote of confidence for their budding semi-independence. Each was dependently hungry for praise and the accorded value of becoming an individual who possessed opinions of his/her own. Both wanted the deep support of parental approval as they began the departure into their own life.

Both Bob's and Sue's depressed and dejected feelings persisted for several weeks, painfully long enough for them to recall the incidents many years later.

It was clear why Bob and Sue experienced their teenage depressions. Each held the necessity belief that their mother must appreciate and agree with their newly found discoveries. When this acceptance and agreement was not forthcoming, each was awash with the terrible feeling of depression. Each had tied his or her self-value too tightly to their mother's approval, and when they did not receive it, a depression resulted.

Another patient, Mary, had experienced bouts of extreme depression including thoughts of suicide. Her family had always been inconsistent, sometimes close and at other times distant and cold. She was particularly vulnerable to the distancing times, feeling left out, unloved, and discounted, and it hurt terribly. Tearfully, Mary explained that families should not be like hers. "Families should be close and always supportive and loving of each other," she insisted. "That's how families should be." Yet the reality was that her family did not always fit her tightly held necessity belief.

In spite of this reality, Mary desperately held on to her belief. Each time she was not included by the family, or she perceived they had distanced from her, she crashed into depression. Mary realized that to cure herself of the depressions, she needed to let go of her necessity belief about her family. She needed to be more tolerant and understanding of them and not require so much. She would have to accept reality and accept it fully, acknowledging a truth she already knew: they were not the way she wanted them to be.

Undoing the Necessity Belief

Part of this convoluted dynamic is first experiencing a situation or conclusion that has a different outcome than what you believed was necessary. This different outcome actually serves as proof that your belief was not necessary, even if it was very important. Second, although you know another outcome or conclusion is possible, you still refuse to let go of your necessity belief or accept that the different reality did occur, stubbornly holding onto the belief and further empowering it, instead of accepting or acknowledging the truth. The result is the pain of depression. In a way, it is like hiking up the trail of life and trying to drink from an empty milk bottle. The reality is simple: the empty container cannot feed you. No matter how many times you try to drink from it, you keep coming up empty and thus are depressed. Fight against the truth of reality, and you create a pain—in this instance, depression. The truth is stronger than your necessity belief. When you accept the truth, even with some reluctance, you will quit feeling depressed; maybe you'll be disappointed, but not depressed.

Mary could now get rid of her passivity and wish. She could invite the family to get-togethers and to parties. She could arrange times with her sisters and mother to go shopping. She could make it better by initiating mutuality with her family. The other family members were independent also and had their own lives and agendas, so their schedules couldn't always jive, but they could sometimes. That was the realistic, most successful, least disappointing, non-depressing way to proceed.

A Case with Suicide Feelings

A few years ago, a thirty-year-old woman under my care in a hospital struggled with suicidal feelings, despair, and depression. During therapy I described necessity beliefs, and she interrupted, "That's me! That describes me to a T." She believed in a variety of self-imposed expectations, including being a perfect devoted mother, a housekeeper who maintained a spotless house, a loving wife, and a caring neighbor who gave selflessly when she could. On top of this, she worked full time. Only grudgingly did she acknowledged she tried too hard to be perfect. Not surprisingly, it was a revelation to her that her perfectionist ideas were unrealistic, and her high expectations could not be maintained. She needed to hold her high expectations more loosely, perhaps as guiding ideals but not as absolute mandates and indicators of her self-worth. The truth was that she had begun to see and understand this on her own before hospitalization, but she felt guilty about softening her self-view. At the same time, she still ardently believed in some of her impossible expectations and fell further into depression after concluding she could not completely fulfill them. Fortunately, once hospitalized she listened to reason and accepted that she had transformed her ideals of being perfect into necessity beliefs. After exposing these necessity beliefs as unrealistic, she was filled with insight, discovery, and the recognition of the truth. This gave her the power to discard her necessity beliefs, and the depression disappeared.

Smaller Depressions

Remember in the chapter on self-power, both Chelsea, the manager, and Bill, the writer, reacted when I asked, "When have you been able to accomplish more than you were able to do"? Chelsea was unable to get any of her planned work done because of personnel problems, and Bill felt dejection at not being able to do his rewrite in less time. Each turned their plan and expectation into a necessity belief and briefly felt depressed when they could not accomplish it. The question, "When have you been able to accomplish more than you were able to do?" interjected enough reality to show them the ludicrous nature of their expectations and how they empowered that into a necessity belief. Humor and reality helped solved their depressed feelings and gave them a hint about what to watch out for in the future. Believing something is necessary when it is not can cause depression, a big one or a little one.

Chapter Summary

1. You create long-term remorse when you hold onto a self-punishing feeling for an action you did long ago. The logical error, the violation of the truth, is to mix up the past and present viewpoints, which causes the illogical pain of long-term remorse.

2. When you have long-term guilt, check the validity of your guilt belief. Have you violated an old agreement you had with a person, principle, or promise? If so, determine whether it is better to reaffirm the old agreement or change it in light of the current circumstances. If you aren't violating an old agreement, then you are magically and irrationally assuming that you are the cause of an unwanted result, inappropriately seeing yourself as the negative cause. This is inappropriate self-blame, the purpose of which is to try to magically undo the unwanted painful result that has already happened. Obviously this is impossible.

3. To remove depression, notice your thinking. Are you holding onto a necessity belief (a belief of how things are supposed to be) that is different from what actually happens sometimes, on a subject that is very important to you?

4. When you create minor depressions, your necessity belief is usually about planned expectation of moderate importance that is held onto even though the reality of the experience unfolds differently than the held-onto expectation.

5. You create a bigger depression by failing to accept the real result and holding onto the different but hoped-for result, believing it is necessary. This creates the psychological depression. It is ridiculous to hold onto the empty belief and refuse to accept the truth of reality. Instead, accept the truth.

6. You occasionally can change the necessity belief to a hoped-for ideal that you yourself might be able to bring about when you have power, but of course not every time.

CHAPTER 18

———◆━◆╳◆━◆———

Overcoming Early Devastation

Early devastation is the most common dysfunctional and pain-producing pattern that hurts intimate relationships; it wastes years of good relationship and life possibilities. If you have it, it is very important to learn its nature, how to release it, and grow beyond it.

There is an evolutionary drive within us to handle and master both the impediments and opportunities that impact us. This drive is an important improvement force because it allows us to handle disasters and even prevent future ones. The drive to overcome vexing problems or devastations leads to actions. Collectively, these drives and actions may be referred to as anti-devastation maneuvers. However, they do not always work as intended, and they can easily go awry and produce negative, even disastrous actions.

The Nature of Anti-Devastation Rescue Patterns
A young boy watches his family and the families of friends, all members of his small mining town, struggle with fear, uncertainty, hope, and then anguish. The news about the cave-in deep in the mine just turned bad.

Nine men—fathers, brothers, sons, and husbands—will not come home again. The boy sees the families' helplessness and experiences his own powerlessness, though he does not know what to call it. He desperately wants to help, but all he can do is try to offer comfort.

Thirty-four years later, Jim feels triumph as his broad-sweeping mining safety legislation passes. His work as a mining safety engineer gave him the knowledge and the reputation he needed to get the laws enacted. Some inner motivation from long ago drove him to succeed, yet strangely, at this satisfying moment, he senses an unexplained sadness and wonders why.

In another family, halfway across the country, Jill watches her younger brother gasp for breath and struggle with the slightest exertion. Like the other kids, he can run and play, but he tires quickly and is not very strong. His fellow second-graders make allowances for his physical limitations, but Jill feels sorry for him, knowing her brother will never have a real chance at a full life. His congenital heart defect is improved by surgery, but his long-term prospects are limited. Her empathy and care are touching and make a significant difference to him and the rest of the family. Years later, they proudly watch as she graduates from medical school, headed for a prestigious cardiology residency. While receiving her diploma, she feels some sadness while wishing her brother could follow in her footsteps.

Negative Examples in History

Adolph Hitler was reported to have reacted to his early helplessness and family shame by creating the Third Reich, a power base for imposing his near-delusional and grandiose scheme of the master race. When it was finished, his quest for world domination cost many millions of lives. Benito Mussolini, the dictator of Italy and Hitler's ally, also was said to have been driven to overcome an early sense of helplessness from devastation resulting in an overreacted striving for power and dominance. The anti-devastation maneuver was operative in both as a large cause of their power strivings that were so destructive to the world.

Hitler's early shame came from being poor and disadvantaged. His father was often out of work and was abusive to young Hitler, physically and psychologically. Hitler in turn became cruel to animals and tortured them. His father died when he was fourteen, his mother when he was eighteen. Orphaned, he sought a sense of identity through ant-Semitic sentiments in Vienna, and later through socialist reform movements and eventually Fascism that adhered to totalitarian rule by one group, the so-called master Aryan race. He felt humiliated by Germany's WWI defeat. These anti-devastation motivation factors, plus his skill at oratory and manipulation, made him the leader he became. The world paid a heavy price when he unleashed his rage.[15]

Mussolini was also poor. His father was an idealist and was often out of work, and he instilled revolt against societal injustices and the existing Italian government in his son. He also was a drunkard and womanizer who harshly disciplined Benito. Benito became a bully and actually stabbed a student with a penknife, and he apparently used it more than once. He eventually found his calling as a political writer, then a rebelling fascist leader who had excellent oratory skills, eventually becoming Italy's fascist dictator.[16]

The Rescue Fantasy

There is a depth psychology concept, the rescue fantasy, that elucidates a particular form of the anti-devastation maneuver. We see it often in our society: it gives strong drive to many useful and helpful motivations and actions. The rescue fantasy is often a component in the career choices of people in health-care professions—medicine, nursing, psychology, and social work. Sensitivity to pain, suffering, illness, and a sense of helplessness are prerequisites. The strong desire to rescue the sufferer and overcome problems is born of our natural caring and nurturing instincts. When these elements are combined with a personal childhood experience of powerlessness and pain, it may give rise to a powerful adult complex, a pathological rescue pattern.

This complex type of anti-devastation maneuver has an equal ability to cause great good or significant harm. It can trap the rescuer into a pattern of compulsive, "no exceptions allowed" rescuing. It can set up relationships between the rescuer and the person being rescued that are inefficient and wasteful, in effect stunting the psychological growth, development, and opportunities of each. Before this anti-devastation pattern can be successfully neutralized, it must be fully understood, released, and then replaced by a stronger and healthier pattern.

The pathological rescue pattern is often seen in the lives of sons and daughters of an alcoholic parent. They marry an alcoholic even though their own lives were at times a living hell because of an out-of-control alcoholic's abuse. Why? They want to rescue their alcoholic spouse from his or her disease, and in doing so make themselves whole. In essence, they perform a substitute cure on the parent stand-in, their current spouse. They unconsciously want to change their own past of helplessness and confusion by changing the life of the alcoholic spouse, as if this present hoped-for cure would mysteriously cure their problems in the past by even changing (retroactively and magically) their alcoholic parent. Of course, it cannot be done. Worse, they can never cure the alcoholic by marrying him or her. The alcoholic must cure him or herself by abstaining from alcohol. Yet hope springs eternal, and this anti-devastation rescue maneuver is tried over and over again. Why do people keep trying?

The Search That Produces the Answer

To look for an answer, we must go deep and must understand that only when one is armed with the answers can the pathological rescue fantasy be released. Why release it? Because it obligates and enslaves our relationship motivation, conscripting it into a constantly attempted set of actions and behaviors that never ultimately work. Not only does it waste energy and wear us out, but also it causes even more pain and frustration—and in futility is still unable to cure the past, the reason it was intended in the first place.

An Illustrative, Revealing Example

The hidden keys to solving and releasing the pathological rescue fantasy lie in understanding what it is trying to produce. William, a mental-health professional in his early thirties, married Linda, a depressed woman who was sometimes suicidal. Linda believed she never received the family support she needed to reach her potential and succeed in life. She wanted that missed love and support from William. For him, this request for support was irresistible.

Before they married, William discovered that Linda suffered a long and debilitating childhood depression, resulting in a self-imposed isolation that made her even more lonely and depressed. His heart went out to her, and he loved her very much. Besides, as a therapist he knew how to help, so he believed he would be particularly good for her. He liked that she was uninhibited and impulsive. She dared to take risks like driving dangerously, experimenting with drugs, and being particularly adventuresome in lovemaking. These qualities were in contrast to his own more cautious, inhibited nature, and he found they made her even more attractive. Not surprisingly, their marriage failed after four years, and William ended up in my office, trying to understand what had happened.

He felt sorry for Linda's childhood depression and its frequent reoccurrence as an adult. He felt even worse because he had not been able to help her more. When her depressions worsened and her anger over the past become unbearable to tolerate, he distanced emotionally from her. Prior to his pulling back, she viewed him as controlling and felt pressured by his need for her to do better. She was often mad at him for that. When he distanced, she felt unsupported and less loved, and she accused him of being like everyone else. Perplexed, he felt he could not do anything right and did not want to even try anymore. Their marriage did not last because it was based, at the surface, on her being rescued and by him doing the rescuing. But underneath, there was much more.

During therapy I learned that early in William's life, his mother suffered bouts of depression. He felt sorry for her and suffered greatly at seeing her constant sadness, anguish, and, at times, despair. He worked at ways to cheer her up and was sometimes successful. What he had no way of noticing, because he was a child, was the helplessness, loneliness, and the lack of nurturing he himself experienced during these episodes of his mother's depression. She could not care for him because of her own self-absorbing psychological pain. He covered over his own devastation without realizing it, by reaching out to help her, and then later helping clients as a professional. I also learned that William failed to gain weight in his second year of life. Pediatricians could not find anything physically wrong, but this failure to thrive occurred at the same time his mother struggled with a difficult depressive episode. In all likelihood, William was suffering his own childhood depression but covered it over with his projected sensitivity to others' depressions and need to help them.

Until William was able to understand the origins and the intentions of his pathological rescue fantasy, he still tried to hold onto Linda, feeling sorry for her, even though they agreed on divorce.

William was attracted to women who had been depressed in childhood. He had deep empathy for them, just like for his mother—and even more unconsciously, for his own childhood depression.

The Cause, the Wish, and Why It's Hard to Let It Go

Eventually William could see the anatomy of his pathological rescue fantasy and its multiple elements. First, he wanted to rescue his mother, and when he made her well, she would then for the first time love and nurture him, which in turn would allow him to go through childhood without the childhood depression. Ultimately, the rescue was for a self-rescue. Until he got the job done of getting his mother out of her depression, he could not cure his own childhood depression. Later as an adult, he couldn't abandon his old childhood self and needs; to do so would be to be a bad parent. Neither could he ignore Linda, who had a childhood depression and childhood neediness. His was a complex of mistaken identities and impossibilities; he needed to cure Linda as if she were his mother, so she would (magically, unconsciously) raise him again, minus the depression. Second, he had to cure her childhood depression, which he was equating with his own. The unconscious strategies of using mistaken identities and unrealistic, impossible solutions were at the source of his pathological rescue fantasy. In the end, William saw the truth of what he'd been doing and its unrealistic and convoluted nature. He was then able to release this powerful binding complex. Later, he made a new, wise marriage choice and today has a healthy and successful relationship.

Could You Have This?

Pathological rescue fantasies and the resulting actions reside in a significant minority of people, not just those who marry alcoholics or are therapists like William. How do you know if you have one operating in you?

The Tip-off and the Start of the Dance

The most prominent tip-off is that you are attracted to someone who has some problems, deficiencies, or depressions, and you feel a strong desire to help, to rescue that person from the problems he or she has not been able to overcome by self-effort. Usually these people in distress signal their painful problem perhaps through hinting, or they present worrisome dilemmas to the potential rescuer, a lure of sorts. The rescuer takes the bait, and the two connect, and romantically dance for a while, sometimes for as long as seven frustrating years, though usually shorter. Why? The ones wanting rescue are dependent and gain energy and supplies for life from luring others to give it. They do not handle life by strong, responsible, capable, self-actualizing behavior; instead they seek the answer and strength from the rescuers, who have their own hidden childhood devastations.

The Cause, and Its Failure to Cure

These rescuers' hidden childhood devastations sensitized them to the sufferers' pain. As time goes by, the rescuers become frustrated because their rescue efforts do not help much, and even though asked for, they are often resented by the dependent partners who lure through suffering. Of course the deeper elements of the purpose of the rescue attempts never get addressed and cannot possibly work out. The rescuers eventually tire and leave, unsatisfied and uncured, and then seek new rescue opportunities, as do the luring sufferers. It usually takes two or three attempted and then failed rescue relationships, before the rescuers begin to see that there is something wrong with their type of attractions and love choices. Their inner mental attraction software is stuck in this powerful, pathological pattern and foredooms each to repeat the problem over and over again, until psychotherapy or fortunate insight changes the pattern and purpose of the love choice. Then and only then can better choices be made based on appreciated and valued mutual strengths, and responsible behaviors for living and handling life. The old software is a powerful tyrant until replaced with wiser and more adaptive, new software based on logic and objective appraisal of the loved person's capabilities. Strength plus strength works in mate relationships, not strength plus weakness.

Each type of partner—the rescuers who do not know of their hidden motivating childhood devastations and the cunning dependent ones who lure from attractive helplessness—have to come to know and then give up these patterns, or they will never have successful and durable, mutually enhancing, mature, long-term relationships. The lure to rescue and the lure to be rescued are wasteful perversions rather than healthy patterns. They are, however, extremely powerful and are fueled by intense motivation.

In my experience, these anti-devastation maneuvers are quite common; they make up the majority of the dysfunctional marital patterns I see in my practice, and they're probably one of the main causes of divorce.

The other main cause of divorce is the unfortunate marriage of people who are so different from each other that they cannot hold the bond together for long; these are people who should never have been married in the first place but who were blinded by their romantic attraction. With awareness and them taking responsibility to change this as a basis for the relationship—that is, quit rescuing—this problem can be worked out.

The rescue maneuver, a pernicious motivator, is an ill-fated attempt at solution for the early devastations of missed nurturing, just as the dependent-luring maneuver. The ones who lure through being dependent, distressed, and helpless also experienced childhood devastations but decided (or found out early) that persistent portrayal of helplessness got them something, so they stuck with it. They do not realize how ultimately destructive it is to their life.

What to Do about It

Readers who are fortunate enough to see either pattern in their mate-seeking behaviors and attractions, especially early enough to prevent several relationships from failing, can seek professional help to understand and change these before they go very far in adult life. Some might be able to see the reasons for their choices from what I have presented in this chapter and modify their attraction software while at the same time discovering their own childhood devastations that sensitized them. They can then come to grips with their past and release the need to rescue or lure. It will be more difficult for the dependent sufferers because they have never taken the full responsibility to independently handle their own life, but they can do it. The rescuers have taken responsibility—and in the area of rescuing, too much responsibility—so they merely have to see and then pull back from their pattern, come to grips with their guilt for not nurturing, and release it. Then they will be open to seeking healthier relationships.

When a couple discovers they are locked in this type of pattern, they can both seek psychotherapeutic help and work to create a more healthy basis for their relationship, giving it a far better chance to survive and flourish. Recognition is the key; without it, there is no reason or power to change the pattern.

Chapter Summary

1. We all have a drive that allows us to handle disasters and even prevent future ones. The drive to overcome vexing problems or devastations leads to actions. Collectively these drives and actions may be referred to as anti-devastation maneuvers. However, they do not always work as intended, and they can easily go awry and produce negative actions.

2. This complex type of anti-devastation maneuver has an equal ability to cause great good or significant harm. It can trap the rescuer into a pattern of compulsive rescuing. It can set up relationships between the rescuer and the person being rescued that are inefficient and

wasteful, in effect stunting the psychological growth, development, and opportunities of each.

3. We need to release a pathological rescue fantasy because it obligates and enslaves our relationship motivation, conscripting it into a constantly attempted set of actions and behaviors that ultimately never work. Not only does it waste energy and wear us out, but also it causes even more pain and frustration and is still unable to cure the past.

4. As time goes by, the rescuers become frustrated because their rescue efforts do not help much and, even though asked for, are often resented by the dependent partners who lure through suffering.

5. The rescue maneuver, a pernicious motivator, is an ill-fated attempt at solution for the early devastations of missed nurturing, just as the dependent-luring maneuver. The ones who lure through being dependent, distressed, and helpless also experienced childhood devastations but decided (or found out early) that persistent portrayal of helplessness got them something, so they stuck with it. They do not realize how ultimately destructive it is to their life.

6. If you notice a rescue pattern in yourself, ask yourself the following question: "What early devastation or major hurt in my life have I covered over and forgotten that has sensitized me to want very strongly to help others with similar or like situations?"

7. When you discover your hidden vulnerability, you can more carefully decide, when trying to help others, whether or not you are feeling too obligated or are giving too much, whether or not you are trying to symbolically rescue yourself or someone else in your early environment.

8. Temper or restrain your zeal to overcome, or to help until you can understand your hidden motivation. When you fully understand your inner, anti-devastation cause, you will make more informed, balanced, and wiser use of your desires to help and overcome.

CHAPTER 19

———◆◈◆———

Regaining Meaningful Purpose

As you may already know, life does not feel good for very long without a sense of meaningful purpose. If you have lost this valuable element, you can learn how to reach within yourself to rediscover your unique form of it.

We all need a sense of meaningful purpose to guide and focus our desires and intentions on doing what is important to each of us; this gives our lives a sense of value. Meaningful purpose is a very important motivation to our life's direction. It gives meaning, useful motivation, even passion to life. When it is lost, we feel flat, meaningless, and upset; we also feel empty, confused, or befuddled.

Life without purpose is painful and wasteful of our life opportunity because its lack and seeming indifference can cause us the pain of anguish and the almost despairing sense of meaningless and uselessness, the feeling of "Why try?" We usually cannot bear this feeling for long. In general we are purposeful beings, organized to seek, to challenge, to master; purpose is in our bones, so to speak. We are probably hardwired for it, as are many of the world's life forms (see the chapter on motivation). We experience this when some prior purpose seems to have run its course or is no longer important to us. However, the sense of meaningful purpose about something remains important to our life—hence the pain at its loss.

Fortunately, most of us have many purposes, large and small. These purposes include finishing school, careers, taking care of family, and the responsibilities of modern living. We rarely lack for this kind of purpose. Yet as time passes, we begin to contemplate the larger, more inscrutable questions about life and purpose. We ask ourselves, "What is my true purpose? Is there a greater purpose to my life? What is truly meaningful to me? What is most meaningful to me? How can I give my life more meaning?"

The Philosophical Life Crisis

Not surprisingly, many therapy patients arrive at my office after colliding with what I call the Great Gray Wall of Now What? Most but not all are male and are usually in their forties. They are experiencing a philosophical crisis revolving around the idea of purpose and meaningfulness in their lives. For the most part, each has already attained a measure of economic success and provided well for his or her family. While continuing to work hard, they have achieved many goals associated with success. They have nice homes, two cars, kids in good colleges, and well-established and respected careers. By early midlife, they have reached the goals they set out to accomplish, but now they wonder what is next. They often feel flat, lost, and strangely without direction. They do not know where to turn or what might be worthwhile. In the rush to achieve their goals, they did not have the time or energy to consider the larger ideas of meaningfulness and purpose of life. Often the result is a brooding uneasiness and a sense that something is wrong or missing.

An Eliciting Scenario

After listening to these complaints and yearnings, I often say to patients, "Imagine you are lifted up from Earth, and someone gives you fifty million dollars, tax free! You can do anything you want with the money. You can also decide where you will be returned to Earth, and even what relationships you will continue or discontinue." I then ask, "What is the first thing you would do?"

First Things

Invariably, people first focus on taking care of their desires for more material things—grander homes, a special car, luxury items they always wanted but could not afford. They would pay off debt, invest wisely, and take care of their extended family, providing fully for their parents and establishing trust funds for children. Many would provide spouses with a considerable sum of money, no strings attached. To my surprise, the vast majority would keep their same relationships, even those with some trouble, and most would be returned to Earth where they lived.

Next ask, "After you have taken care of all material and family considerations, what then?" I ask. Most would travel for a year or two, having adventures and discovering new places. Some would return to a favorite place, now with more time and greater resources. Many would immerse themselves in something they had always wanted to do or perhaps start anew with something they had done when they were younger; things like sculpting, painting, photography, music. Some want to pursue hobbies like astronomy or writing and possibly turn them into second careers.

Then ask, "Now that you have done this for a year or two," I continue, "and you find yourself fully satiated, you discover you are looking for something else ... something more? What is it you would do?"

The response of one patient, Don, a clinical psychologist, is fairly typical and indicative of the power that purpose and meaningfulness represents. Perhaps because of his profession, Don had a pet interest in stress reduction. After building a new home on a hill, sending his parents on a world tour, and putting his kids into Ivy League schools, he would purchase a twenty-acre spread in a nearby mountain valley, next to a spring creek, and build an institute for stress seminars.

Don would fly in corporate executives and leaders from around the country and hold week-long seminars. There would be ample opportunity for participants to have individual sessions with instructors and experts. Don would handpick the best professors and clinicians and would involve graduate students and fellows. With this generative fantasy, Don hoped to stimulate better executive health, promote more efficient and productive work with less stress, and have his institute serve as a place of innovation for better stress-reducing techniques. Personally, Don's institute would fulfill and actualize his strong sense of purpose.

Another patient, Nancy, a single, surgical nurse, said she would buy a large yacht and sail the Mediterranean, staying at favorite ports and entertaining people she'd meet in her travels. She would invite old friends to cruise with her. Eventually, when Nancy wanted something different, she would open an art gallery on an Italian isle and collect Mediterranean and classical art objects. She would surround herself with friends and acquaintances and enjoy her gallery. Ultimately she would set up an art school and bring visiting painters to teach and lecture. Nancy felt very enthused and even grand about this whole endeavor.

Without exception, when patients are asked to imagine this freedom-from-financial-concerns scenario, they move quickly to areas that are deeply meaningful, worthy, and purposeful to them. Based on unique skills, talents, and interests, each person possesses an inner sense of what is truly meaningful to him or her. The imaging scenario has the power to bring this valuable answer to the surface. It is worth noting that each person wanted to share, to educate, and to provide others of like-minded interests an opportunity to pursue and share in what was meaningful.

Getting Back in Touch with the Meaningful

With assistance and understanding, the Great Gray Wall of Now What? disappears and a valued direction emerges. People get in touch with what is meaningful beyond economic necessity. Few of us will ever experience the freedom and power of a Bill Gates, but all of us can give audience to our inner voice of purpose and meaningfulness.

Each of us has an inner, central essence of what is meaningful; it is an expression of our unique gifts, talents, interests, and passions. We can create something with it and gain a real and true sense of renewed purpose. Don obtained research grants, mentored graduate fellows, traveled occasionally, and gave seminars. Nancy took a long vacation to the Mediterranean. She worked part time at an art gallery back home and eventually took private art lessons. She plans to open an art gallery soon. Following their lead, each of us can find ways to get in touch with our own sense of purpose and meaningfulness. We all have something to give and to share if we are not doing so already.

Incidentally, having great resources does not alter the importance of the search for purpose and meaning. I have had wealthy patients, friends, and acquaintances, and from my observations they have the same need and desire for meaning and purpose. They, too, need interests, passions, new discoveries, and goals. They may have greater degrees of freedom and opportunities based on their resources, but their interest and passion is still predicated on what is uniquely meaningful to each of them. Purpose and meaning are expressions of the soul, so to speak; there is no need to wait for financial success to let your soul's song be heard. How do you get started? Ask yourself one of several questions. "What have I let go of doing that I have often thought about doing, but have never really immersed myself into? What did I used to tell myself I'd do when I had more time? Is there an unexpressed passion I have to do, something besides my everyday work and other activities?" Use the eliciting scenarios earlier in this chapter, study the examples to see the method applied, and then use it on yourself.

A Really Grand Gift

Just for fun, imagine you have been gifted with immortality. Along with this gift comes an ever-increasing knowledge and wisdom. What would you do? Over the years, I have posed this question to many patients and associates, and here is a synthesis of the answers. "I would study, learn, discover, and create. I would explore new ideas and solve many problems. I would create new opportunities for myself and others. I would not want to be alone. I would want to unlock the mysteries of the universe and discover how it works, and why, and for what purpose if any. If I could not find out the purpose by doing this, I would postulate one. Life without purpose doesn't go well."

If we analyze the ingredients needed to create such a grandly fulfilling eternity, we might find the following. We desire to increase in strength, power, knowledge, capability, and wisdom. We want to unlock mysteries and enjoy the pleasure of discovery. We want to do good for others and ourselves. We want to create new opportunities. We want to observe our accomplishments and enjoy the good feeling they give us. We want to have created something that will benefit all. We want to relate intimately, soul to soul, with those we treasure.

I have concluded that the above ingredients are universal, and in order to make them become realities, it is important to keep them in mind and then act on them if you are not already doing so. Ask yourself these questions: "What is most meaningful to me? What do I value highest? And, what would I love to do more than anything else?" In your answers, you will find fulfillment, purpose, meaning, and value.

Chapter Summary

1. When you find yourself feeling flat or purposeless, imagine this scenario: You are lifted up from Earth, and someone gives you fifty million dollars, tax free. You can do anything you want with the money. You can also decide where you will be returned to Earth and the relationships you will continue or discontinue. Then ask yourself, "What is the first thing I would do?"

2. Then imagine one to two years have passed and you have completed what you set out to do, and you find yourself wanting to do something more (the process of increase). What is it that you want to do next? Keep asking the question until you have completed at least two or three projects and have many things going that you feel very good about.

3. Imagine you have been gifted immortality. Along with this gift comes ever-increasing knowledge and wisdom. Ask yourself what you would do.

4. Your answers to the questions raised in this chapter will help you find fulfillment, purpose, meaning, and value. Start doing a realistic and possible form of whatever inner essence emerged from your look into your inner creative self.

CHAPTER 20

◆━◆◈◆━◆

How to Understand and Face Despair

Despair has an exact formula and contains a hidden growth message that allows you to master it, if you so choose. If you master it, you will develop greater personal strength and a more solid sense of self, rather than totally giving up and dying. You need to know both its truths and false beliefs to empower yourself or others to remove it and move beyond it.

Despair is the most dangerous and potentially deadly condition we experience. If you have not experienced it, there is a good chance you will one day. For people suffering depression, despair can occur. Suicidal attempts occur only at times of despair. These individuals see no way to obtain relief from their anguish and psychological pain—their personal hell—other than giving up and taking their own lives. Nevertheless, the real truth or message we can learn from despair is that it provides a rare opportunity for producing great inner strength and resolve, the opportunity to own our own life as never before.

People who face despair successfully can be identified by their fierce determination to live the rest of their lives well. They solve problems quickly and decisively, facing hardships directly and learning from them.

In a way, despair is akin to the concept of trial by fire, a dangerous and deadly experience through intense anguish and turmoil that ultimately transforms into a source of great strength and determination. Those who accomplish the trial are willing to meet all that life brings and find some way to handle and master it.

Unfortunately, those who do not face despair often die by their own hands or continue to stumble forward in life. They are very vulnerable, riding the support of others and not having decided fully yet which way to go. They are safe for the moment, but at any time that could change. The state of despair with its all-consuming anguish, in large part from a lack of feeling any harmony with anything in life, is so painfully soul-wrenching and devastating that we cannot remain there for long. Despair forces action: we either deal with it or it consumes us. Each person makes that decision.

Carolyn's Despair Example

Carolyn became psychologically depleted over a two-year period because of depression, relationship breakups, a job loss, and the death of her mother, on whose strength she greatly relied. Carolyn began thinking very negatively and wondered if there was not something terribly wrong with her, for all these negative things to happen in her life.

Despairing, Carolyn attempted suicide twice by overdose and was hospitalized both times. As a result, she was placed on appropriate psychiatric medications and had a course of electroshock therapy. These treatments, alone or in combination, are usually successful, but in her case did not work. Carolyn had chosen death through suicide each time she experienced total despair, not knowing what else to do. She was approaching this dangerous place again when she sought treatment with me.

The Causes

After a careful review of Carolyn's treatment history, I concluded that there was little hope a new medication or repeat electroshock therapy would help.

Her problem seemed to be one of inadequate self-determination and self-reliance. The clues were that after her mother's death two years earlier, her world began falling apart. She lost her job because of performance problems, obtained another, but then her new company downsized and she was one of the first to go. Next, she experienced the breakup of a close relationship for reasons that were not totally clear to me. She did not feel like going on and wanted to end her life. "Life just is not worth it," she sobbed, "it's too painful!" Carolyn was in a crisis of will and in great pain.

I decided to meet her despair head-on, confronting her omnipotent, unrealistic negative ideas that she caused or brought on all her problems by being such a failure. I attempted to get her to take responsibility for only what she had caused, and further to acknowledge all the things outside her control that impacted her—the weak job market, her mother's death, her boyfriend's choices.

For the next three weeks we worked on her dependency upon her mother, who apparently held the family together and upon whom Carolyn and her family depended too much. After the mother's death the family fell apart, frequently attacking and blaming each other when problems arose. They were unsuccessful at rearranging and remodeling the necessary elements of a new family system that could support them all. Carolyn tried to carry the standard of her mother's role in the family but could not pull it off; she was either not adept enough or the family just could not accept her in that role. Carolyn felt she was honoring her mother by continuing with her patterns and believed her mother would be pleased with her. Sometimes she felt her mother's presence and believed she was being a good daughter and receiving her mother's approval. Carolyn had a spiritual belief that God was with her through all this.

The Nature of the Choices in Despair

During one session, she described a crisis with a noisy, intrusive neighbor. She sought help from her landlord, but nothing was done. She had been fearful of the neighbor and was passive in dealing with him. She was feeling defeated and thinking of giving up. I attempted to show her that despair was an opportunity and a choice. "One path is to kill yourself," I told her, "and you will die with your loyalty to your old and current self, intact. You will take with you the repertoire of life-handling capabilities you possess now, the capabilities that are no longer sufficient to allow you to master your current situation." I paused to let that sink and then went on. "Or, you can make a choice to grow new capabilities at this time of great uncertainty and pain. You can own your own life and go on with courage and determination." She quietly listened to me. I added, "In order to go on, you will have to dare to develop new ways and new capabilities." She told me she was not sure she could or wanted to do that. I advised another hospitalization for safety until the despair dissipated. Carolyn was at a critical point and had to make her own choice. She did not want to go back to the hospital, but she would think about all I said and would call me if she could not handle it herself.

I did not receive a call. At the next session she described how she stood up to her neighbor and did not back down; she informed her landlord and neighbor she would call the police the next time. Carolyn felt better and seemed far less despairing. At the next session she came in sobbing feeling very uncertain, and she related how she and her father had fought. Carolyn turned some of her father's blaming comments into self-deprecating themes, and she was hovering at the edge of despair again. She considered hospitalization but decided against it. She felt defeated and this time forsaken—even by God. "Why doesn't anything ever work out? Why doesn't God answer my prayers?" She informed me she was considering moving to a neighboring state and starting over. "There is nothing for me here anymore."

"A new start might help you," I concluded. "It would get you out of the bad patterns and away from family problems … but you would still have to increase your reliance upon yourself. You still need to develop better patterns or you'll fall into despair again sometime in the future."

Carolyn's Choice

I was relieved and somewhat excited to see a marked change during her next visit. She was no longer despairing and had chosen to make her life work—to live it and to handle what came. After she had left our last appointment, she again considered hospitalization or moving away. She prayed but still felt forsaken. She visited her mother's gravesite, feeling compelled to go there and looking for solace. While sitting next to her mother's grave, it came to her: "I must be what I choose to be, not what anyone else wants. It's my life. Mother, I cannot be you, and I cannot replace you. I want to live, and I will." Her words possessed firmness and conviction. Carolyn had chosen for life and for going on. In her view, just at that decisive moment, she felt God come back into her life. Now she was determined and positive, even assertive. She enjoyed this new feeling of self-determination and the power it gave her. She had fully faced her dilemma alone. She had choices, and she made the one to live and go on, mastering as she went. Her despair was gone.

The Dynamics of Mastering Despair

With despair, the choices are to live, or give up and die with a loyalty to life-handling abilities that will not work anymore. When you resolve to pull yourself forward and create new abilities or awareness, the despair disappears. Despair has a false belief in it—that you can't do anything more to help yourself. That is dead wrong.

I have worked with many people in the throes of despair and seen similar results. It seems there comes a point in many people's lives where they must shed a dependency that they have unknowingly allowed to restrict their future growth. Their developed capabilities and established patterns of dealing with life do not work anymore, so they must make a choice themselves while feeling terrible despair: to live no matter what comes next, or to give up. If the choice is to live, they must use their will and determination, even though filled with uncertainty, to develop new ways to solve problems, face hardships, and pull themselves forward. Despair offers us a crisis of self-choice: to die with the old dependencies and capabilities or to boldly go on, dedicated to developing new workable capabilities. Despair tests the strength of our will to live. If the choice is to live, we come through it with strengthened autonomy. I call it the self-owning of the self, a self-baptism, to face and live life no matter what, to fully own one's lifetime space. It makes one as strong as stainless steel.

When you feel despair, ask yourself, "What have I been relying on that no longer works, at least at this time?" Then tell yourself, "I must give up on that reliance and pull my own self up to form some new abilities, to take new action even though I feel extremely uncertain and full of anguish. I will attempt and live my own future and give it all I have. I'm willing to face all that life brings, now and in the future, and to keep evolving and increasing." After you make such a statement with strong resolve, not false hope, your despair will disappear, and you will have mastered this difficult life episode.

We all need to understand that sometimes very important and strongly held values and loyalties hold us back. They keep us from handling the new challenges we have to face in life. Most people ultimately choose to live their life and go forward, strengthened in will and inner conviction, never feeling suicidal again unless they have biological depression with severe relapses. Even in those circumstances, many who have conquered despair once do not fall as far into that state ever again. They have performed a baptism of the self, by the self, into their new, autonomous life.

When Depression Is Too Immobilizing

Of course, some people become totally overwhelmed by depression and cannot think well enough to analyze the dilemma I have presented. They may need the safety and expertise of a psychiatric hospital to evaluate and treat their depression and despair-induced suicidal urges. They can be kept safe from themselves, and with the support of family, friends, and hospital staff in a stress-free environment, they can be encouraged to develop the change of heart (and mind) to choose life over death by suicide. The changes required for their life to be workable and worth it, to stay around and live it, can be discovered and implemented with a treatment program of psychotherapy, and probably psychiatric medications.

Despair can come from a variety of tightly and desperately held dependencies that can no longer work for life to go on. People who have lost important relationships in childhood (a mother or father, for instance) may believe life is not worth living if during adolescence a "first love" relationship breaks up, or even later in life if they are divorced by a spouse. Suicide attempts are often desperate attempts to keep the person depended on from leaving. Job losses, physical impairments, and monetary losses are among the perceived things with which people believe they cannot deal. They do not have to be spiritual or believe in God to believe that life (as they have wished it should be) has forsaken them. The point is, the forsaken feeling comes from the absence or inability to access that which has been so strongly and importantly depended upon. Of course, when life and mastery is chosen, and as the newly developed set of capabilities gives new opportunity, the forsaken feeling disappears, and once again harmony with life and its processes and a new belonging comes about. One now has a more developed self, ready to venture further.

If you are experiencing despair, think through what you have just presented, considering it carefully and truthfully as you ponder your dilemma. If you are a family member or friend of anyone who is despairing, talk with that person about the nature and composition of despair and its life-giving mastery opportunity.

If you are a therapist, I suggest using this with your clients if they become despairing. I always do. It cuts to the heart of the matter and is usually refreshing and helpful to my patients. This direct, no-nonsense approach to a dangerous situation unmasks despair, promotes open discussion, and shows a way for relief through the most appropriate actions. My patients become more cooperative and trusting when they know I can clarify the elements of their desperate dilemmas. They feel safer that I understand despair and can guide them by outlining the choices and tasks confronting them, and that I can explain the logic (the nature) of the despair experience and its purpose. This encourages them to choose to master it and live on more ably.

Chapter Summary

1. Despair is the most dangerous and potentially deadly condition we experience. However, despair provides a rare opportunity for producing

great inner strength and resolve, the opportunity to own our own life as never before.

2. Despair tests the strength of our will to live. If the choice is to live, we come through it with strengthened autonomy. I call it the self-owning of the self, a self-baptism to face and live life no matter what, to fully own one's lifetime space.

3. Most people ultimately choose to live their life and go forward, strengthened in will and inner conviction, never feeling suicidal again unless they have biological depression with severe relapses. Even in those circumstances, many who have conquered despair once do not fall as far into that state ever again.

4. Some people become totally overwhelmed by depression and cannot think well enough to analyze the dilemma. They may need the safety and expertise of a psychiatric hospital to evaluate and treat their depression and despair-induced suicidal urges. They can be kept safe from themselves and be encouraged to develop the change of heart and mind to choose life over death.

5. People do not have to be spiritual or believe in God to believe that life has forsaken them. The forsaken feeling comes from the absence or inability to access that which has been so strongly and importantly depended upon. When life and mastery are chosen, and a newly developed set of capabilities gives new opportunity, the forsaken feeling disappears.

CHAPTER 21

———◆◆◆———

Accepting and Integrating Undesirable Past Actions into the Present

When we carry hidden shame, we are vulnerable to the fear that people will find out or remember past actions of which we are not proud. Because they are hard to face, we mentally try to hold them away from ourselves as if they never happened. When we acknowledge these actions and integrate their memories into our identities, we strengthen ourselves and remove our vulnerability to others. We can then be at peace with ourselves.

The crown of successful growth and development is the achievement of an autonomous identity. It results from integrating all the elements of our past (through the process of understanding our prior motivations and actions), then accepting and, if necessary, forgiving ourselves so we can use our earned wisdom to guide our present and future.

Often I hear, "I'm so ashamed," or, "I feel so guilty for what I've done in the past," or "I didn't become what I should have." The person who says this is showing a problem that needs working out if they are ever going to be able to feel a cohesive sense of personal identity and say, "This is who I am, and I accept and acknowledge it."

The "This is who I am" statement can only be made when all aspects of oneself can be accepted, self-owned, and brought into the inner circle of awareness and agreement. Integrating the disparate aspects of ourselves, including the things we do not like about ourselves or did not like about our former actions, gives us a sense of knowing who we are and a greater acceptance of ourselves. It makes us stronger, with far less vulnerability.

Why is this important? What does it do for us? What will we miss if we do not get it done? Moreover, what keeps us from being able to do it?

If we do not integrate, accept, and acknowledge all aspects of ourselves, we will remain divided by failure to fully accept the truth of everything we have done. When we fight this truth, we feel shame, guilt, or failure for not living up to ideals we believe in but have not achieved. The end result is that these failures will have power over us. The following is an example of a way to find self-acceptance.

The Act of Understanding and Accepting

People often say, "I did that then, and now I wish I had done this." Looking back and remembering, "What was my purpose then? Where was I coming from?" gives us the basis on which to understand and then accept those actions with grace and forgiveness instead of shame. We know what we were trying to do for ourselves and the way we tried to do it. With our greater knowledge about life now, we know our past performance was not the best way for us. But that is where we were and how we thought back then. At the time, that is what we desperately wanted for our needy former self. We now know differently, so we now do differently. We can now say to ourselves, "I can accept each aspect of myself, even at differing times."

The Key

The key to integrating and acknowledging the truth of what we did formerly that we now do not like, and coming to acceptance of the truth that we "really did it," is to analyze and understand our motivation, the purpose for doing it back then. Remember, motivation consists of the purpose for the action and the worth-it-ness assessment. Therefore whatever it was we did we had a purpose then, and we concluded that it was worth it!

Old Dependencies

The purpose may have been to gain acceptance from others, and we believed that acting a certain way would bring it about. If so, we were still dependent on acceptance from others. Perhaps it was something we did not get enough of earlier in life. When we reach maturity and autonomy, we quit being so needy and giving our power away to others. By maintaining or retaining our own power, we accept ourselves, and then we can master the problem. If we are still too willing to give our power away, we are still trying to feed that hunger for acceptance—we are still too dependent. To cure this we must instead see the value of accepting our self and better define who we are; we must shed the belief that we have to please others and gain their acceptance to be okay. The belief that we must please others does not work as a final way of gaining our self-identity, though it is useful in childhood and adolescence before we mature and create our own autonomous identity. The old saying, "We have to be successfully dependent in order to become successfully independent," is true. Successfully independent really means being autonomous, able to stand alone with self-integrity, or able to interrelate and mutually depend on others, and they on us, so we can accomplish mutual goals.

Fear and Dependency

If the purpose for hiding a prior action that we are not proud of—or are possibly still ashamed of, or are still strongly embarrassed—about is being fearful of others being disappointed in us or of condemning us, we have not yet gained a full identity. It means we still have other people set up in our minds as authorities over us. Realize instead that the mature way to live and the most important reason for doing things is that it works for our lives both now and in the future to produce the best quality and most inner peace. The unwise way is to still give power away to perceived authority, to let *them* pass judgment on us.

No wonder we are still afraid. We keep ourselves in a dependent position, like a frightened child who knows or fears that he or she has displeased a parent and will likely be punished. What does a child usually do in that circumstance? He or she lies to the parent, hoping the perceived unacceptable action will not be discovered. In like manner, by not accepting and acknowledging our prior actions and their original motivating purposes, we are lying to ourselves. In this way we keep ourselves divided, lacking integration and solidification; our identity remains incomplete. We must win this battle, and dare to self-choose, and momentarily stand on our own, or else we will not solve this problem. If we do not, we will instead keep having pain because we will not see the full truth about our self (the past and present), and we will still be fighting it. Instead we close our eyes to it, look away, and retain it in ourselves secretly, not wanting to face it. Once again, pain— in this instance embarrassment, guilt, or shame—is the pointer to truth undiscovered or fought against, if known. We can count on it.

The Value of Accepting and Acknowledging

What does accepting and acknowledging all our past actions do for us? First, it frees us from obligatory and desperate dependence upon others, wanting them to see us in a certain way, so we aren't ashamed or humiliated and hiding it. When we accept it, we take the power of being vulnerable to others' opinions out of the situation. It gives us freedom from the pains of not accepting the actual reality of what we did or for not living up to an ideal we now value; it removes the old shame from the old actions. Instead, a good way is to create our future and own way of functioning, based on the truth and actual reality of who we now are and accept ourselves to be. We have learned from our own mistakes and successes, and we can be thankful for them, because they have both taught us well on who to be, now and henceforth. That is the real truth of how to function at our best.

James kept finding attraction to so-called damsels in distress, and the relationships wouldn't last. Frequent marriages ended in divorce. His old college social group would usually tease him about this part of his past when they got together. He used to be embarrassed about it, but at age forty, he sought in-depth psychotherapy to see why this pattern kept occurring. He was at first astounded to learn that he had a rescue complex. Then he learned to remove it and make a new, clear, better marital choice that lasted. No longer vulnerable to his rescue pattern, he could joke and tease with his old friends, laugh at himself, and at serious moments advise them to get help for any stumbling blocks in their lives. "After all," he said, "how can you know before you know?"

This aspect of fully acknowledging and accepting all aspects of our self, past and present, brings peace and a feeling of freedom. It also brings the opportunity to be unified in ourselves to care well and responsibly, even lovingly, for the life opportunity we have been given. The wise use of the past, learning from it rather than having regrets, is the way that works best for us.

If we do not make the steps to fully create our own autonomous identity by integrating, accepting, and acknowledging all our prior behaviors and then guiding our life wisely, we will remain divided and in pain. We will fight the truth, hoping for something that will never come, passively wishing something would get better rather than making it better by effective action (e.g., wishing a better job would come along rather than taking extra training to improve job skills and employability). Choosing this path is a great waste, a squandering of opportunity.

If a parent indulges a child constantly, never placing limits on the child's requests or behaviors, the requests soon become demands, the demands become tantrums, and the child becomes an enfant terrible. By nurturing the child's demands rather than teaching self-control through demonstrations, discussion, rewards, and punishments, a parent can help create a monstrous child that nobody wants to be around.

The Wages of Fear

Fear is the gap signal that we are not at a preferred place. If we hang onto the dependency as the preferred place, there will always be a gap between us and wise living, knowing what is the truth of best functioning but never obtaining it—our reward will be fear, pain, and missed autonomous opportunity.

Ultimately, fear keeps us from having an autonomous identity. Fear born of a hungry, needy dependence, and based on the belief of having to be acceptable to others, keeps us enslaved to its tyranny. It is a belief that is not adequate for handling life well. *When we nurture an inadequacy, we create a monster.* The avoidance of the autonomous step and the empowerment of dependencies will remain our monster.

Magnified Self-Deprecating

So often during my psychiatric work, patients finally begin to share things they have hidden—especially from themselves—out of embarrassment or shame. They fear the worst, that I will believe they are a terrible person. These secrets cause them so much pain that it is only the hope of relief that allows them to take the chance to reveal them to me. Generally they have built these secrets up so negatively that they see themselves as monstrous. They carry these secrets deep within themselves, not wanting to face them because that might mean they must face the conclusion that they are a terrible person. They admit, "I'm a terrible person, not the person I'd like to see myself as being." This assessment keeps them from resolving the problem and moving toward a life with less pain and one more integrated. Instead, they keep their shameful deeds secret, as if they were foreign objects. By keeping them separate or foreign, they partition them off and play a childhood game of making believe they do not exist.

An Illustrative Case

Jewel, an accomplished pianist and master's-level nurse, came to me for depression and anxiety. She had done well as a concert pianist earlier in life, touring North America several times. Later, she went back to her nursing career and become a nurse manager at a local hospital. Now in her mid-sixties, she eventually revealed a wild and raucous life in her late thirties, during her concert touring years. She met and socialized with the rich and famous, engaging in many sexual liaisons, drug highs, and parties; she rarely slept, going from party to party, often the celebrated belle of the ball. She had many marriage proposals and actually had two brief marriages. She eventually gave up that life, became religious, went back to graduate nursing school, and embarked on her second career. When she confessed her prior life to me, she was red faced and looked away. She cried a little and made deprecating comments about herself.

Jewel went too far in blaming those past behaviors as the cause of nearly every disappointment in her life since then, including not getting a management position for which she applied. Some of Jewel's old self-elements (her thirties' life) were being rejected rather than accepted by her now changed and more mature self. She was in battle with herself. Her failure to integrate these seemingly disparate elements caused emotional and psychological pain every time she thought about them.

At this point, I pointed out that she was feeling embarrassed, ashamed, and then guilty *in the now*, the present time, because her prior behavior did not fit her current values. She agreed that she would not do such things now, that they were foolish and even risky. She was much wiser now, having learned from experience what worked well and what did not. However, when younger she had different motivations and aspirations. She wanted to experience the power that her beauty brought, particularly the power to attract men. She reveled in this, probably somewhat naturally and partly to compensate for a disadvantaged childhood with a frequently absent alcoholic father who traveled the rodeo circuit, barely making enough money to support the family he rarely saw. Her motivations were understandable. She had fame, beauty, and power, and she moved in all the right circles. The benefits turned out to be somewhat illusory, but she had a high time for several years.

The Cure

I focused on the fallacy in her thinking. She was condemning herself from her present, significantly evolved viewpoint—that of someone in her sixties. Her earlier motivations and actions were accepted and desired at the time, but not now. I told her, "Anything different from accepting and acknowledging that it was okay then would be kidding yourself, distorting the truth of the way it was. If you were to do those same actions now with your current values, then it would be appropriate to feel guilty, having transgressed your agreement with yourself and the values you now uphold. Then was then; now is now. If you mix the two up, you'll have pain, shame, and guilt caused by violating the psychological truth of actual time sense: past is past, present is present, and past cannot be present." She got the point and let go, accepting the actual truth of the two different times and their differing motivations and values. Her pain was gone. Occasionally she would mix these up, feeling guilty, but she'd realize her error of logic and then be at peace with herself.

At times people may do things they highly suspected were dumb to do or may cause them trouble, but it was fun enough at the time they threw caution to the winds and did it anyway, only to have it backfire and cause them problems they later regretted. Still, in the present they can say, "I am wiser now, and I wouldn't take the chance. It is in the past, I did it, and I paid the price. Now it's over and done with. I will go on being smarter and using better judgment."

Bill's old friends and he were having lunch together after they had all retired. They were talking about a time in their twenties when they had unmercifully teased and made cutting remarks to Bill about his being engaged to two different women in a short six-month period of time, then breaking up with each. He recalled how uncomfortable he had felt, how he had tried to hide his hot cheeks of embarrassment and sense of shame. The guys apparently had sensed his shame, which increased their teasing. For several years they still brought it up, and he'd still feel embarrassed and try to pass it off as nothing. Yet it still bothered him in his thirties, when they still brought it up. Now as a retiree, he knew he had done well in life, had an excellent marriage and a meaningful extended family. He really was no longer bothered by their comments. He could laugh at his prior attempts at mate selection, joke about that in front of them, and conclude that all that practice helped him finally get it right. He wouldn't change that past for anything. He truly was no longer vulnerable to them, and he was accurate that those two earlier engagements had taught him some important things in his future picking of a wife with whom he was very compatible. His prior two engagements had proved to not be undesirable after all, just part of learning about life.

For Those Who Have Been Sexually Abused

In more serious clinical situations, when unfortunate people who have been sexually abused in childhood or early teens start to recall those traumatic memories, they often try to put them out of their conscious mind. "It's so painful, and I don't want to face it," is a frequent response. Yet face it they must, if they want to rid themselves of the piled-up, painful emotions including rage, guilt, powerlessness, humiliation, hidden pleasure, and overwhelmed feelings. The choice they do not realize until later is that they must face and work through their feelings, or else suffer distorted self-views such as "I'm bad," or "It happened to me; there must be something wrong with me," or even, "I'm dirty, I'm sinful." Of course, to work with such situations clinically, there is much unraveling to do after therapeutic trust is established. For full identity integration, the past situations eventually must be faced and understood in their context, and appropriate emotions evoked and understood: outrage and chagrin at being used, at trust being violated, at being victimized. Then, the victims can experience current life relationship patterns with healthy emotions, including love and trust.

The Result: A Better Life, a Better Future

Our lives and our knowledge of truth are ever evolving. We will move into our futures unencumbered and free when we understand and accept our past, truly coming to know who we are. Then by choice, as we live and further develop our capacities, we can greet the future with quiet confidence and optimism. After all, it is our future. Each of us is unique and distinctive; there is no one else exactly like us, so it is up to each of us to manage our own futures.

Once we have made the important step to own our past and integrate our identity, we are not vulnerable to others who might bring up our past and attempt to criticize or demean us. We will not have to hide in shame or fear. We can retain our power and say, "Yes, I did that, and I understand why." How nice it is to arrive at this place of having solved these vulnerabilities. We cannot have full, continuous, abiding good inner quality of life until we do.

Chapter Summary

1. Are there still things you feel ashamed of or embarrassed about, even though they may have happened long ago? The best way to face and acknowledge these situations and bring them into yourself is to recall the purpose of what you did then. Remember how you were thinking then and what your intentions were. They are probably different now.

2. Next, identify how you now view those situations from your current perspective and greater wisdom. Notice what you have learned, how you have become different, and how you have increased from the prior time.

3. Accept the true differences and acknowledge the past from a past perspective, the present from a current perspective. Understand that both perspectives are yours, but you have greater wisdom and different purposes now than then. When you bring your former self's mistakes and even shameful actions into your present self's acceptance, you will have integrated them and will be much stronger. You will not have to be apologetic (unless you have wronged someone; then make amends), and you will be far less vulnerable to others—they will not be able to evoke your old shame to get power over you.

4. If we do not integrate, accept, and acknowledge all aspects of ourselves, we will remain divided due to our failure to fully accept the truth of everything we have done. When we fight this truth, we feel shame, guilt, or failure for not living up to ideals we believe in but have not achieved. The end result is that these failures will have power over us.

SECTION 7

Have and Enjoy Excellent Ongoing Quality of Life

CHAPTER 22

The Arrival of Trusted Life-Handling Capability

You can enjoy peace and ease in your life after learning to remove your painful obstructions, which will allow you to take any newly arising uncertainties smoothly and in stride.

My writing consultant recently told me he knew of only two people who seemed to be consistently calm, smooth, and unruffled in their demeanor. According to him, these two individuals embraced every situation and problem energetically and with optimism. Both were confident, knowledgeable, and seemingly without worry or a hint of being *crucial*. They never showed a tendency for excessive striving, but both were high accomplishers. If this were not enough, they were easy to be around, laughed a lot, and often saw humor in dilemmas. "They seem to be masters at living," he said, with a note of reverence. "Any idea what made them this way?"

"Well, I really can't say," I started. "I don't know enough about them. Perhaps if I had more information, I might be able to give you an educated guess."

"You *should* know," my consultant added wryly. "You're one of them."

I was surprised and a little stunned, and I felt some pleasure at his unsolicited assessment. Before I could respond, he went on, "How did you become that way?"

"You know," I said, slightly taken aback, "I really can't say because I can't really see myself as you see me. I can't self-observe that accurately. I appreciate your observations, and I do have a sense of what you are saying. I wish I had some simple answer to your question, but I really don't know. I can, however, describe how I feel internally most of the time now; it's quite different from how I felt many years ago. Perhaps how I feel is a corollary to how you see me."

Over the next few days, I thought about what my consultant told me. He was not the first person to tell me something similar. I recalled how the nurses at my hospital twenty years ago saw me. One told me, "Dr. Wallace, you're the only doctor we know who doesn't get all stressed and pressured. You never order people around when there's a problem, and you laugh a lot." That was the first time I realized I had very little, if any, self-pressure or personal stress. I had become automatic about not getting *crucial* and absolute in my thinking and motivational self-statements (chapter 1). I had mastered the ability to use truth and logic most of the time, seldom slipping into the false logic of crucial and absolute *have to* and *must* types of thinking. I felt calm and used my energies well, and apparently it showed.

I also recalled how I once sought *being into being*, a term used in the 1970s and 1980s. Being into being is a state of mind and self-sensing that feels calm and soothing; it is actively tranquil, accepting, and liberating. Striving for goals was no longer necessary—goals, yes, but striving, no. Previously I discovered the times I felt the elusive state of being into being was usually after I accomplished some gain or developed a new capability. The good feeling it generated would last for only a few days, and it was peaceful and enjoyable, but soon new problems or new discoveries beckoned. The uncertainties of new situations and the lack of know-how took the feeling of being into being away. When I made sufficient gain again, the good feeling came back for a brief stay.

I realized I had not been *thrown* by an uncertainty in a long, long time. I take uncertainties in stride now, where formerly they caused me distress and confusion; they seem minor and part of the reality of living. I accept them and have confidence I can master them if I so choose. My sense of self, I surmised, was much stronger and more capable than it had once been. It was large now because I had successfully experienced many things in life. Today, each new task, discovery, or problem I encounter is small compared to the larger self I have developed. I no longer have to put all of my attention and energy into not being thrown.

Some time back, I forgot about trying to attain a constant sense of being into being. It came about quietly within me, and though I was not aware of it until later, at some point I achieved it. I concluded my knowledge of the varieties of uncertainty and how I smoothly handled them gave me a sense of gratitude and appreciation. I now understood how everything I experienced and learned gave back to me. I attained a state of constant and automatic gaining and increasing, and it was truly good to be alive. I understood the natural order of things and could even accept death without fear.

I considered how to explain all this to my consultant but realized I could not offer an exact, step-by-step formula because so many things contribute to the process. One important thing I knew I would tell him was how I had passed through despair and various other hardships but still made a choice to embrace and affirm life. At a certain point, I had decided to meet, accept, and handle whatever happens. Most important, I would emphasize that I accept reality and truth easily and well; I realize and appreciate their value. Using reality and truth precisely saves energy and makes us efficient, automatically putting our energies to use in a manner that works best.

At our next lunch meeting, I followed up with what I had been thinking, summarizing many of this book's discoveries and psychological truths. "It had taken a long time," I told him, "a twenty-year quest." He listened, and when I finished, he asked, "Could you have achieved it all sooner?"

I thought, *He is probably also asking if he could achieve this sooner.* "Certainly, someone could achieve it in less time if he or she had access to identifying and understanding the psychological truths I have discovered and how they work in life." I reminded myself that I found out most of these things for myself, in a long progression of growth and discovery, aided by the myriad of problems my patients presented and the many solutions we worked out together, and the discussions, proofs, and applied experiences with which I credited my think tank. We spent many hours over a thirteen-year-period discussing the workability of the concepts I proposed. I said to my consultant, "Someone could probably learn this much faster, if they had enough life experience." I stopped and considered what I had said, and then added this caveat. "Until you've reached the age of uncertainty—the point you have to start making all of your own decisions and taking all the responsibility for your life—it may not mean a lot to you."

To that point, I told him about a continuing education class on the material we were now discussing, which I had taught at Westminster College, a local liberal arts college, in the early 1980s. Some of my bright high school patients and their friends attended, as well as many adults. Most of the older students saw the material as very helpful; some even said it was profound. On the other hand, the high school students just saw it as good common sense and obvious. I had to chuckle, realizing they had not reached the age of uncertainty yet or dealt with many of life's complexities. I recounted this experience to my consultant and further told him how my own daughters had rejected the idea of releasing mental pressure when they were in high school, saying they wouldn't do their work without it. How different they are now that they are nearing the middle of their lives. They now love the concepts they had earlier rejected and use them in their daily lives. They are excited to talk about discoveries, both theirs and mine.

After lunch my consultant told me he was curious about something. "What keeps you going?" he asked, knowing I had just turned sixty-seven at the time. "You are still working full time. You are writing a book. You have many interests. You are always enthusiastic and excited."

"Much in my life is meaningful and filled with purpose," I started. "For me, I cannot think of any higher good than assisting my patients and utilizing my faculties to the fullest. The work is always interesting and filled

348

with psychological detective work and discovery. I love to see people get better, to make discoveries for themselves, and to improve their current life quality. It excites me. I get to learn all the time—and it's a heck of a lot better than golfing or fishing all the time."

I realized I have always had a burning desire to *know*. Knowing makes me seek; it is the impetus for my life's quest. Since childhood I had always sought the answer to what makes for quality of life, and it motivates me. I understand the ingredients of change, each requiring new additions to keep quality high and even improve it. As we age, interest, novelty, and involvement are important to keep us going. Discovery never gets old even though we do. Lately, I found that my explorations of psychological truth and the increased knowledge I have gained from this fascinating and vast subject excites and enlivens me. I have found that these truths unify many things about the human psyche. Truth is the supreme force, our psyche's highest organizer. It has even given me a full and workable psychological definition of good and evil, and a comprehensive consideration ethic that guides and governs me.

"I guess what really makes me tick," I said, "is appreciating the grand workability of the ideas and concepts of psychological truth. Each idea, each concept stands for itself and will improve functioning and increase wisdom in people throughout their lives. Each time we make a gain in capability, we perform thereafter with more wise authority and clarity. We gain every step of the way, long before we've attained being into being. Life is set up for gain. We cannot help but increase."

That's what excites me and motivates me to write—the sharing and the wish to help, to stimulate, and to impart what I believe is useful knowledge. I also get joy and fulfillment when I receive feedback that these truths and concepts have helped lives and even stimulated some individuals' personal quests.

Philosophically, I have always been an optimist. Now I have knowledge and capability to back up my optimism. I could not be anything different knowing what I know. I marvel in wonder at the elegant truths of the human psyche plus our capacity to observe, understand, and appreciate them.

Chapter Summary

1. Keep handling situations and applying psychological truths until you are able to live without mental pressure and are not easily thrown by new uncertainties that arise.

2. Each concept stands for itself and will improve functioning and increase wisdom in people throughout their lives. Each time you make a gain in capability, you perform thereafter with more wise authority and clarity.

3. When you have handled enough situations and discovered enough truth, you will no longer be thrown by new uncertainties—you will take them in stride.

CHAPTER 23

———◆◆◆———

How to Create an Enduring Psychological and Emotional Quality of Life

Excellent, durable quality of life comes when you apply psychological truths effectively. Then you can live well. Here are examples of people who have learned to live well, with or without adversity. There are truths you can learn from them.

When things go relatively well, and the way we want them to go, we feel good and tend to believe that for now our quality of life is good. However, as we know far too well, things do not always go our way. When the unwanted happens to our relationships, health, or economic securities, psychological quality of life may suffer. If we want to develop a long lasting and resilient quality of life, we must go beyond simply relying on current prevailing circumstances and situations. Obviously, we must look elsewhere.

Though there will always be aspects of life we have little control over, to a large extent we can have significant control over our personal capacity for handling life. I have known a few people who seem to have a gift for always having good quality of life. These individuals have a consistent attitude that includes a resilient, ongoing optimism, acceptance of whatever life

351

deals them, gratitude for the opportunity to live, and a genuine love of people. Perhaps they are born this way, carrying a genetic predisposition. Perhaps they have learned some valuable lessons along the way.

I have seen an increasing number of people become adept at creating ever better quality of life as they gain deeper understanding about their own life and develop abilities to handle anything they encounter. Contrary to the few "naturals" I have known, these people have changed their life's quality from often painful to consistently good, simply by learning how to do it. One cannot tell them apart from the naturals, except they are perhaps more aware, precise, and discerning; they have had to develop these functions in order to build their abilities at life-handling.

By specifically focusing on the goal of developing excellent and durable quality of life, we can identify which developed powers and capabilities are most likely to produce this goal.

Enduring good quality of life is always an individual, unique matter, and no two people have the same recipe or ingredients for producing it. We all have a unique mix of interests, experiences, and genetics. Yet the general principles are present and available for each of us to utilize.

The Great Quest

Good psychological and emotional quality of life is something we seek on a continuous basis, and we frequently evaluate our lives from its perspective. Not surprising, for all the time and energy we spend obtaining it, few of us seem to achieve it for very long. It is usually lost when circumstances change, or our inner sense of what it is changes. As we evolve, increase, and change, so does the sense or definition of what constitutes quality of life. Our lives are so complex that elements of our lives may have excellent quality, whereas others may be in disarray. Usually these troubled aspects include health, mood and emotional problems, difficulties in relationships, concerns about children or grandchildren, and problems within us or within our friends' lives.

One person's valued quality of life may be meaningless to someone else. Some people find the bustle of city life of the highest quality, and others value the quality of the quiet solitude of the countryside. I do not presume to know what creates or constitutes quality of life for others, but I do know my own evolving formula. I also know that it is both subjective and elusive, most immediately and consciously felt when things go how we want them to, and it is quickly lost when we are sick and feeling poorly—but it's reclaimable as we feel better and our energy returns.

Major Elements That Compose Excellent Quality of Life

Quality of life pertains mostly to how we sense and evaluate our inner emotional and experiential life—what means most, what is most satisfying, and what gives us meaningful purpose, fulfillment, continuing satisfaction, and the perception of being of value. This inner quality of life sense for many may be buttressed to an extent by possessions, means, and access to quality experiences. Such things as art appreciation, labor-saving appliances, leisure time, and material goods like boats and automobiles help a little, but they are not sufficient in and of themselves to create quality of life. For a deep, abiding sense of quality of life to develop, there must be more.

The Ingredients and Descriptions: Three Naturals I Have Observed

I have observed what appears to be a durable and abiding sense of quality operating in a few select individuals. These individuals seem to show a high sense of acceptance of whatever comes, an acknowledgment of all reality, and a genuine appreciation for all experiences, particularly encounters with people. They supply something magical in the encounter, something respectful, positive, and reverent to others. The recipient comes away feeling their lives have been enhanced. It seems that these few people supply and stimulate others, and have been able to personally change or transform their attitude about living into an ever-positive gain. They demonstrate a quiet confidence and smoothness as they go about the business of living. Though I do not know the inner workings of their minds or their private lives, I do perceive a definite resiliency and, it seems, trust about life's processes. They seem to have an appreciation and gratitude for all that life is. They have a reverence for the opportunity to live the wonder of existence. This attitude transcends the problems of life and gives a pervasive support and protective immunity. We all probably know someone like this. I can think of three naturals who exemplify these characteristics.

Ken

Ken was a family man and corporate executive who volunteered for years to teach a weekly class to high school youth in my hometown. I heard good things about him before I attended his class. During junior high, I enjoyed the fun association of one of his children. I was not prepared for the impact of one of his first lessons—it rocked my soul, as it did so to others. There was not a dry eye in the group when he finished. He told the story of a tavern owner in Kansas City that he knew who placed a sign in his window, "It's always Christmas at Jim's."

Jim had a big heart, and he cared for skid row down-and-outers, supplying them with food and lodging any time of year, not just at Christmas time. He did other good things too. Yes, it was always Christmas at Jim's. Through stories like this, Ken reached us. We wanted to identify with his attitude of caring and his ability to see the good in people. He was an inspirational leader to youth, and we treasured him.

Ken challenged us with his quiet, gravelly voice and often asked us questions. What could we do? What would we do if ...? Could we be as good as Jim? Tavern owners did not carry a great reputation with the community, but Ken asked us to take a deeper look at Jim and see the good he did, and then he challenged us to see if we were doing something comparable in our own lives. Ken had a way with words and a way of reaching us. He had reverence and looked beyond prejudice. He saw the good in each of us and helped us to feel valued. We all felt understood by Ken, as if we had some importance to him. He provided great service, at least to us. Ken had a profound effect on us. Young adults who had graduated and gone away to college always came back to his class when they returned for the holidays. They wanted to rekindle the special feeling they had for him. Ken was also an excellent administrator in his job and advanced up the corporate ladder. No matter what arena he was in, he treated people well. He showed remarkable resiliency to adversity; nothing seemed to ruffle him, not even a diagnosis of cancer that his later surgery cured. He seemed to love life and could be playful as well as serious. To us, he exemplified how to live a quality life.

Ken took me fishing once and imparted some of his wisdom about life, particularly how important it was to not lose the way of purpose, value, and service. When work took him to another state to live, I visited once, playing golf and enjoying a lighter time with him. I never saw him again, and I'm quite sure he has long since died. Yet, I cannot forget him. *How did he do all of this so well?* I have often wondered. He was a great role model for living a full and quality life.

Genevieve

Genevieve is a neighbor of mine, now almost ninety years old. She has a smile and sincere greeting for everyone. She is still socially active, is mentally sharp, and she walks daily even though she had a heart attack three years ago. Genevieve is a person of great service. She raised two superb step-daughters who lost their mother early in life. One of these was a sweet friend of mine back in high school, and she exhibited the respect and care Genevieve taught. Genevieve not only has children of her own, but her step-daughters love and admire her so much that they honor her publicly with large birthday parties and awards even though they live out of state. I recall with fondness how she gave such loving, respectful care to her late husband during his last years, which were complicated by a debilitating illness. When she was unable to turn him in bed she would ask for my help and was so grateful for whatever I provided.

Genevieve has a transcendent attitude, able to accept and improve everything and everyone that she touches. Nothing seems to ruffle her; she responds to everything with a smile, and if it is a difficult situation, she gives it a touch of wry humor and twinkle of her eye. We all marvel at how she does it. Like Ken, she is an optimist. Some recent psychological literature postulates that for some, optimism is genetically based. I have my doubts and feel I would have encountered many more than I have, if this were so. As science further elucidates this subject, we will better understand the possible extent of genetic influences. Of course, genetically predisposed or not, we all still must consciously make day-to-day decisions and choose our attitudes as we proceed in life.

Allie

The most constantly happy and upbeat person I know is Allie, a married woman in her sixties who always has a little laugh and a fond, warm greeting. She comes the closest of all to possibly expressing optimism on a genetic basis. According to lifelong friends, she has always been fun-loving and happy, even in childhood. Even so, she often says in the face of an adverse outcome, "Well, you can't do anything about it, so why fight it?" She has consciously learned to make such decisions. She accepts all outcomes because she is such a good realist, yet she certainly has her opinions and expresses them without hesitation. I have never seen her worry, fight reality, or be down. Her husband, who wishes he could be more like her, has never seen her worry. Her upbeat attitude, her realistic appraisal, and her acceptance of whatever occurs make it a joy to be around her. Being this way is all very logical to her. "Why should I be any other way?" she says. She is without guile or prejudice. Everybody lightens up and laughs more when Allie is around.

You Can Become Like the Examples

If you are not already a natural, you can learn to be like one. There are ways to achieve this abiding and durable attitude for good quality of life. You can create the ability to produce it by mastering the attributes and components that can bring it about. Also, identify and overcome the roadblocks that routinely take it away. The following examples illustrate the general principles needed to provide the framework for good quality of life.

Their Characteristics

All three of my naturals show these characteristics.

1. They love people and treat them with genuine care and empathy.
2. They involve themselves in service to others as an expression of love and caring.
3. They see the best in others but do not automatically give their power away and become too dependent, or allow themselves to be vulnerable to others. They instead retain their self-power and use it well.
4. They are good realists and accept whatever life brings, rather than dwell on hopes unrealized or fight against unwanted happenings or misfortunes.
5. They have resiliency.
6. They love life and its opportunity, and they have gratitude for that opportunity.
7. They have a sense of purpose about life.
8. Though humble, they try to be a value to themselves and others.
9. They don't let things stop them for long. They acknowledge, understand, and deal with obstructions and adversities.
10. All things difficult are viewed simply as realities and part of life, to handle in the process of living.

Allie does this particularly well. She knows to not give power away, as some do when using such views as, "Oh no, all is lost!" or, "Why does this happen to me?" She understands that unwanted circumstances—as well as wanted and fortunate circumstances—can occur at any time. Rather than let circumstances rob quality or conclude she is a victim, she prefers to solve the problem and remove the impediment.

Gains That Create Quality of Life

People would be wise to be more like Allie because they can learn, gain, and discover from their experiences. They can come to know that psychological and emotional pain-inducing experiences are positive signals that point to a psychological truth, that *pains are the pointers to truths undiscovered or capabilities not used or not yet developed.* This psychological truth helps develop new abilities and helps create an attitude of willingness to handle life well. It pays dividends of both shortened pain time and increased pleasure and exhilaration from greater numbers of new discoveries. This process and attitude becomes self-perpetuating, aiding resiliency and producing optimism.

Earlier, we saw how uncertainty can cause confusion, fear, and avoidance, all of which rob quality from life. Instead, we need to view uncertainty as part of our mastery mechanism and the mind's increase drive. It is a true force that stimulates adventure, discovery, and eventually new mastery. The ability to use uncertainty well and gain life-handling power puts us far more self-in-charge and can give us confidence. The result is a greater quality of life.

When we fully see our self-power and learn to own it, we quit being so dependent, weak, vulnerable, or easily threatened. Instead we make liaisons with people or decide not to, based on our conscious decisions, with ourselves, of agreement or non-agreement. Additionally, for ongoing quality it is important to continue learning and exploring the nature of anything that exerts influence on us.

A Valuable Tool to Use throughout Your Life

I recall Desiree, who strongly overreacted to the authority and perceived secretiveness of her treatment program director at a specialized eating-disorder facility. She gave her power away to her administrator, felt victimized, often complained, and was frequently frustrated. She hung on every word the program director said, either fully embracing some or strongly fighting others. She focused far too strongly upon what she perceived the director meant and what her actions were, whether accurately or wrongly perceived. She was like an overly dependent adolescent, blindly following or vocally rebelling, often threatening to leave treatment. She had made good progress but now was letting her reaction get in the way of further success.

I asked, "Why, are you giving this so much power, letting it affect and upset you so much after you've made such good progress?" Desiree trusted me because of our established therapeutic rapport. After a pause, she blurted out excitedly, "I've been giving my power away to her, as if I were the same helpless victim in early childhood when my older brother controlled and repeatedly victimized me. It seemed similar, without my realizing it, but of course it isn't. You're right—I don't need to give it any more of my power. I can let it go and get on with my treatment." She did and succeeded admirably.

We discussed how she now had a valuable tool she could use. I counseled, "Every time you're influenced by something that is causing you uncertainty and pain, but you do not fully understand it, you'll quite naturally give your power away to it. That should be a signal to discover and understand its nature. You can then give it power or not, use it or not, depending on your choice. You have power over it from then on."

This can be a valuable tool for us all. Certainly it has been for me. Anytime we overreact with frustration or complain too loudly, or feel threatened and lash out emotionally, we are giving our power away to something we do not understand, to something we have not mastered yet and that continues to exert influence on us. Our quality of life will be periodically robbed until we catch on and learn enough about these to be able to minimize their negative effects and quickly understand them. Eventually, when they are mastered we will not even notice the process occurring; it will have been absorbed by our capability.

How We Continue to Gain: The Process

As we increase our ability to discover away pain, creating pleasurable states of satisfaction, fulfillment, and joy, our quality of life increases. And when we dare to face the uncertainties and increase in capability, our quality of life gains again. The more adroit we become, the greater our psychological agility becomes. We can evaluate and handle situations we encounter, which leaves us more time for quality pursuits to which we can apply our increasing set of capabilities.

When we acknowledge that actual reality is our strongest force and use it well, rather than fighting it, our psychological pain, particularly the stubborn victim or "poor me" attitudes, evaporate. Ideas such as "I'm a failure" have little or no credibility. The reality of what truly happened, regardless of cause, serves us without fail. Acceptance and acknowledgement are the only good, workable self-actions. Employing actual reality transforms previously viewed failures into the realization that the results are successes to the extent the attempts worked. If you make it halfway to completion, you got half of it right. On your next attempt, you will be concerned with getting the remainder right. The "I've failed" endeavor is actually a success to the level that it worked. For example, when we finally figure out a Rubik's cube puzzle, do we consider all our prior attempts failures? These attempts were necessary to obtain the experience needed to reach the solution. The kind of thinking that respects reality and acknowledges its truth makes life go smoother. This kind of thinking produces resiliency and gives a far greater sense of clarity.

The Value and Valuing of Supportive People

Having the support of people we care about and who care about us adds to our feelings of quality. For me, the revered, special moments of excited sharing and telling conversation punctuate my life with natural highs. Discovery and valuable information occurs during these conversations, and each person leaves with good feelings, believes they have been of value, and values the other.

The quality of understanding and recognizing others' unique motivations, aspirations, and intentions (i.e., having empathy) engenders an attitude of respectful valuing. In turn, the recipient is often stimulated to reciprocate these attitudes. This passing back and forth graces human relationships, adding a powerful element to our quality of life.

The Value of Good Self-Care Practices

It has been said that we have to love ourselves before we can love others. I do not believe it is true; I think it is far easier to love others, to express positive feelings outwardly toward others than inwardly toward ourselves. Certainly our quality in life disappears during times of self-loathing, self-castigation, and self-hate. If we treat ourselves with respect and caring, avoiding too much self-sacrifice, we come closest to a practical idea of loving ourselves. Some excellent ways of good self-care are an adequate amount of leisure, sleep, and good health practices. It is important to give ourselves exciting new interests and sufficient time to engage in our passionate and meaningful pursuits; then life has zest, and we look forward to each new day with its opportunities, surprises, and anticipations. These good practices make it easier to trust, to be an optimist, and to enjoy the pleasurable anticipations of positive uncertainty and the spirit of adventure. The practices and attitudes promote the pleasure of an optimistic outlook. The rewarding pleasure of an optimistic outlook, in turn, creates the desire to maintain and produce ongoing optimism. It becomes self-perpetuating. Optimism, good self-care practices, and increased capability produce a quiet, inner confidence and a trust in the belief of our ability to live well.

Using Our Predominate Attributes

Perhaps the greatest power source for our drive to succeed is our unique set of predominate attributes. The leader is a leader because he or she has leadership qualities. The artist paints, the writer writes, the musician plays, the good mother raises her children well, the scientist studies and reveals, the teacher teaches, and the healer heals. How are these successful doers able to do?

Some of our predominate attributes are inborn, some are trained, and some are added by the opportunity to apply and test ourselves. Eventually we find a fit for our unique set of abilities; a place they can play out our life's purposes for our personal benefit and that of society as well. We come to know ourselves as others know us, by our predominate attitudes and functioning.

We produce our greatest successes and most exhilarating involvements when we elaborate on the things we are best at doing. If we are fortunate enough to use these unique attributes in making a living or fulfilling some major role in life, we are all the more rewarded by the pleasurable and more far-reaching accomplishments our talents produce.

When I was a boy, I heard the sage advice to choose an area for making my living that I liked or loved, because I would be doing it at least eight hours a day. It was good advice, but it stopped short of saying that I would also be more productive and fulfilled. We have all experienced the absorbing pleasure and timelessness of being involved in endeavors we love; hours slip by as if minutes. It is great to be typecast for our jobs or roles. Here are some examples of how some peoples' predominate attributes have made them who they are.

Examples of Good Use of Predominate Attributes

Ginnie raised her family and taught them well. She received many awards during her career as an elementary school teacher and has continued her successful ways as a beloved grandmother. She teaches as she plays with her grandchildren, understanding each for his or her unique qualities. She reinforces her belief that everyone wants to feel important and recognized by offering praise and acknowledgment to each child. Needless to say, she is beloved, respected, and sought after.

Karl made a successful career by assisting businesses to connect with other businesses. He facilitated meetings and connections for the mutual benefit of all. He supported and advertised fledgling businesses on his radio show. Karl was always upbeat, friendly, and interested in people. He was willing to listen to peoples' stories and introduce them to people who could assist them in succeeding. His efforts have been recognized with awards and presentations. His predominate attributes of being able to discern good fits, make connections, and not of least importance, helping the little guy succeed served him and others well. He not only loves to do this, but it is good for his own quality of life.

Hal writes novels and nonfiction books as well as publishes other writers' works. He enjoys people and cares tenderly for his friends and his loyal pets. He teaches creative nonfiction writing at a local university and treats his students in the same respectful way. His novels show the same personal sensitivity, respect, and love for nature that he internally feels. He looks out for those friends who are less fortunate, champions causes against inhumanity, and facilitates students and authors who want to express their valued soul offerings. Hal is known and recognized for the very attributes that have made him successful; he cannot be any other way.

Big Jim is a friendly, caring, and considerate man whom everyone respects. Even acquaintances feel they are his good friend. He listens well and treats people with respect. Though big in stature, he speaks softly. Separate from this friendly and warming way are his excellent analytical and mechanical skills; he is great at fixing things. Both of these attributes—the friendly and confidence producing, and the analytical and mechanical—combine to serve him well in his career of real-estate sales and project management.

Jill is a young woman whose interests include homemaking, mothering, travel, sports, and physical conditioning. She has been a travel agent and still does some of this work from home. Although multitalented, her predominate purposes are raising her children well, teaching family values, and organizing her children's and husband's home life. Her devotion, strong motivation, and expertise in these areas are easy to identify. These interests and involvements give meaningful purpose to her life.

Paige is a former career woman with editing and management skills who found something was missing and not fulfilling enough in her life. She was not fully using all of her interests and talents in her job. In her mid-thirties she embarked on a new career goal as a research scientist, going back to college and then graduate school, where she is pursuing studies in statistical genetics and brain science. Always curious and with excellent math skills, she wants to make satisfying discoveries and important contributions to the human family through a research career. She now feels her dream is the right thing to fulfill and satisfy her life desires, and to best express her valued attributes.

George is a forty-five-year-old married man without children who works in a supermarket as a grocery checker. He had difficulty in school because of some learning problems that were probably secondary to an early childhood illness of meningitis and encephalitis. In spite of this, he has always been friendly and caring, and had many acquaintances and a few good friends. He won "employee of the month" more than once through the years because of his friendly and helpful manner. His line at the check stand is always the longest—people want his line so they can have brief and enjoyable exchange with him. He makes people feel good. One night a week he volunteers at the local juvenile detention center. He knows about adversity, having overcome his own. He has helped many mixed-up teenagers see a better path. His capability for relating well with people constantly buoys his spirits and provides the basis for his self-expressed good quality of life.

Sally, in her late thirties, has a successful career producing and providing quality evaluations of her company's financial software program productions. She is called on frequently to discover glitches and solve problems. She often receives compliments from her bosses, including the company CEO. She has the attributes of precise, logical, and careful thought, which serve her well. In addition to her work attributes, she has a sensitive, gentle, caring love for animals. She champions their cause and currently provides a home for a family of abandoned cats. She volunteers at her nearby veterinarian's clinic and sometimes provides care at a small-animal shelter. Though these things give a good sense of quality, she has gained greatly, she says, from learning to use the discoveries, concepts, and techniques in this book. She has learned to stop creating mental pressure and now better owns—and more frequently fulfills—her valued preferences rather than give into others' as she formerly did. She safely moved through some momentary feelings of despair during a failed relationship a few years ago.

Robert, a successful professional, has strong drives to provide service and give leadership. He has been president of many organizations and is admired by many. He is bright and somewhat of a philosopher (his major in college), and he enjoys problem solving. He gives his clients clear choices and good advice. Robert has solved most of the problems that take away personal quality of life by using concepts and truths incorporated in this book. He credits the psychological truths, concepts, and techniques with making his life "continuously the best of times since 1989." He says, "The psychological truths work and have remarkable power to remove pain and give one the opportunity and abilities to always function well. They have greatly increased my ability to handle life."

Robert achieved national prominence in his profession by handling key cases, teaching seminars, and advising colleagues. He is also a spiritual leader in his church and serves his family, friends, and neighbors admirably. He is content moment to moment and has peace rather than the constant mental pressure he once experienced. He comprehends how actual reality works and uses it well, rather than fighting it and producing pain. He now functions smoothly where he formerly had impediments that resulted in constant expressions of anger. Once, he had anxiety attacks, but now he's free of them. His former pains are now gone, replaced by discoveries he has turned into mastery. He now knows how to live well, and does.

Into Our Futures

Where do we go with life? It is a good question for each of us to continue to pose and continue to answer. I've asked this question many times through a life mostly lived. The enduring answers, the directional pointers that continue through and beyond each life stage and its tasks, can be summarized below.

"Follow your passion," is good advice. "Follow your art," as one friend said.

I started using the following three lines thirty-four years ago at a time when I understood them far less than I do now:

- Know who you are.
- Know who you were.
- Become who you will.

My friend and massage therapist Dennis, also a man listed in the Martial Arts Hall of Fame and highly respected for his skills, says it another way. "Stick with what you're good at. By all means, build up your insufficiencies and shed your excesses. But most important, find out what you're good at and stick with it. If you set your heart on things you are not made for, you will only end up in failure."

As we follow these general aims, learn to clear our pains, increase our efficiency, and continue to develop better life handling skills, where then do we go?

Continuations and Advancements

Continue to seek new challenges and further increase your mastery and ability. Keep discovering and asking why. Ponder your questions and uncertainties, and keep comprehending new truths to deepen your realizations. Know what you value and what gives you meaningful purpose. Fulfill your promises and agreements instead of creating impediments for others. Produce the beautiful hum of responsibility well taken. Share your life and grace your relationships. Have empathy and give care, concern, and consideration to others. Give what you know is of value to others. Become an ever-increasing source of value, and see others in that light. Always desire to live well and have gratitude for all that life is and brings.

Chapter Summary

1. Follow your passion.
2. Excel in your areas of special talent or aptitude. You will find out what these are through experiencing life and trying things out.
3. Accept and acknowledge reality as it occurs.
4. Learn, know, and apply your many psychological truths intentionally, with conscious awareness.
5. As the case vignettes demonstrate, these attitudes and actions add to the quality of life:
    ◦ Learn how to communicate clearly and considerately with others.
    ◦ Treat people with respect, dignity, and appreciation for their uniqueness.
    ◦ Enjoy people and let them know how they matter positively.
    ◦ Have gratitude, feel it, and express it often.
    ◦ Greet life as an ever-evolving adventure.

EPILOGUE

Looking Back and Looking Forward

These trustable psychological truths, discovered during my personal and professional journey, have produced excellent quality of life for others and for me. They are powerful and reliable. These truths have continued to provide new discovery, greater comprehension, further accomplishment, increased understanding, and wisdom for all who have used them.

As I contemplate the completion of this book, my thoughts return to its inception in 1971. I am heartened to realize that my original belief is as valid and true today as it was in its beginning. This belief revolves around the idea that we can grow new capability, outgrow problems, and overcome obstacles or stumbling blocks. I'm not sure just when I got this idea, but I do recall clearly a mental image of climbing a rock face and being stopped by an overhang. I was convinced that with enough understanding, growth, and new learning, I could move up and over the overhang and continue on my way. Each time I was stopped, I would inquire as to the nature of the block and why it stopped me. By pursuing answers to these questions and following the leads to their origins, I learned enough to master the block or problem and would grow on.

I learned that many obstacles or stumbling blocks I encountered were my own uncertainties. Whether it was not knowing what something was or not being familiar with it, I set out to explore its true identity and learn what it really was. Sometimes the obstacle was the uncertainty of not knowing how to handle something, so I responded by developing new techniques for dealing with it. Each time I faced uncertainties this way, my repertoire of life-handling abilities increased. The same problems that once stopped me cold could not stop me anymore. Additionally, I discovered that the psychological-emotional pains such as bewilderment, confusion, depression, or great pressure that once obstructed my progress could be dealt with or eliminated in the same way. Once I understood the meaning and structure of each of these types of pain, I could then release them, having gained new knowledge to move beyond their specific impediments. As I moved forward, I began to trust the process and realized that my uncertainty signals were telling me what needed mastering for me to advance further. When I learned this, I knew I could use my developing skills and my increasing certainty knowledge to master the new uncertainties I encountered. Each time I conquered an uncertainty, I added a new certainty, a new capability, to my ever-growing repertoire of life-handling skills.

By putting these techniques into action, my understanding grew broader and deeper. As I conquered more uncertainties, I grew more confident, and I sought discovery with zest and enthusiasm. I found myself repeating a phrase: "Excitement exists at the edge of the new unknown." I embraced uncertainties instead of shying away from them; they beckoned with new adventure and intriguing mystery. I made inroads into the frontiers of my own mind—and in a larger sense, the human mind—and discovered a reliable way of continued growth. I called this development "conscious aware capability." Then, over the years I made more discoveries, such as the mind's signaling systems and the psychological truths revealed in this book.

The question arises, "How early in life can these truths be taught? Could they influence educational systems positively when taught age-appropriately? How much stronger psychologically, and how much more capable, will those be who know the psychological truths than those who do not?" It would also seem these many truths can be adapted to many different fields of endeavor—business, education, philosophy, and more. After all, these truths function on our minds and our decisions, our central information that applies to all our fields of focus.

By the mid-1980s, fifteen years after starting my discovery trek, I had gained enough strengths, polished skills, and comprehension that uncertainties no longer threw me. In fact, I took them in stride and no longer had mental pressure or personal stress. I often felt joy. I had a clear and released free feeling, as if I were on an extended vacation, even when working. Today, a few minor irritants that I have not yet mastered can take the good feeling away. A large number of interrupting calls on my pager in a short period of time, or frequent managed-care calls during which medical insurance company clinicians would permit or remove financing for patient care depending on their criteria and not mine—these things can still bother me. If I'm not careful, I can still give these things power and negative significance, even though they are facts of life that I cannot control. When I do acknowledge and accept the truth of their existence and don't fight against them mentally, I quickly regain my desired quality of life. These bothersome irritants amount to less than 1 percent of my time. I would also like to master these, and believe I will someday.

This method of increase in capability, growth by mastery, and developing new certainties and abilities—which continues to this day—has brought me a large treasure. I strongly believe that for those inclined to discovery, these truths and methods work. Each of us can push back any frontier and keep pushing it back, continuously learning more. Yes, excitement does exist at the edge of the new unknown. The mystery is waiting there for us, and the solutions just beyond.

One of the exciting new exploration tools of our brains functioning during behaviors, meditation, mood problems, and other psychiatric syndromes, addictions, and problem-solving thinking is the functional MRI brain scan. That and other specialized scans show the metabolic and electrical activity of the brain and the places where the activity is located. As my clinical experience has shown, our psychological truths and the entity that is truth appear to be the supreme organizers in the mind. Where and how they act to do this, would, I presume, show up on such a brain scan during the operative time of the particular truth while it is exerting its reorganizing influence in someone's mind and life. What would these scans show that would be different from the scan of a brain of a person not using the psychological truths?

Nonetheless, the important point is that we can and will continue to develop new knowledge and capability as we discover and think. When we use the power and value of psychological truths by choice and with awareness, we will greatly increase our personal evolution and influence society's evolution in wise ways.

Endnotes

1. R. J. Brand, R. H. Rosenman, R. Sholtz, and M. Friedman, "Multivariate Prediction of Coronary Heart Disease in the Western Collaborative Group Study Compared to the Findings of the Framingham Study," *Circulation* 53 (1976): 348;

2. M. Friedman et al., Recurrent Coronary Project Study. *Circulation* 66 (1982): 83.

3. T. Holmes, Presentation, "Life Stress Events," Psychiatric Grand Rounds, University of Utah Medical Center, 1965.

4. H. Benson, *The Relaxation Response* (New York: William Morrow and Company, Inc., 1975, revised 2000).

5. K. M. Flegal et al., "Prevalence of Obesity and Trends in the Distribution of Body Mass Index Among US Adults, 1999–2010," *Journal of the American Medical Association* 307, no. 5 (2012), 491–497.

6. Center For Disease Control and Prevention, "443,000 Smoking Related Deaths in US Per Year" (updated January 24,2012). *Morbidity and Mortality Weekly.* http://www.cdc.gov/mmwr/preview/mmwrhtml/mm5745a3.htm (accessed January 31, 2012).

7. L. E. Hung, H. Gu, Y. Yang, T. J. Ross, B. J. Salmeron, B. Buckholz, G. K. Thaker, and E. A. Stein, "Association of Nicotine Addiction and Nicotine's Actions with Separate Cingulate Cortex Functional Circuits," *Arch Gen Psychiatry* 66, no. 4 (April 2009): 431–444.

8. D. L. Hilton Jr., "Can Pornography Use Become an Actual Brain Addiction?" (Forward Press Publishing, January 20, 2011), www.forwardpress.org.

9. N.D. Volkow et al., "Addiction; Pulling at the Neural Threads of Social Behaviors," *Neuron* 69, no. 4 (2011): 599–602.

10. G. F. Koob and N. D. Volkow, "Elaboration of Reward Circuitry in Brain That Mediates Responses to Natural Rewards (Food, Sex) Under Normal Conditions and How This Circuitry Is Corrupted by Chronic Exposure to Drugs of Abuse," *Neuropsychopharmacology* 35, no. 1 (2010): 217–238.

11. M. Yucel, N. Solowij, C. Respondek, S. Whittle, A. Fornito, C. Pantelis, and D. I. Lubman, "Regional Brain Abnormalities Associated with Long-Term Heavy Cannabis Use," *Arch Gen Psychiatry* 65, no. 6 (June 2008): 694–701.

12. K. Lorenz. As reported in *Comprehensive Textbook of Psychiatry* 1, Fifth Edition, 336–337.

13. E. Erikson, "Identity and the Life Cycle," *Psychological Issues* 1 (1961): 1.

14. G. Chapman, *The Five Languages of Love* (Chicago: Northfield Publishing, 2010).

15. S. N. Garfinkel and I. Liberzon, "Neurobiology of PTSD: A Review of Neuroimaging Findings," *Psychiatric Annals* Vol. 39. No.6 (June 2009): 370–381. PsychiatricAnnalsOnline.com.

16. "Adolf Hitler," *Wikipedia.* whttp://en.wikipedia.org/wiki/Adolph_Hitler (accessed September 2, 2011); B. Jansen, "How Did Adolph Hitler's Childhood and Youth Influence His Development?" (June 12, 2003). http://www.Epinions.com/content_3337855108?sb=1 (accessed September 2, 2011).

17. "Benito Mussolini," *Wikipedia.* http://en.wikipedia.org/wiki/Benito_Mussolini (accessed September 3, 2011); "Mussolini Biography," http://www.notablebiographies.com/Mo-Ni/Mussolini-Benito.html (accessed September 3, 2012).

Index

certainty; *see also* uncertainty
   applying, 105
   of capability, 120
   dominating need for, 106–7
   false sense of, 124, 125
   flow of, 102–4
   foundations of, 104
   many faces of, 104
   relying on, 105–6
   settling effect of, 104–5
   vulnerabilities to needing, 105–8
change
   and anxiety, 274, 278, 283
   beyond our control, 199
   choosing a new direction, 128–29
Chapman, Gary, 223
children
   depression in, 311, 312
   and discipline, 98–99
   disruptive behavior, 202–4
   exercising self-power, 59
   and expression of preferences, 168
   frightening uncertainty in, 116–17
   helplessness experiences, 309, 311
   lack of nurturing, 311, 314
   and mastery development, 88, 93–94
   overindulged, 92, 336
   parents giving power to, 68–70
   seeking familiarity, 106
chronic pain, 160
communication
   accusations, 187, 221, 226, 235, 236
   care package technique, 236
   clarity of, 229, 231–32
   click of certainty, 232–33
   cross-checking, 232
   defensiveness, 226, 227, 232, 235, 236
   enhancers of, 232

   of expectations, 175
   how things are said, 233–34
   impact of statements, 234–35
   invitational *versus* accusative, 235–36
   misunderstandings, 28, 226–28, 229–31
   principles, 234, 235
   restating, 231, 232
   self-referring, 232, 236
   shifting responsibility, 232, 234, 235, 236
   through emotional expressions, 26
competence, *see* mastery
confusion
   caused by uncertainty, 111
   how to handle, 48
cultural shock, 200, 211

D

death
   and loss of belongingness, 212
   of a loved one, 43, 256, 264, 265
decision making
   and knowledge, 51
   and mental pressure, 9–10
   and uncertainty, 124, 125
delayed gratification, 246
demoralization, 159, 160, 161
dependencies
   and despair, 328, 329
   and fear, 334–35
   on others, 313, 314, 334
   and panic, 53
depression, 6, 64
   and anxiety, 284
   in childhood, 311, 312
   and despair, 324, 329

mattering
  case examples, 255–56, 257–59
  consequences of negative, 253–54
  and depression, 256–57, 258
  and disappointment, 256–57
  expressing, 252, 253
  helpful techniques, 259–60
  how it happens, 252–53
  indifferent, 254–55
  negative, 253
  perceptions of, 256–57, 259
  positive, 251–52, 260
meaningful purpose, *see* purpose
medications
  for anxiety, 277, 284
  for depression, 160, 329
meditation, 7
memories, 105, 126; *see also* past
    experiences
mental acceptance, 11–12
mental breakdowns, 6
mental illness, 7
mental pressure, 3–4, 134; *see also* stress;
    thought patterns
  and acceptance, 11–12
  and anxiety cycle, 12–13
  awareness of, 14
  causes of, 5, 7, 8–9
  compounding, 10–11
  dependence on, 5, 18
  emotional pain from, 39
  experiencing, 5–6
  in high achievers, 9–10
  mastery over, 15–16
  and motivation, 5, 16, 17, 19
  physical symptoms of, 6
  release of, 4, 8, 13–15, 16–17
  resistance to changing from, 18–19
mental pressuring, 7

merger anxiety, 290–91
midlife crises, 318
motivation, 148–49, 334; *see also*
    desires; preferences
  from emotions, 25, 27
  examples in nature, 154–55
  inspirational leaders, 174–76
  inspiring others, 173–74
  and law of adaptive value, 152, 153–
    54, 178
  of mastery mechanism, 88–90
  and mental pressure, 5, 16, 17, 19
  mystery of, 149–51
  obscurity of, 151–53
  and purpose, 151, 154
  purpose problems, 158–59
  resistance to, 176–78
  and volition, 157–58
Mussolini, Benito, 308, 309

N

necessity beliefs, 303–4, 304–5
negative self-assumptions, 73–76
negativity, 259, 326; *see also* pessimists
nicotine addiction, 164–65

O

obesity, 161, 162, 165
obligations, 64, 65
obstacles
  beyond our capabilities, 36–37
  emotional pain from, 28, 36–37
oedipal complex, 152
optimism, 243, 345, 349, 351, 356,
    358, 361

CPSIA information can be obtained at www.ICGtesting.com
Printed in the USA
BVOW011852240912

301262BV00003B/3/P